San Fran

and the Wine Regions

Brian Eads

CW00613867

Mitchell Beazley

THE AMERICAN EXPRESS ® TRAVEL GUIDES

Published by Mitchell Beazley
International Ltd, Michelin House,
81 Fulham Road, London SW3 6RB

Edited, designed and produced by
Castle House Press, Llantrisant,
Mid Glamorgan CF7 8EU, Wales

First published 1990 as *The American
Express Pocket Guide to Los Angeles &
San Francisco*. This adapted and
expanded edition published 1992.

© American Express Publishing
Corporation Inc. 1992

ISBN 1 85732 920 1

The author, editors and publisher join
in thanking the San Francisco
Convention & Visitors Bureau, in
particular Helen K. Chang, Anne
Uyehara, Susan Arthur and Sharon
Rooney. The author also wishes to
thank Judy, his wife and fellow
traveler, and Claes Bratt and all those
in Northern California who shared
their knowledge and insights. Warm
thanks too are due from the editors to
Anne Ryland, Neil Hanson, David
Haslam, Hilary Bird, John Hale, Alf
and Muriel Jackson, Sally Darlington
and Diane Williams.

The editors and publisher are also
grateful to American Airlines for their
generous assistance with the author's
travel arrangements. Details of American Airlines' telephone numbers in San
Francisco and Great Britain are given on
pages 48-9.

FOR THE SERIES:
General Editor:
 David Townsend Jones
Map Editor: David Haslam
Indexer: Hilary Bird
Cover design:
 Roger Walton Studio

FOR THIS EDITION:
Edited on desktop by:
 Eileen Townsend Jones
Associate editor: Sharon Charity
Art editor: Eileen Townsend Jones
Illustrators:
 Sylvia Hughes-Williams,
 Karen Cochrane
Gazetteer: Anne Evans
Cover photo: Alan Williams

FOR MITCHELL BEAZLEY:
Art Director: Tim Foster
Managing Editor: Alison Starling
Production: Sarah Schuman

PRODUCTION CREDITS:
Maps by Lovell Johns, Oxford,
 England
Typeset in Garamond and
 News Gothic
Desktop layout in Ventura
 Publisher
Linotronic output by
 Tradespools Limited, Frome,
 England
Printed and bound in Great Britain
 by HarperCollins Manufacturing,
 Glasgow

Contents

Culture, history and background

Basic information

Planning

Sightseeing

Where to stay

Eating and drinking

Entertainments

Shopping *by Nell Bernstein and Joel Simon*

Ideas for children

Excursions

Wines and wineries *by Bob Thompson*

Maps

How to use this book

Few guidelines are needed to understand how this book works:

- For the general organization of the book, see CONTENTS on the pages preceding this one.
- Wherever appropriate, chapters and sections are arranged alphabetically, with headings appearing in **CAPITALS.**
- Often these headings are followed by location and practical information printed in *italics*.
- As you turn the pages, you will find subject headers, similar to those used in telephone directories, printed in CAPITALS in the top corner of each page.
- If you still cannot find what you need, check in the comprehensive and exhaustively cross-referenced INDEX at the back of the book.
- Following the index, a LIST OF STREET NAMES provides map references for all roads and streets mentioned in the book that are located within the areas covered by the main city maps.

CROSS-REFERENCES

These are printed in SMALL CAPITALS, referring you to other sections or alphabetical entries in the book. Care has been taken to ensure that such cross-references are self-explanatory. Often, page references are also given, although their excessive use would be intrusive and ugly.

FLOORS

We use the American convention in this book: "first floor" means the floor at ground level.

KEY TO SYMBOLS

☎	Telephone
ⒻⓍ	Facsimile (fax)
★	Recommended sight
☆	Worth a visit
♨	Good value (in its class)
i	Tourist information
⬅	Parking
☒	Building of architectural interest
☒	Free entrance
☒	Entrance fee payable
☒	Entrance expensive
☒	Photography forbidden
ⲅ	Guided tour
☕	Cafeteria
✲	Special interest for children
☁	Hotel
☷	Luxury hotel
▢	Cheap
▢	Inexpensive
▢	Moderately priced
▢	Expensive
▢	Very expensive
⊟	Air conditioning
ⒶⒺ	American Express
☒	Diners Club
☒	MasterCard/Eurocard
ⓋⒾⓈⒶ	Visa
☒	Secure garage
☒	Quiet hotel
☒	Elevator
☒	Facilities for disabled people
☐	TV in each room
☒	Telephone in each room
☒	Dogs not allowed
☙	Garden
∿	Swimming pool
⪜	Good view
⫫	Gym/fitness facilities
☒	Conference facilities
☒	Minibar
☒	Bar
☒	Restaurant
☒	Luxury restaurant
☒	A la carte available
☒	Set (fixed-price) menu available
☒	Good wines
☒	Disco dancing
☒	Nightclub
♫	Live music
☒	Dancing
☒	Adults only

HOTEL AND RESTAURANT PRICE CATEGORIES

These are denoted by the symbols ▢ (cheap), ▢ (inexpensive), ▢ (moderately priced), ▢ (expensive) and ▢ (very expensive). They correspond approximately to the following actual local prices, which give a guideline **at the time of printing**. Naturally, prices tend to rise, but, with a few exceptions, hotels and restaurants will remain in the same price category.

Price categories	Corresponding to approximate prices	
	for **hotels** *double room with bath; singles are slightly cheaper*	for **restaurants** *meal for one with service, taxes and house wine*
▢ very expensive	over $210	over $65
▢ expensive	$160-210	$45-65
▢ moderately priced	$110-160	$35-45
▢ inexpensive	$60-110	$30-35
▢ cheap	under $60	under $30

About the author

Brian Eads was born in Lincoln, England and educated at Cambridge University. For many years he was a foreign correspondent, writing variously for *The Observer, The Economist, The Washington Post* and *Newsweek,* living and working out of Paris, Bangkok, Hong Kong and Los Angeles. Currently he is on the staff of Granada Television, making current affairs documentaries. Home is now in the hills of Derbyshire in the northwest of England, but he spends part of each year in California.

Bob Thompson, who contributed the WINES AND WINERIES chapter, wakes up at night wondering if he has become a monomaniac. Since 1967 he has written — in round numbers — ten books, a hundred magazine pieces, and a thousand newspaper columns about wine. Titles he has written include *The Californian Wine Book* with Hugh Johnson, *The Pocket Guide to Californian Wines* and this book's ancestor, *The American Express Pocket Guide to California.*

Other contributors to this edition were **Nell Bernstein** and **Joel Simon** (SHOPPING) and **Jonah Jones** (ARCHITECTURE).

A message from the series editor

In designing *American Express San Francisco and the Wine Regions* we aimed to make this brand-new edition simple and instinctive to use, like all its sister volumes in our new, larger paperback format.

The hallmarks of the relaunched series are clear, classic typography, confidence in fine travel writing for its own sake, and faith in our readers' innate intelligence to find their way around the books without heavy-handed signposting by editors.

Readers with anything less than 20:20 vision will doubtless also enjoy the larger, clearer type, and can now dispense with the mythical magnifying glasses we never issued free with the old pocket guide series.

Months of concentrated work by our editors, together with the author and contributors, have been dedicated to ensuring that this edition is as accurate and up to date as it possibly can be at the moment it goes to press. But time and change are forever the enemies, and in between editions we very much appreciate it when you, our readers, keep us informed of changes that you discover.

As ever, I am indebted to all the many readers who wrote during the preparation of this edition. Please remember that your feedback is extremely important to our efforts to tailor the series to the very distinctive tastes and requirements of our sophisticated international readership.

Send your comments to me at Mitchell Beazley International Ltd, Michelin House, 81 Fulham Road, London SW3 6RB; or, in the US, c/o American Express Travel Guides, Prentice Hall Travel, 15 Columbus Circle, New York, NY 10023.

David Townsend Jones

San Francisco
and the Wine Regions

America, only more so

It is an odd thing, but anyone who disappears
is said to be seen in San Francisco.
(Oscar Wilde)

San Francisco is certainly too odd for some people. The unpredictability, eccentricity, tolerance, libertarianism, and preciousness that underpin the city's popular identity sometimes exasperate its more conventional citizens. But seldom, if ever, is their irritation enough to undo their civic pride. San Franciscans are capable of disagreeing about almost everything, except their universal devotion to the city itself.

It has been called "the land of Oz by the Bay." As Dorothy, the heroine played by Judy Garland in the movie "The Wizard of Oz," puts it to her dog, Toto: "I've a feeling we're not in Kansas any more."

San Francisco is like muesli. Take out all the fruit
and nuts, and all you're left with are the flakes.
(Anon.)

The message is that we are now somewhere altogether different; somewhere magical, weird, unpredictable, maybe sometimes a little scary or a touch ridiculous, but often lots of fun. A place where the constraints of buttoned-down, clean-cut America can be shrugged off. Where the parameters of what is acceptable, indeed of what constitutes reality, are mobile.

I have heard San Francisco described as "a city in love with itself," and "parochial in its cosmopolitanism." But neither of these slights has come from a native San Franciscan. Maybe the first native you meet will hate the place, but I doubt it. The city is small enough and compact enough to be intimately knowable, manageable and lovable.

LIVING WITH THE FAULT
Curiously, living with the San Andreas fault seems to be a positive factor in San Francisco's identity. Like any shared adversity, memories of the most recent apocalyptic earthquake, and the prospect of another, make for great community spirit. In 1906, earthquake and fire killed 2,500 people and destroyed 80 percent of the city, leaving 400,000 people homeless. Rebuilding began while the ruins were still smoking. Nine years later, the splendidly reconstructed city hosted a glittering International Exposition. In 1989 an earthquake centered on the Bay Area did $2 billion worth of damage. But, as befits a city whose flag features a phoenix rising from the ashes, San Francisco once again dusted itself down rapidly and bounced back.

There is an uncommon solidarity and devotion to the City among its diverse inhabitants. They, or sometimes their ancestors, often labored long and hard to reach the shores of the Pacific Ocean. Even those who arrived in comfort came to change their lives. And they are proud of what has been built out of opportunity and, in the early days at least, hardship.

CITY OF GOLD

Visitors need some awareness of history to appreciate this peculiar *esprit de corps*. And few cities revel in their history as much as San Francisco. Flying in today from London, Tokyo or New York might not be as exhausting or as romantic as those earlier voyages. But it is still possible to share the exhilaration recorded by earlier travelers. Traversing the western slopes of the towering Sierra Nevada 120 years ago, "The Amateur Emigrant" Robert Louis Stevenson felt the weariness of the arduous journey from his native Scotland slip from his shoulders.

"At every turn we looked further into the land of our happy future. At every turn the cocks were tossing their clear notes into the golden air and crowing for the new day and the new country. For this indeed was our destination... this was 'the good country' we have been going to for so long."

The 19th-century Gold Rush set the tone. If the 1930s Hollywood "dream machine" can be said to have framed the self image of Los Angeles, then 1849 was the benchmark for its northern neighbor. The era is burned into the collective psyche of San Francisco. The area of the city proper is 49 square miles. Its hugely successful 49ers football team is named after the fateful year. The "scenic drive" is mapped around a precise 49 miles.

Not for nothing was it called a "rush" for gold. Anything went in the miners' shanty that was Gold Rush San Francisco. Inevitably, it attracted dreamers, mostly young, who were fired by ambition, opportunity or greed. Many came equipped with the energy and enterprise to turn dreams into reality. As the biggest port on the West Coast, "The Barbary Coast" in the 19th century, and a toehold on the "golden land" that was California, the city continued to attract adventurers and explorers, ruffians and runaways.

ALTERNATIVE SAN FRANCISCO

This frivolous inheritance has not always sat easily with the straight-laced burghers of San Francisco, the solid blue-collar working class who built its industrial base, or the "new money" anxious for respectability. But it has proved an irresistible magnet to those in search of personal freedoms, prosperity, or lifestyles alternative to those on offer in Kansas City, Calabria, Canton, County Cork, or Cholon. They are still arriving.

Of course, San Francisco's reality is not a seamless tapestry of raffish beat poets, racial harmony, economic prosperity and sexual licence. In the not-too-distant past, poets have been censored, the significant Chinese and Japanese minorities have been discriminated against, coherent "village" communities of Irish, Italian and Hispanic origin have fragmented, the head count of beggars has grown to rival that of a Third World city, political leaders have been assassinated, and the AIDS epidemic has taken, and continues to take, a shocking toll.

San Francisco claims to be one of the four sunniest cities in the United

States, but the weather is not nearly as benign as that of Southern California. Indeed, Mark Twain wrote that the coldest winter he had ever known was one summer in San Francisco.

Mostly, however, the city of San Francisco is peopled by the kind of cheery, life-enhancing optimists for which the State of California has a worldwide reputation. Theirs is a Pacific culture, far from the leaden skies and inhibiting chills of the North Atlantic coast. It is also a major international port, with all the freewheeling cosmopolitanism that this brings.

A PROSPEROUS DIVERSITY

Through the centuries, San Francisco's opportunities for work and play have attracted — and continue to attract — wave after wave of immigrants: Hispanic, Anglo Saxon, Southern and Eastern European, Armenian, Arab and Asian. The range of cuisines and entertainments on offer reflects this diversity. And this vibrant mix of humanity works as hard, perhaps harder, than it plays. San Francisco already ranks as one of the financial centers of the Pacific; "Wall Street West," in fact. Not far away are powerhouses of the aerospace and computer industries.

Recession across the United States in recent years has taken some of the gloss off even the sunbelt boom industries. But, as an agricultural and economic power, an independent California would still rank in the world's top ten most prosperous economies. And for many, San Francisco would be the first choice as its capital city.

San Francisco's destiny looks set to be even brighter in the decades to come. To the east lie the natural barriers of deserts and mountains, and beyond them, the memory of less sun-kissed lives. The physical and psychological orientations of the city and its inhabitants face firmly toward the west. San Francisco is a city of the Pacific Rim. And, as economic pundits continually remind us, we are approaching the "Pacific century," with booming economies from Tokyo to Vancouver, Singapore to San Diego, accelerating a spiral of rising prosperity.

Of course, there is a downside: pollution, drug-related crime, pockets of severe deprivation. There are areas of the city, such as the Western Addition and the "Tenderloin," that can be dangerous after dark.But the human traffic is still moving towards California. And, some would say, the cutting edge of the future is already being honed in nearby Santa Clara's high-tech Silicon Valley.

It is hard to ignore the contrasts between San Francisco and Los Angeles. To those repelled or intimidated by the urban giantism to the South, San Francisco is the very model of a small, user-friendly, old-fashioned, "European" city, complete with tasteful turn-of-the-century architecture. Were it not for the live-and-let-live tolerance common to both, the cities could almost be on different planets. Whatever you do, do not tell a San Franciscan that your favorite city is Los Angeles. There is little love lost between the two, for reasons to do with history, climate and terrain.

San Francisco was already a thriving city when Los Angeles was little more than a pioneer encampment. Los Angeles has wide skies and horizons, whereas San Francisco spends forever looking back upon itself up and down its hills. And while Los Angeles basks in (almost) year-long summer, San Francisco has four identifiable seasons, and is reminiscent of Southern Europe.

Like Europeans, San Franciscans value continuity. They also care passionately for the natural environment, view their city as a western outpost of refinement and sophistication, and pride themselves on their civic devotion. Famously, they feel free to challenge conventional aspirations. Not for nothing did the "beat generation," the hippies of Haight-Ashbury and the gays of the Castro district make their home in San Francisco; although, very possibly, home was nothing more radical than a gingerbread Victorian town house. Nowadays, in line with these free-spirited ideals, San Francisco is the center of ecological activism in the United States. Greenpeace, Friends of the Earth and the Sierra Club all have their headquarters here.

San Francisco gave birth to the United Nations and the topless dancer, LA to Hollywood and valet parking. In short, each city is a vivid tableau of the American Dream. Although, delighting in contradiction, San Francisco considers itself both the more urbane and the more risqué.

Writer and environmentalist Wallace Stegner has observed that San Francisco is "America, only more so." Or, as movie producer and San Francisco resident Francis Ford Coppola put it, more laconically: "I kinda like this place." So do a great many other people. The city is regularly voted favorite destination by US and non-US travelers alike. Maybe it is because the California Constitution provides for the right to "pursue and *obtain* happiness." Elsewhere in the United States, only the right of pursuit is enshrined in the constitution. It is a distinction that makes all the difference.

Eureka ("I have found it")
(California's motto)

Culture, history and background

The city and its people

*I would rather be a broken lamp-post in San Francisco's
Battery Street than in the Waldorf Astoria in New York.
(Turn-of-the-century boxer)*

The city of San Francisco sits like a thimble on the thumb of its peninsula. It has a population of just 731,000, making it only the fourth-lar-
gest of California's cities. However, this figure is misleading; the
population of the nine Bay Area counties approaches 6 million, and
many people commute into the city proper to work and play. And
what diversity they encounter within its intimate scale!

Distances between cultural, linguistic and culinary traditions that
might be a world apart are measured in San Francisco in the width of
streets. The journey from Chinatown to Little Italy is a matter of crossing
Columbus Ave.

It is said that a hundred different languages are spoken by the citizens
of San Francisco. That could be an exaggeration, but only slightly. Official
figures show that one in three San Franciscans come from a home where
a language other than English is spoken. The largest communities
counted by ethnic origin are Chinese, Italian, Black, Hispanic, British,
Irish, and German. But there are many many more. Basques, Filipinos,
Russians, Iranians, Japanese, Vietnamese, Khmers, Ethiopians etc. — the
list of ethnic groups reads like the membership list of the United Nations
General Assembly. Yet, for the most part, the people of San Francisco
enjoy a more relaxed co-existence than do the diplomatic delegates. This
is hardly surprising, given that many of the city's communities have been
learning the art of living together for around 200 years.

There is no mistaking the busy, narrow streets of Chinatown, the ritzy,
monied solidity of Pacific Heights, the Neapolitan ease of North Beach,
or the almost exclusively gay orientation of The Castro. San Francisco is
spared the featureless suburban sprawl of larger, younger or less vibrant
cities.

Among older people and recent arrivals there is sometimes a degree
of linguistic and cultural isolation. Some of the more affluent groups have
chosen to move out of town to leafy suburbs and, as a consequence, the
balance of population in the city proper has tilted in favor of people of
Asian and Hispanic origin. But, for the most part, San Franciscans of all

origins mingle across their cosmopolitan city. The melting pot is simmering and there are few neighborhoods that do not have something to offer the curious visitor.

The lives of these diverse people, unlike those of their neighbors in some Californian cities, are not ruled totally by the internal combustion engine. Certainly, San Franciscans like to drive, and rush hours can be severely congested. But they also take buses, cable cars, and trains; they even walk. A shortage of parking spaces and the liberating joys of valet parking services has something to do with it, as does the comprehensive and affordable public transportation network. But more important is the city's intimacy and human scale.

With the exception of the downtown Financial District, San Francisco has few deep canyons of soulless concrete, nor does it have the seemingly endless featureless boulevards that offer no hope of distinguished architecture or human activity. People walk here because it is a pleasure. And it is a pleasure that pays dividends; the women of San Francisco are said to have the shapeliest legs in California, thanks, perhaps, to all the walking they do.

Even for the first time visitor, the distances and the shapes of the city are easily comprehended and managed. Some of the steeper of San Francisco's 42 hills admittedly require a well-developed set of calf and thigh muscles as well as a strong heart and lungs. But the stunning vistas and ebullient street life ease any pain. And if it is possible to know a city, then walking is the best means of becoming acquainted with its nooks and crannies, and all its diverse pleasures.

"San Francisco has only one drawback," lamented Rudyard Kipling, "... 'tis hard to leave." He wasn't talking about the traffic jams.

BEYOND THE CITY LIMITS

What of areas outside the city? First of all, do not consider even those close by as suburbs of San Francisco. The natives would resent it, with justice. Contrary to what more chauvinistic San Franciscans like to think, however, there is life beyond the city limits. Some of these areas are cities in their own right, and most have a distinctive and engaging identity of their own.

Oakland, due E across the Bay Bridge, is a major manufacturing center with a population half that of San Francisco. Farther up the Bay is the university town of **Berkeley**, which boasts one of the most liberal and highly educated populations in the United States.

South of the Bay, in Santa Clara County, is **San Jose**, unofficial capital of Silicon Valley. It has the heaviest concentration of high-tech industries on earth and perhaps the densest population of whizz-kid boffins to keep it buzzing with innovation.

Other towns, inland and along the coast, are small in comparison. **Palm Springs** (40,000), **Santa Barbara** (80,000), **Carmel** (5,000) and **Monterey** (30,000) are a mixture of elegantly polished retreat and gift-wrapped tourist attraction, sustained by hordes of visitors and wealthy residents. Each has its resident celebrities and a unique, if predictable, charm.

Of the other cities and towns within striking distance of San Francisco, **Sacramento**, the state capital to the NE, has a population of under 300,000. **Los Angeles**, 400 miles to the s, is by far the biggest. Los Angeles City proper boasts around 3 million people, while greater LA has a population of more than 8 million. As for the rest, **San Diego** is the most populous with around 1 million people, making it California's second-biggest city.

It was at San Diego in 1542 that Juan Rodriguez Cabrillo claimed what is now California for the Spanish Crown, and many regard this as the state's birthplace. Like LA, its northern neighbor, San Diego sprawls — 20 miles to north, south and east. A relaxed mix of US naval base, fishing port and beach resort, its closeness to Mexico gives it a marked Hispanic flavor.

It is as if the entire city came from common parents — Scott Fitzgerald and Isadora Duncan. (Anonymous 20thC writer, Hollywood)

The natural setting

From the earliest years of its history, the economic riches of California and its principal cities have been derived from the land: gold in the N, oil in the S, and an agriculturalist's Eden along the length of its Central Valley. This material wealth is matched by the aesthetic richness of the setting.

San Francisco Bay, 450 square miles of water entered through the Golden Gates, is among the world's finest and most visually pleasing natural harbors. The city itself, draped over tumbling hillsides and surrounded by water on three sides, offers an almost inexhaustible range of vistas. The flora of the Bay Area is equally compelling, and in the 1,017-acre Golden Gate Park, complete with lakes, meadows, waterfalls, English country-estate-style landscaping and Japanese Garden, San Francisco has an inner-city recreation area second to none.

It was not always so well manicured. Before the settlers tamed it, the San Francisco peninsula was a raw and barren expanse of rocky hills and sand dunes, swamps, tidal marshes and lagoons. Nowadays, probably the only taste of this former ruggedness is to be found along the cliffs fronting the Pacific. But for those who prefer the natural world red in tooth and claw, there is plenty to aim for.

Beyond the city are mountains, deserts, lakes, fertile valleys, cathedral-high coastlines and rugged offshore islands. From the NE corner of the state, the **Sierra Nevada** mountain range runs S for some 400 miles, a solid granite barrier reaching a height of 14,495 feet at Mount Whitney. Lower down its slopes are forests of giant sequoia, pine fir and cedar. From the NW, the gentler Coastal ranges, with elevations of between 2,000 and 7,000 feet, extend almost to Los Angeles, with northern evergreens giving way to oaks and finally a chaparral of stunted shrubs. Between the two there is the fertile Central Valley, some 40-50 miles wide.

San Francisco's favorite nature playground is probably **Yosemite National Park**, 1,169 square miles of protected wilderness on the western slope of the Sierra Nevada to the SE of the city. Extending from the mountains at the crest of the granite Sierra in the E to the dry foothills where the mountains run into the San Joaquin valley in the W, it is an area of startling beauty that quickly exhausts descriptive superlatives. All the hugeness of wild California is there. Its chain of mountains averages 10,000 feet, there are 429 lakes, canyons, glaciers, forests of oak, fir, maple and pine, and high mountain meadows. The **Upper Yosemite Falls** tumble 1,430 feet, or nine times as far as Niagara! The name "Yosemite" is thought to mean "grizzly bear" in the language of the original Miwok Indian inhabitants. Bears are still in residence, along with around a hundred varieties of mammal, 230 varieties of bird, and 1,200 types of flowering plants and ferns.

One third of California is desert. But it is seldom desert characterized by the monotony of sand dunes. The **High Desert** or **Mojave**, most of which falls within San Bernardino County, and the **Low Desert** or **Colorado** in the SE of the state, can both be unforgiving. Joshua trees, cacti, scrub and man-made oases aside, their flora offers little excitement, and the visible fauna seems limited to an occasional coyote.

Nonetheless, the landscape serves up an artist's palette of colors and shapes that might have been formed by whimsical giants. **Death Valley** offers a tranquility that is hard to duplicate.

Most of the **lakes** are in the N, and Tahoe, the biggest, ranks as one of the world's great alpine lakes. Farther s, the high, man-made **Arrowhead** and **Big Bear Lakes** provide easily accessible playgrounds for LA. Along much of the coast, particularly s of Monterey and N of San Francisco, the Pacific Coast Highway hairpins above majestic cliffs. The views, like the drive along Highway 1, can be literally breathtaking, especially if they include a sighting of migrating whales.

Sea bathing is another matter. N and s of San Francisco, as far as Santa Barbara, the waters of the Pacific Ocean are cold and more suited to well-kitted-out sailors or fishermen. Only s of Santa Barbara does the water become warm and the waves ruler-straight, making it a swimmer's and surfer's paradise.

Early sailors, less well equipped, believed California to be an island. We know better, but islands there are: the four **Catalinas**, the four **Santa Barbaras**, and a dozen smaller ones. Much of Santa Catalina, 27 miles sw of LA's harbor at Wilmington, is preserved, largely unscathed, as "open land."

California in general, and San Franciscans in particular, are more passionate about, and caring of, their natural environment than most. Recently, however, after several years of drought, doubts about the wisdom of mankind's stewardship of natural California have grown. In the Central Valley, intensive agriculture, with its associated toxic residues, overgrazing by cattle, and a sinking water table, have raised the specter of a repeat of the Oklahoma dustbowl disaster. Likewise, the fire that swept through suburban Oakland in October 1991, destroying 1,800 homes, posed questions about the breakneck colonization of rural California.

Transforming California into the richest and most populous state in the United States has involved considerable violence to the natural environment, and perhaps some lessons for the future will have been learned. For now, however, much of it remains generally unspoiled, having proved too big, uncompromising and remarkable even for late 20thC pioneers.

CALIFORNIA

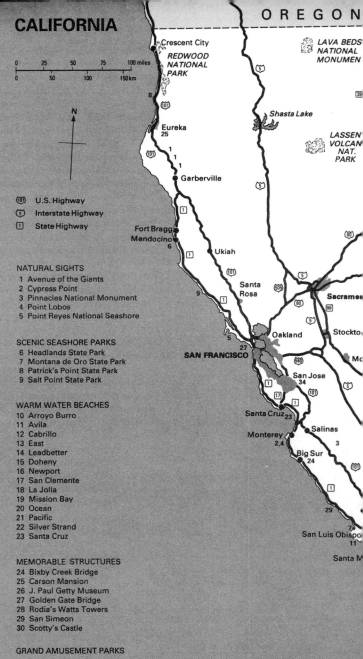

OREGON

Crescent City

REDWOOD NATIONAL PARK

LAVA BEDS NATIONAL MONUMEN

Shasta Lake

8

Eureka
25

1
1
1

Garberville

LASSEN VOLCAN NAT. PARK

Fort Bragg
Mendocino
6

Ukiah

Santa Rosa

9

Sacramen

Oakland

Stockto

SAN FRANCISCO
27

San Jose
34

San Jose

Santa Cruz 23

Monterey
2,4

Big Sur
24

Salinas

3

San Luis Obispo
11

Santa M

29

7

100 miles / 150 km scale

N

(101) U.S. Highway
(5) Interstate Highway
[1] State Highway

NATURAL SIGHTS
1 Avenue of the Giants
2 Cypress Point
3 Pinnacles National Monument
4 Point Lobos
5 Point Reyes National Seashore

SCENIC SEASHORE PARKS
6 Headlands State Park
7 Montana de Oro State Park
8 Patrick's Point State Park
9 Salt Point State Park

WARM WATER BEACHES
10 Arroyo Burro
11 Avila
12 Cabrillo
13 East
14 Leadbetter
15 Doheny
16 Newport
17 San Clemente
18 La Jolla
19 Mission Bay
20 Ocean
21 Pacific
22 Silver Strand
23 Santa Cruz

MEMORABLE STRUCTURES
24 Bixby Creek Bridge
25 Carson Mansion
26 J. Paul Getty Museum
27 Golden Gate Bridge
28 Rodia's Watts Towers
29 San Simeon
30 Scotty's Castle

GRAND AMUSEMENT PARKS
31 Disneyland
32 Knott's Berry Farm
33 Marineland
34 Marriott's Great America
35 Sea World
36 Six Flags Magic Mountain
37 Universal Studios

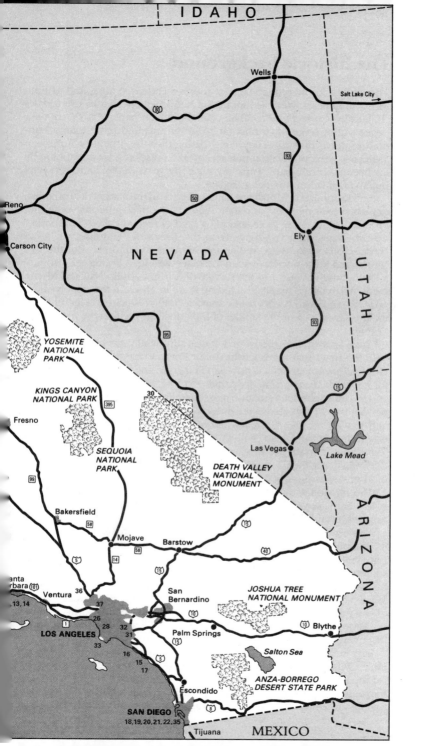

The historic background

The earliest known inhabitants of the San Francisco area, and of California in general, were seminomadic Native Americans (to use today's "Politically Correct" term). They numbered perhaps 150,000 at their peak, with a score of distinct language groups and more than a hundred regional dialects. They fared badly after the arrival of European settlers — their population ravaged by alien diseases, land-grabbing by Europeans, and Indian "wars." By the early years of the 20thC, the total Indian population was put at 16,000.

The European explorations gathered pace in the **16thC**, with Spanish explorers seeking to expand their king's Mexican dominion ever farther to the N and W. They were seeking a land of legend called "California," described as being "...very near to the Terrestrial Paradise." In **1525** Hernando Cortez discovered a land he named California. But the first White man known to have seen the place was Juan Rodriguez Cabrillo, a Portuguese navigator in the service of Spain. Cabrillo National Monument in San Diego marks his landing there in **1542**. In the same year he sighted San Pedro harbor and named it "Bay of Smokes;" legend has it that he saw the campfire smoke of Indian villages within the present LA County.

Then Spanish interest flagged. It was almost 40 years before it revived with the news that the Englishman Sir Francis Drake had anchored his *Golden Hinde* near what is now San Francisco and claimed the new land for England. More thorough Spanish explorations of the coast followed, and in **1602** Sebastian Vizcaino reasserted his monarch's claim. But it was not until **1697** that Jesuits received royal warrants to enter the territory, and it was another 70 years before the first permanent colony was established at San Diego. With the Jesuits out of favor by then, it was left to Franciscan friars and the army to extend the northward penetration. Between them, the Cross and the sword had by **1823** established a chain of 21 missions along 600 miles of the Camino Real or King's Highway. In **1776** a mission, Dolores, and a small military fortress had been founded at San Francisco. One of the first civilian settlements, in **1781**, was Los Angeles, established with 44 settlers.

Earnest development began in the **19thC**. First, in **1821**, Mexico won its independence from Spain and retained California as a colony. Relations between the Californios and their Mexican governors were strained, sometimes violent. But the watershed came in the early **1840**s with a quickening influx of American settlers. The Californios welcomed them; Mexico banned their further immigration. Finally, in **1846**, a small group of yanquis staged the "Bear Flag Revolt," declaring the California Republic. Then, 23 days later, Commodore John D. Sloat raised the American flag over Monterey and claimed California for the US.

The next surge of immigration followed almost immediately. News of James Wilson Marshall's discovery of gold, near what is now Sacramento, in January **1848**, prompted what has been described as the greatest mass movement of people since the Crusades. The previous year, the population had been put at 15,000. By **1850**, when California became the 31st state, it was nudging 100,000. A decade later it was close to 400,000. Many were "'49ers," as the Gold Rush arrivals were called, and much of the growth was in and around San Francisco, which fast emerged as the dominant city on the West Coast.

Ten years after the "Gold Rush," a "Silver Rush" further boosted San Francisco's prosperity and pre-eminence. Now it was a city confident enough to humor a man such as Joshua Abraham Norton, a failed English businessman and eccentric who, in **1859**, declared himself Emperor of the United States, and commanded his San Franciscan subjects to build bridges. In due course they did and, at the end of his 21-year "reign," 30,000 people attended his funeral.

By comparison, it took the completion of the transcontinental railroads — the South Pacific in **1876** and the Santa Fe in **1885** — to begin the transformation of Los Angeles from a sleepy pueblo. The people of the Mid-West began boarding trains and heading for Los Angeles and the newly irrigated farmlands around it and, by the **1880s**, it was the center of an hysterical property boom.

San Francisco, with its cable cars, enclaves of wealth and style and cosmopolitan sophistication, continued to overshadow the southern city until the turn of the century, when two things happened which altered the relationship. One was the discovery and commercial exploitation of oil in the LA area, which led to rapid economic expansion and population growth. The other was the San Francisco earthquake on **April 18, 1906**. In the fire that followed, 500 died or went missing and 5 square miles of the San Francisco area were destroyed.

Reconstruction plans were being drawn even as the ruins smoked, and within three years 20,000 new buildings had been constructed. A more thoughtful, more elegant San Francisco emerged from the trauma. But meanwhile Los Angeles had been accelerating ahead. Oil, the movies (the first motion picture studio opened in **1906**), the increasingly busy port of San Pedro, and agriculture fed by the astounding engineering feats of William Mulholland, all accelerated LA's growth. By the end of the **1920s** the population stood at 1.2 million, and already the city sprawled.

Post-quake San Francisco did its best to bounce back. The opening of the Panama Canal in **1914** boosted trade and manufacturing industries, and a year later celebrated the city's recovery with the Panama-Pacific International Exposition.

Immigrants continued to arrive — in the **1930s**, refugees from the Mid-West Dustbowl, many traveling down the famous Route 66; in the **1940s**, Europeans fleeing war and tyranny, and tens of thousands of servicemen demobilized on the West Coast after World War II; in the **1950s**, Blacks from the s and NE; and, through the decades, a rainbow of races, people from the "rustbelt states," from Eastern Europe, Indochina, the Middle East, Central America, seeking the better life so temptingly portrayed by Hollywood. Every wave fed San Francisco's greatest resource — the ambitious, enthusiastic, innovative, enterprising minds of its people.

In the **1960s** the social, political, cultural and sexual upheaval that changed the shape of American life took its lead and direction from

California. Henceforth it was said that what happened in California yesterday happens everywhere else tomorrow.

The demographic and political fulcrum had also moved. In **1980** Ronald Reagan, former Hollywood movie star and Governor of California from **1967-73**, became US President and served for two terms. It seemed to set the political seal on what West Coast people already knew; San Francisco and the other great cities of California had not only arrived, they were the vanguard of the nation's economic and cultural life, with their front door on the Pacific, the ocean of the future. Now they *must* be taken seriously.

Landmarks in California's history

San Francisco did not evolve in a vacuum. It is part of the wider historical experience of the State of California. The following chronology reflects this.

1510: "California" received its first mention, in Montalvo's fiction *Las Sergas de Esplandian*. **1542:** Sailing from New Spain (Mexico), Juan Rodriguez Cabrillo discovered San Diego Bay and claimed it for Spain. **1579:** Sir Francis Drake landed near San Francisco, named what he saw "New Albion" and claimed it for England.

1769: Father Junipero Serra established Spain's first California colony at San Diego. Gaspar de Portola's expedition reached San Francisco Bay. **1776:** As the American colonies declared independence from Great Britain, a Spanish mission and *presidio* (fortress) were founded at San Francisco. **1777:** Felipe de Neve made Monterey capital of California. **1781:** Pueblo (civilian settlement) founded at Los Angeles.

1796: First US ship, Ebenezer Dorr's *Otter,* anchored in a California port. **1812:** As the US fought the War of 1812, Russian fur traders established a colony at Fort Ross on the Sonoma coast.

1821: Mexico achieved independence from Spain, keeping California as a colony. **1828:** Jedediah Smith became the first White man to cross the Sierra Nevada. **1845:** Mexico ineffectually banned immigration of US settlers into California. Mary Peterson and James Williams became the first Americans to marry in California. **1846:** American settlers who overthrew the Mexican Government of General Mariano Vallejo in Bear Flag Revolt at Sonoma were put out of power within weeks as the US declared war on Mexico and seized California. Yerba Buena became San Francisco.

1848: John Marshall discovered gold in American River at Coloma, setting off the Gold Rush of **1849**. **1850:** California became the 31st American state. **1854:** Sacramento became the state's permanent capital.

1861: As the US was consumed by Civil War, California remained little more than a bystander, its sympathies divided between Union and Confederacy. The state's first vineyards were planted with 1,400 varieties of vines shipped in from Europe.

1868: The University of California was established at Berkeley. **1869:** The first transcontinental railroad was completed at Promontory Point, Utah, linking California with the E and ending the era of Pony Express and clipper ships around Cape Horn. "Emperor" Norton commanded bridges built across San Francisco Bay. **1872:** End of the Modoc War, the last major confrontation with the Indians of California.

1873: The first San Francisco cable car began operating. **1900:** Major oil discoveries in Los Angeles produced an economic boom there. **1904:** A.P. Giannini created the Bank of Italy in San Francisco. Eventually it would become the Bank of America.

1906: The Great Earthquake and Fire leveled much of San Francisco. Rebuilding began almost immediately. Beverly Hills was founded, along with the first motion picture studio. **1908:** The first commercial motion picture was filmed in Los Angeles, beginning the phenomenon of Hollywood.

1913: The 250-mile Los Angeles Aqueduct, bringing water from the distant Owens Valley, was completed. It allowed LA to annex the entire San Fernando Valley. **1915:** Panama-Pacific International Exhibition held in San Francisco. First transcontinental telephone call.

1928: Daily San Francisco-LA passenger flights began. **1932:** San Francisco opened its Opera House, and Los Angeles staged the summer Olympic Games. **1935:** Donald Douglas' great airplane, the DC-3, ushered in the age of air travel and launched California as a center of aerospace technology. Construction of the Central Valley Project began. **1937:** The Golden Gate Bridge was opened. **1945:** As World War II drew to a close, the United Nations founding assembly was held in SF.

1955: Disneyland opened, the forerunner of a host of theme parks and symbol of California's playfulness. **1958:** Planar technique of producing transistors devised by Fairchild Semiconductor, an electronics company in Santa Clara Valley, to the SE of San Francisco. This paved the way for the silicon chip, cornerstone of the microelectronics revolution. Major league baseball arrived with the San Francisco Giants and the Los Angeles Dodgers. **1960:** The Winter Olympics were held at Squaw Valley.

1964: California surpassed New York as the most populous US state. John Steinbeck won the Nobel Prize for Literature. **1967:** Ronald Reagan was elected State Governor, the *Queen Mary* was moored at Long Beach, and *Rolling Stone* magazine began publication in San Francisco. **1968:** The Summer of Love: hippies discovered sex and drugs and rock 'n' roll.

1971: Earthquake in the San Fernando Valley killed 64 people and caused more than $1 billion in damage. **1981:** The Mediterranean fruit fly (Medfly) infested Santa Clara County and neighboring areas, ushering in tight agricultural controls on the state's borders.

1984: LA staged the summer Olympic Games for a second time, matching the record of Athens, Paris and London. **1989:** Ronald and Nancy Reagan retired to Bel Air. The US's second worst earthquake hit the Bay Area causing more than $2 billion in damage. **1991:** California imposed water rationing after five years of drought. **1992:** Fire swept through Oakland at a cost of $1.5 billion. In the spring, violent rioting erupted in Los Angeles and fanned out across the United States.

The arts

Not unlike New York in its essentially European notions of what constitutes "culture," San Francisco takes itself seriously, at least some of the time. The arts have a long history here. One hundred years ago the city already had a population that was more cultured, literate and well educated than any other in the US. It mattered not that they had acquired these qualities elsewhere; they brought them to San Francisco. The city also had the wealth and the inclination to sustain the arts. Local historians like to recall that even in 1850, amid the bordellos of the Barbary Coast, the city boasted at least 15 legitimate theaters. Today, in the performing arts, the range and quality of theater, music, opera and dance, both mainstream and avant garde, are worthy of much bigger and older cities. And they benefit from the multitude of cultural traditions on which they are able to draw. The choices on offer range widely from classical performances at the **American Conservatory Theater** (ACT) to the wild iconoclasm of **Club Fugazi**, and the highly regarded **San Francisco Ballet**.

The same is true of the city's museums and galleries. The first San Francisco Arts Association was founded in 1871. Today the **M.H. de Young Museum** is among the West Coast's leading cultural institutions and boasts impressive collections of art from Europe, Asia and Africa as well as a notable American collection.

San Franciscans read books passionately and in inordinate amounts, and if they have a cultural Mecca it is the **City Lights** bookstore at North Beach. The Columbus Ave. shop, owned by poet Lawrence Ferlinghetti, took off in the 1950s and 1960s, publishing the works of Jack Kerouac and Allen Ginsberg. It became unofficial HQ for the San Francisco "**Renaissance**," an anti-establishment movement of poets, writers, jazz musicians and artists. Today, the beatniks are long gone, but Ferlinghetti is still there, and the cluttered shop carries an eclectic mix of literary, political and spiritual books and periodicals.

A bold, outspoken, convention-busting style has distinguished the literary life of this part of California since the Gold Rush days. It is to be found in the works of **Mark Twain, Jack London, John Steinbeck** and **Upton Sinclair**, and in books by **Dashiel Hammett, Henry Miller** and **Jack Kerouac**. Social criticism, articulating the views of the underdog, and poking fun at the greedy, pompous and corrupt are the norms to which fiction writers, as well as journalists, still aspire. As befits the city's sometimes wild and wooly past, San Francisco's artistic and literary scene feels perfectly at home in a metaphorical silk top hat, but insists on wearing it at a decidedly rakish angle.

An hour or three spent leafing through the arts and entertainments supplements of San Francisco's newspapers will give a taste of the explosive vitality of the city's cultural life. Name another city of 700,000 people with 80 theater companies! The richness of San Francisco's artistic scene is vitally important to its sense of identity and well being — not least because of the intense rivalry in this, as in most other things, with its bigger and brasher southern neighbor, Los Angeles.

THE MOVIES

Any consideration of the true literature of California cannot ignore motion pictures. From D.W. Griffith's *The Birth of a Nation,* through Orson Welles' *Citizen Kane,* Mike Nichols' *The Graduate* and Roman Polanski's *Chinatown* to Robert Towne's *Tequila Sunrise,* they and hundreds of other movies tell a vivid story of each generation's distractions and preoccupations. Whether it be sexual mores, the violent struggle for control of water, cocaine trafficking, or the latest trends in designer pasta, nowhere has had its social and cultural history more closely, creatively and entertainingly documented on film.

BACKGROUND READING

There is no shortage of significant literature preceding and paralleling the movies. Richard Henry Dana's *Two Years Before the Mast* contains excellent descriptions of southern California in the years before it was settled. Mark Twain's *The Celebrated Jumping Frog of Calaveras County* is only one example of his brilliant reporting of the Gold Country and early San Francisco. Robert Louis Stevenson's essays, collected as *From Scotland to Silverado,* tell wonderfully evocative tales of life in 1879-80, from crossing the Atlantic in steerage to the beginnings of the Napa Valley wine country. Even more romantic is Helen Hunt Jackson's *Ramona,* a sentimental novel that in its day captivated millions of Americans.

CALIFORNIA WRITERS

Among the first California-born writers to command more than local attention was Jack London. His early works *Tales of the Fish Patrol* and *John Barleycorn,* set in his native San Francisco Bay Area, contradict Stevenson's idyllic descriptions. John Steinbeck goes even farther in *The Grapes of Wrath,* and his story of the San Joaquin Valley establishment resisting an influx of impoverished farmers in *East of Eden* is one of the grimmest views of California on record. Steinbeck offers a more comic view of Monterey in two books, *Tortilla Flat* and *Cannery Row.* Nathanael West's *Day of the Locust* and Evelyn Waugh's *The Loved One* each provides in its different way a sharp-eyed, sharp-tongued exploration of southern California, in West's case through Hollywood, in Waugh's, inimitably, through the funeral industry.

However, the literature of LA and San Francisco probably reached its apogee in two writers who perfected a home-grown genre — that of the hard-boiled private eye. Dashiell Hammett's *The Maltese Falcon* and Raymond Chandler's *The Long Goodbye, Farewell My Lovely* and *The Big Sleep* are unequaled in their evocation of the moods, styles, geography and underlying realities of the cities. Inevitably perhaps, their works were turned into memorable movies.

More recently, Tom Wolfe's *Electric Kool-Aid Acid Test* and *The Pump House Gang* chronicle the Flower Power era in much the same kind of personal journalism that Mark Twain practiced on an earlier Californian society in upheaval. Ray Bradbury captures the essence of the sun-kissed society in one of his Martian tales *Dark They Were and Golden Eyed.* Gore

Vidal's *Myra Breckinridge,* for all its rather heavy-handed symbolism, is an entertaining romp through multilayered Californian illusion. Joan Didion's *The White Album* and *Play It As It Lays* offer penetrating insights. And the works of thriller writers Robert Campbell and James Ellroy offer a chilling contemporary vision of LA's "mean streets".

PICTURES AND PAINTERS

In California, photographs are to paintings what motion pictures are to plays. The photographs of Ansel Adams, from the 1930s onward, have given the world images of the Californian landscape (most notably of Yosemite National Park and Death Valley) that are as potent and memorable, if not more so, than those of Albert Bierstadt, the state's most celebrated landscape painter. Photography in California began with the Gold Rush and provides a wonderful historical record. Interest in photography as an art form here is such that outstanding prints can command prices comparable with those fetched by paintings and drawings.

Among contemporary artists, the British painter David Hockney has done something to redress the balance. His seemingly clichéd paintings of deep-blue swimming pools, flanked by palm trees, and cube-shaped buildings in desert colors, capture a unique reality that is at once both commonplace and central to the experience of southern California. Also prominent on the extremely fertile art scene are internationally acclaimed artists such as Mark Rothko, Diego Rivera, Robert Graham, Richard Diebenkorn, Ed Ruscha, Billy Al Bengston and Charles Arnolds.

If you're alive, you can't be bored in San Francisco
(William Saroyan as a half-starved young Armenian writer
during the Great Depression)

San Francisco's architecture

Nothing characterizes San Francisco's complex ethnic groups and its location in the Pacific Basin so much as its architecture. The various races have each laid down their respective styles: Spanish Mission churches, Central European Baroque civic splendor, Hispanic and Italianate frontages, Chinese and Japanese temples, Victorian "gingerbread" houses that are so reminiscent of England.

Rising from the Marina shoreline on the Bay, the grid pattern of terraces climbs the undulating hills, the houses mostly without enormous distinction but never without gems in their midst. If the grid appears to offer no nodal point of high interest like the Paris Arc de Triomphe or London's Trafalgar Square, the various neighborhoods each offer landmarks of especial interest. The nearest to a focal point is the **Civic Center Plaza**, including the two-blocks-square **City Hall**, modeled on the Capitol in Washington and even exceeding the height of its dome. This merging of its significant architecture into its streetscape bestows a certain domestic ease about the place, and when the 1980s' rash of Manhattan mania threatened to engulf the downtown area in skyscrapers, the city fathers introduced legislation to curb it.

The Baroque **San Francisco City Hall** (1915) by Arthur Brown Jr and John Bakewell Jr was built as part of the superb Civic Center following the 1906 earthquake and fire. The Civic Center is regarded as the finest grouping of Beaux Arts architecture in the US.

The original Hispanic-Mexican flavor of San Francisco was gradually overlaid in the 19thC with the spread of "Victorian" domestic building to cope with the Gold Rush of 1849 and the huge volume of subsequent immigration. In the relatively cool climate, European and New England

29

Bank of Canton

styles predominate. Bay windows, handsome portals and "areas" in front of houses are typical. But there are also more affluent styles, originally introduced to satisfy the rising bourgeoisie round the turn of the century.

The beautiful terrace of matching houses known as the "**Painted Ladies**" is the much-photographed jewel of the 14,000 examples of Victorian residences built between 1850 and 1900. About half this number have been maintained or restored by a populace keen to keep faith with its past. The richest remaining Victorians are to be found w of Van Ness Ave., with a smaller share in the Mission district South of Market, the fires that followed the 1906 earthquake having been responsible for the virtual devastation of 514 blocks of the northeast side.

Gradually, real estate has risen in value in the city proper, since the peninsular nature of the city inhibits spread, and apartment blocks now house a large section of the population. These blocks are redeemed by a variety of styles, Art Deco, Brownstone, post-Corbusier glass boxes and now Post-Modern, each style cherished by the occupants, for eccentricity is a virtue in San Francisco. The curving facades of **Sea Cliff** terraces with their view over the Pacific are now enjoyed by the wealthy only.

Places of worship abound in San Francisco. The oldest, naturally, belongs to the early Spanish settlement, and the **Mission Dolores** (pictured on page 58) dates from 1776. The Neo-Gothic **Grace Cathedral** dominates the Huntington Park district near the center, and is perhaps most notable for its bronze doors, from casts taken of Ghiberti's *Gates of Heaven* in the Baptistry in Florence. Only a city with such a strong Italian contingent could earn such a privilege.

The highly Italianate church of **St Peter and St Paul** merits attention, and depending on whether your reaction be favorable or hostile, the **St Mary's Cathedral of the Assumption** (pictured on page 75), described as "hyperbolic paraboloid" in form, and the creation of international architects Pietro Belluschi and Pier Luigi Nervi, may be well worth the trip up Geary Boulevard.

Civic Center architect Arthur Brown Jr. was responsible, too, for the **Temple Emanu-El**, and the marked contrast between the two, massively domed buildings pinpoints Brown's versatility.

The **California Palace of the Legion of Honor**, in its parkland setting, excites both architectural and visual arts interest, since it houses an illustrious art collection and is itself a replica of Napoleon's edifice housing his *Légion d'Honneur* in Paris. Despite its temporary closure for restoration and seismic upgrading, it can still be admired from the outside.

The **Coit Tower** near the lower end of Lombard Street offers a fine panoramic view over the Bay and city and is in itself an imposing structure, commemorating one of the city's more famous eccentrics, Lillie Coit, who left enough funds to the city to thus remember the volunteer firemen of old San Francisco. The angular **John Hancock Building** (1959) reacts against the rash of glass cubes and is a sturdy example from the Chicago school of Skidmore, Owings and Merrill, while their more recent (1980) **Louise M.Davies Symphony Hall**, with its wrap-around auditorium, is an exercise in curve and light. Downtown, the 1980s **Marriott Hotel** calls to mind a giant Wurlitzer and has earned itself the epithet "Jukebox Marriott" from local wags.

Vedanta House

Another structure likely to excite love or hate, and nothing in between, is the tallest building on the San Francisco skyline. It is the **Transamerica Pyramid** (pictured overleaf), which had the curious distinction of being designed by Los Angeles architect William Pereira. More obelisk than pyramid in profile, it pierces the sky with needle-sharp audacity.

One of the most significant Post-Modern complexes is the **San Francisco Shopping Centre** on Market Street, from the city's own Whisler-Patri stable. It has a fine, if inevitable, atrium, and the justly famous spiral escalators, engineered to a Mitsubishi design.

The Oriental connection is emphasized in many places. The famous **Dragon Gate** (pictured on page 56) marks the frontier of Chinatown, at Grant Ave. and Bush St. Eyes should be raised from store-window level to take in the full splendor of the decorative arts of China that are emblazoned on so many buildings. The oldest (1909) oriental-style building is a three-tiered "temple." Now occupied by the **Bank of Canton**, the building once housed the Chinatown Telephone Exchange.

An even more bizarre influence is evident in **Vedanta House**, Joseph Leonard's tribute to Hindu tolerance, its towers topped by a fantastic rook and a turban. The strong Japanese presence in San Francisco is affectionately remembered by the remarkable **Peace Pagoda** (pictured on page 57) in the **Japan Center**, a gift from the Japanese people. Designed by Yoshiro Taniguchi, it rises 100 feet and perpetuates a commemorative tradition that goes back 1,200 years.

In the hinterland beyond San Francisco, one of the world's most flourishing viticultures in the Napa Valley and Sonoma bears exciting remnants of the old Mexican-style California, with further eccentricities such as Samuel Brannan's clapboard and Gothic fantasies, the rustic wineries built by the original wine buff Count Haraszthy, or Beringer's Belgian Art Nouveau mansion in St Helena.

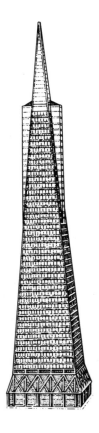

The **Transamerica Pyramid**

The only city I'd be sorry to leave in the United States is San
Francisco, where I have a feeling of being near home.
(Graham Greene — an Englishman resident in France)

Basic information

Before you go

DOCUMENTS REQUIRED

British citizens except those from Northern Ireland, and citizens of New Zealand, Japan, and all Western European countries except Greece, no longer need a visa to visit the US, provided that their stay will last for 90 days or less and is for vacation or business purposes. If arriving by air or sea, the visitor must be traveling with an approved carrier (most are) and must have an **onward or return ticket**. (Open or standby tickets are acceptable.) If entering overland from Canada or Mexico, no visa is required. An unexpired **passport** is also essential.

British subjects will need to obtain a visa, as will any British citizen who wishes to stay more than 90 days for whatever reason, has a criminal record, has suffered from tuberculosis, is suffering from AIDS, is HIV-positive or has previously been refused a visa. The US embassy in London has a useful recorded message for all general visa inquiries (☎ *(0898) 200290)*. If you need a visa, it is wise to allow plenty of time.

You must show a valid **driver's license** and, unless you are a US citizen, a passport, in order to rent a car. For visitors from most countries, an international driver's license is not required. Some firms ask to see your return ticket. Most rental companies will offer to sell you short-term insurance and it is wise to take it, unless your own policy gives adequate coverage. If you are arriving by private car from other states or countries, bring the **car registration document** and **certification of insurance**.

TRAVEL AND MEDICAL INSURANCE

US medical care is good, but expensive, and medical insurance is strongly recommended. UK travel agents have the necessary forms, and tour operators frequently include medical coverage in their packages. Baggage insurance is recommended in case of theft. American Express offers baggage insurance to card members, as do automobile clubs.

MONEY

The basic unit is, of course, the dollar ($). It is divided into 100 cents (¢). Coins are: the penny 1¢, nickel 5¢, dime 10¢, quarter 25¢ and half dollar 50¢. Bank notes (bills) in general circulation are in denominations of $1, $5, $10, $20, $50 and $100. A few $2 bills are in circulation. Any amount of money may be imported or exported, but when the total exceeds $10,000 you must register with the US Customs Service.

It is wise to carry **cash** in small amounts only, keeping the remainder in dollar **travelers checks**. Those issued by American Express, Bank of America, Barclays, Citibank and Thomas Cook are widely recognized, and MasterCard and Visa have also introduced them. Make sure you read the instructions included with your travelers checks. Note separately the serial numbers and the telephone number to call in case of loss. Specialist travelers check companies such as American Express provide extensive local refund facilities through their own offices or agents. Many shops accept dollar travelers checks.

Charge/credit cards are welcomed by nearly all hotels, airlines and car rental agencies, and most restaurants, garages and shops. American Express, Diners Club, MasterCard and Visa are the major cards in common use. While personal checks drawing on out-of-town banks are seldom accepted, many hotels will cash small amounts in conjunction with a charge/credit card.

American Express also has a **Moneygram®** money transfer service that makes it possible to wire money worldwide in just minutes, from any American Express Travel Service Office. This service is available to all customers and is not limited to American Express Card members. See USEFUL ADDRESSES on page 48.

CUSTOMS

Returning US citizens present themselves and their luggage to a single officer for inspection. All others must first clear passport control, collect their baggage and then move on to a customs official. Although the process has been streamlined, the combination of three Jumbo jets disgorging at once and government concern over smuggling can slow things down to a crawl. It may take no more than 30 minutes from plane to street, but an hour or more is not unusual.

Nonresidents can bring in any items clearly intended for personal use, duty-free, with the exceptions noted below.

Tobacco goods   200 cigarettes *or* 50 cigars *or* $4\frac{1}{2}$ lbs (2kg) tobacco. An additional 100 cigars may be brought in under your gift exemption (see OTHER GOODS below).

Alcoholic drinks   Adults over 18 are allowed up to 1 quart (1 liter) of spirits.

Other goods   Nonresidents may also import up to $100 in gifts without tax or duty if remaining in the US at least 72 hours. Returning residents are granted a duty-free allowance of $400, on goods brought back personally. Families traveling together can pool their allowances to cover joint purchases. For more information on customs regulations, a brochure entitled *US Customs Hints* can be obtained from US embassies and consulates, or directly from the Department of the Treasury, US Customs Service, Box 7407, Washington, DC 20044.

TOURIST OFFICE

American Visitors should make contact with the **San Francisco Convention and Visitors Bureau** *(201 3rd St., Suite 900* ☎ *974-6900)*. Visitors from the UK can obtain much useful information from the **US**

Travel and Tourism Administration, P.O. Box 1EN, London W1A 1EN (☎ *(071) 495-4466)*.

GETTING THERE

San Francisco International Airport, 14 miles S of downtown on US-101, *(map 9 F3)*, is served by nearly all major national and international airlines. It is the fifth busiest airport in the US and the seventh in the world, handling 1,300 flights a day and served by 34 major scheduled carriers. The North Terminal and South Terminal handle domestic airlines; the International (Central) Terminal handles overseas flights. Arrival is at the lower level, departure at the upper level.

A free **shuttle service** is available within the airport. There is protected short-term parking for some 7,000 vehicles, but it is often full. Valet parking is also provided. Facilities within the airport include a communications center *(upper level, International Terminal)* for long-distance calls, a choice of restaurants and bars, gift stores and newsstands. For reservations and up-to-date flight information most airlines have toll-free (800) numbers detailed under "Air Line Companies" in the *Yellow Pages*.

For general flight information ☎555-1212. For information on services for disabled travelers ☎573-9688. See also the list of airlines on page 48.

Ground transportation to San Francisco and other parts of the Bay Area includes buses from the lower level, outside baggage claim areas (reservations recommended before collecting baggage), taxis from stands on the lower level, and limousines by prior reservation. San Francisco is sufficiently compact to make taxis affordable in a way that they are not in Los Angeles.

ALTERNATIVE AIRPORTS

San Francisco International is the biggest but not the only airport in the Bay Area. There are smaller airports that could be a more convenient alternative for flights within the US.

Oakland International Airport   Doolittle and Airport Way
☎839-7488
San Jose International Airport   1661 Airport Blvd. ☎(408)
277-4759

BY CAR

For drivers, five major interstate freeways ("I" routes) connect California to points S, E and N. Scenic N-S routes running through San Francisco are US-101 and SR-1. They merge near the Golden Gate bridge and continue as one into Marin County. However, the SR-1 coastal route can be subject to fog. A quicker N-S route is the I-5, running to the E of the city. It runs from San Diego in the S through the length of California and up to the Pacific Northwest, and is kept open all year, although drivers can be subjected to delays in winter, when snowstorms blanket the Siskiyou Mountains on the California-Oregon border.

The main approach from the E is along the I-80 from the Sierras. This route crosses some of the higher parts of the Sierra Nevada and the Rocky

Mountains before ending at San Francisco. It is also kept open all year, but there can be snowstorms between October and April.

For information on **highway conditions** ☎557-3755.

BY TRAIN

Amtrak, the subsidized passenger rail service, runs daily trains on three interstate routes from San Francisco and Los Angeles (☎*(800) 872-7245)*. One daily train connects both San Francisco and Los Angeles with the Pacific Northwest. The second connects San Francisco with Chicago via Reno and Denver. The third connects Los Angeles with points NE and SE including Las Vegas, Phoenix, Houston and New Orleans. Rail services to San Francisco terminate in **Oakland** at the 16th St. Station. Passengers are carried on the final leg of their journey by bus to the city's Transbay Terminal at 1st and Mission Sts.

BY SHIP

Dozens of oceangoing steamship lines and cruise vessels serve San Francisco.

CLIMATE

California's climates are as varied as its people and its cuisines. In San Francisco and along N coastal areas, warm summers are tempered by cool sea breezes and persistent fog, while winters are generally wet. Average temperatures vary between 54-65°F (12-18°C) from March to October and from 48-59°F (9-15°C) from November to February.

Elsewhere in the state, inland areas have drier, hotter summers that are less oppressive on the hills than in the valleys.

It is said that the temperature rises 10° with every 10 miles you travel away from the city. When it's a comfortable 65° in San Francisco, it will be 80° to the N in Marin County, to the S on the peninsula or to the E, while 88 miles away in Sacramento, the mercury will have risen to 100°.

Winters are both colder and drier than on the coast. Southern deserts are warm in winter but often intolerably hot in summer. Mountain regions enjoy four distinct seasons: fine, cold winters; warm, sunny summers; and changeable springs and falls.

The famous San Francisco fogs provide the city with its own air conditioning, but neither the coolness nor the fog will necessarily last for more than a few hours.

Fall is the warmest season; the foghorns sound most often July through September; the Golden Gate never sees snow.

For daily **weather information** ☎936-1212.

CLOTHES

What to wear will be dictated by exactly where you are going, given the variations in temperature described above. San Franciscans themselves are most comfortable in a wardrobe of spring clothes — knits, light wools and worsteds — which can be worn throughout the year. An all-weather coat may be needed for the cooler evenings, and lightweight summer clothes are very much an optional extra.

San Francisco is an intensely fashion-conscious city and visitors will feel most comfortable if they dress "up" and not "down." Men should expect to wear a tie and jacket at lunch or dinner in many of the city's best restaurants. Many clubs now frown on "sneakers," and elsewhere, the not uncommon notice "No shoes, no shirt, no service" speaks for itself.

Other tips: women may find a headscarf to be the best protection against Pacific breezes and summer fogs; and remember to pack some comfortable shoes, as you should expect to do a lot of walking.

MAIL

Visitors choosing not to receive mail in care of their hotels can use US Postal Service General Delivery (poste restante), addressed to any small town post office. In cities, only one post office, usually the main office downtown, is equipped to handle General Delivery. The address for such mail in SF is: Main Post Office, San Francisco, CA 94103.

The main **Post Office** is located at 7th St. and Mission, just s of Market St. (☎ *556-2500, map 6 D8).*

For **telegram, telex or fax**, contact **Western Union** (☎ *392-7785),* or *International Telephone & Telegraph (* ☎(800) 922-0184).

Stamps can frequently be bought in hotels and drugstores.

Getting around

BUSES FROM THE AIRPORT

Airporter   To downtown, every 20 minutes 5am-midnight, less frequently throughout the night ☎495-8404.

Door to Door Airport Express   To downtown, every hour 5.30am-10.30pm, reservations required ☎775-5121.

Francisco Adventure   24-hour shuttle from downtown to San Francisco and San Jose airports, plus sightseeing tours throughout N California ☎821-0903.

Marin Airporter   To Sausalito and Marin County destinations, every 30 minutes 6am-midnight ☎461-4222.

Supershuttle   Door-to-door throughout San Francisco, around the clock ☎871-7800, (415) 558-8500.

Yellow Airport Shuttle   To hotels and door-to-door throughout San Francisco and Bay Area, around the clock, reservations recommended ☎282-7433.

PUBLIC TRANSPORTATION

San Francisco's public transportation network is probably the most user-friendly in California. This is mainly due to its **Municipal Railway** ("**Muni**") *(for route information* ☎*673-MUNI),* which blankets the city with bargain-priced light rail, trackless trolley, bus and cable car lines. Better still, take advantage of the one-, three- or seven-day "Muni Pass-port." Passengers are entitled to unlimited rides throughout the Muni system, and the savings are enormous. The passport, available widely and through Visitor Information Centers, also brings discounted admission to more than 24 visitor attractions.

You should always carry the exact fare, as drivers do not give change. Timetables are available from Metro station booths, AC Transit booths, and on Muni trolleys and buses.

Cable cars run on three routes: the Powell-Hyde line from Powell and Market Sts. to Victoria Park near the Maritime Museum; the Powell-Mason line from Powell and Market to Bay St. near Fisherman's Wharf; and the California line from Market St. to Van Ness Ave. All-day passes are available. Buy your ticket before you board.

Ferry services include **Golden Gate Ferries** (☎ *332-6600), from* the s end of the Ferry Building at the foot of Market St., crossing the Bay to Sausalito in about 30 minutes; **Red & White Fleet** (☎ *546-2896),* from Pier 43½ to Sausalito, in addition to tours from Pier 41; and **Blue and Gold Fleet** (☎ *781-7877),* running Bay tours from Pier 39. Tours circle Alcatraz and pass beneath both the Golden Gate and Bay Bridge.

The **Bay Area Rapid Transit** (**BART**) is a modern light rail system with lines running s from Market St. to the Mission district and Daly City and E to Oakland, Berkeley and other East Bay cities (☎ *788-2278; runs Mon-Sat 6am-midnight, Sun 9am-midnight).* Excursion tickets are available. However, BART is more useful for travel to and from the suburbs than within the city proper.

See also page 61 for buses and trains beyond San Francisco.

BUSES

There are bus connections from the **Amtrak** depot at 16th St. in Oakland to the Transbay Bus Terminal on 1st and Mission Sts., map **6**C9. Other bus services:

Greyhound Lines   Depot at 101 7th St., one block s of Market, map **6**D8.

Trailways, Inc.   Depot at 1st St. and Mission St., map **6**C9.

AC Transit   ☎839-2882; bus services to East Bay cities such as Berkeley, Oakland and Treasure Island, as well as other cities in Alameda and Contra Costa counties via the Bay Bridge.

Owl Service   Buses take over from Muni Metro from 1-5am.

Golden Gate Transit   ☎332-6600, runs from the Transbay Terminal at First and Mission Sts. into Marin and Sonoma Counties.

TAXIS

The comparatively small size of San Francisco makes for taxi rides that remain affordable. Taxis maintain stands at most major hotels, and additional companies are listed in the *Yellow Pages.* Or try:

City   ☎468-7200
De Soto   ☎673-1414
Luxor   ☎282-4141
Pacific   ☎776-6688
Sunshine   ☎776-7755, with Chinese-speaking drivers
Veteran's   ☎552-1300
Yellow Cab   ☎626-2345

LIMOUSINES

Limousine services are available for sightseeing tours or general transportation for individuals or groups. Some names to try:

Chauffeured Limousines   ☎344-4400, (800) 338-8200
A Classic Ride   Vintage limousines ☎626-0433
First Class Limousine   ☎261-5213
Golden Gate Limousine   ☎487-0531
Milt's Livery Service   ☎952-0466
San Francisco Sightseeing & Tours Inc.   ☎777-0102
Visit USA Bureau Inc.   ☎391-0500, (800) 722-0872

RENTING A CAR

Perhaps the best way to travel. Major car rental firms include Airway, Avis, Budget, Dollar, Econocar, Hertz, National and Thrifty. All have a downtown office, and a depot near San Francisco International airport; many have them at the smaller airports too and have toll-free (**800**) numbers through which reservations can be made. Advance reservation is recommended.

It is worthwhile shopping around, even among the major car rental firms; rates can vary and managers will often negotiate. Fly-drive packages, available through airlines, may offer the most favorable rates for renting a car. Rent-it-here/leave-it-there arrangements are available, but they can be expensive. In addition, major cities have cut-price firms such as **Rent-a-wreck**, offering old but sound vehicles at relatively low prices.

Most car-rental firms offer insurance packages additional to those required by law. Given the high costs of medical care and the potentially astronomical costs of litigation, these are well worth considering. The especially cautious should consult their insurance broker before leaving home. Limousine services are widely available as a relaxing alternative to rental cars.

Alamo Rent-a-Car   Cars and vans at competitive rates ☎882-9440
Autoexotica   Top-name sports and luxury cars ☎885-6655
Avis Rent-a-Car   75 locations in s California ☎885-5011, (800) 331-1212
Budget Rent-a-Car   American and prestige European cars, convertibles ☎875-6850, (800) 527-0700
Dollar Rent-a-Car   Late-model economy and luxury American and Japanese cars ☎771-5300, airport 244-4130, worldwide 1-800-800-4000
Hertz Corporation   Ford cars, with special group and convention rates ☎771-2200, (800) 654-3131
Rent-A-Wreck   Used cars, vans, trucks at rates up to 50 percent below competitors (after a short closure for relocation, Rent-a-Wreck will reopen later in 1992: check *Yellow Pages* for new details)
Thrifty Rent-a-Car   Convention rates ☎673-6675, (800) 367-2277

TOURS

Agentours Inc.   157 West Portal Ave. ☎661-5200, half-day sightseeing with multilingual guides.

Alcatraz ☎546-2896, (800) 445-8880, from Pier 41 from 8.45am, reservations recommended in summer. Map **5**A7.

American Express Travel Service Office 237 Post St. ☎981-5533, (415) 981-6293, map **6**C8, 4-hour narrated tours of Sausalito and Muir Woods, 8-hour visit to wine country, all-day tours of Monterey Peninsula and Carmel.

Ami Tours 808 Post St., Suite 1430 ☎474-8868, map **5**D7, city and out-of-town tours including Victorian houses, wine country and coastline, plus customized tours.

Bargain Bus ☎533-0874, 7-hour tour of garment district; designer clothes at discount prices, hotel pick-ups.

Cable Car Charters Inc. 2830 Geary Blvd. ☎922-2425, map **4**D4, narrated tours of San Francisco from Pier 39 and Pier 41.

Carriage Charter Pier 41 at Powell and Jefferson Sts. ☎398-0857, map **6**B8, horse-drawn carriages around Fisherman's Wharf, North Beach from 1pm.

Commodore Helicopters 240 Redwood Highway, Highway 101 ☎332-4482, city, Bay, bridges and wine country from the air.

Express Tours Unlimited PO Box 77267, San Francisco 94107 ☎621-7738, (800) 535-3500, city tours plus Monterey, Reno, Yosemite (May-December), by reservation only.

The Gray Line Inc. Powell and Geary Sts. ☎558-9400. Bay Area tours including Alcatraz, Sausalito, San Francisco-by-night, Monterey, Carmel, Marin County, wine country.

HMS Tours 1057 College Ave., Suite 206 ☎(707) 526-2922, (800) 331-6086, wine country tours and hot-air balloon rides, hotel pick-ups.

Otis Spunkmeyer Air Tours North Field, Oakland International Airport ☎667-3800, (800) 634-1165, 1-hour tours by restored Douglas DC-3 with in-flight refreshments.

San Francisco Bay Tours Inc. 2690 3rd St. ☎550-8954, map **2**D5, city, Berkeley, Monterey, Carmel, Yosemite, with Japanese-speaking guides.

San Francisco Gourmet Tour 1550 California St., Suite 6164 ☎781-TOUR, map **5**C7, the city's best restaurants by limo.

Scenic Cycling Aventours PO Box 583, Ross 94957 ☎453-0676, 4-hour tours of San Francisco and Marin County, bicycles and picnics provided.

Super City Tours Inc. 2143 Powell St. ☎391-9805, map **6**B8, multilingual tours of San Francisco and Bay Area by day or night.

Ticketeasy 50 Joice St., Suite 7 ☎956-1765, map **6**C8, unusual, inventive tours of San Francisco at affordable prices: churches, theaters, factories, private homes. Lunch/dinner included.

Trancisco Tours 601 California St., Suite 704 ☎477-9706, map **6**C8, wine and dine on a mini-vacation aboard the *Sierra 49er Express*. Packages include luxury train rides and hotel accommodations at Lake Tahoe, Reno and mountain ski resorts.

DRIVING

San Francisco proper is of such a manageable size that visitors may not wish or need to drive. This is fortunate; parking and rush-hour congestion can be a problem, for this is not an automobile city like Los Angeles. Taxis are relatively plentiful, distances unlikely to tax the wallet, and public transportation is excellent.

But, if you do wish to drive, the grid system of streets makes the city reasonably easy to navigate, and only the widespread one-way systems frustrate the simplicity of it all. The main thing to remember is to turn the wheels of the car toward the street when parking uphill, and when parking downhill to turn the wheels toward the curb. This is not just good advice to guard against runaway vehicles on the city's steep hills; it is also required by law.

Laws on stopping and parking are quite strictly enforced. See LAWS AND REGULATIONS on page 46. If your car is towed away, you must obtain a release from the nearest district police department, then collect your car from the towing company.

Independent excursions into neighboring counties are best undertaken by car, and many of the routes (especially the northbound Pacific Coast Highway) afford spectacular scenery. Within the city the only really compelling reason to be auto-mobile is the "49-Mile Drive." Originated for the 1939-40 International Exposition, the half-day drive snakes through the city past major points of architectural, historical and scenic interest, including the splendid Golden Gate Park. The route is well signposted, and the Visitor Information Center (see USEFUL ADDRESSES on page 48) provides free maps.

The **California State Automobile Association (AAA-California)** is located at 150 Van Ness Ave. (☎ *565-2012, map* **5** *E7, members only).*

Contact the **Department of Motor Vehicles** *(*☎ *(415) 557-1191)* for a copy of the *California Driver's Handbook,* summarizing traffic regulations.

GETTING AROUND ON FOOT

It is best to cross only at pedestrian crossings — usually at traffic lights and intersections. When there are pedestrian signals, cross only when the light reads "Walk" or a small walking figure appears. At crossings without traffic lights, traffic is supposed to (but doesn't always) stop for pedestrians. Walking along or across freeways is prohibited. Walking alone at night should be avoided in some neighborhoods (see WALKING, below).

WALKING

Do walk. Although some of the steeper hills can be taxing, and a handful of neighborhoods, such as the Tenderloin, the Mission district and Haight-Ashbury, can be intimidating after dark, the city's compactness and climate make walking a pleasure. The best approach is to identify a few destinations and an approximate route, then just ramble; there are few streets without something to interest or delight, be it an unusual building, a dusty bookstore or a chic café.

Otherwise, structured walking tours — many of them free — are available: Civic Center, North Beach, Japantown, Market St. etc. by

Friends of the Library (☎ 558-3981); Chinatown by the **Chinese Cultural Foundation** (☎ 986-1822); the **Chinatown Walk 'n Wok** guided tour, including kitchens (☎ 355-9656); Golden Gate Park by **Friends of Recreation and Parks** (☎ 221-1311); the Victorian and Edwardian mansions of Pacific Heights by the **Foundation for San Francisco Architectural Heritage** (☎ 441-3004); and the **Maltese Falcon Tour**, an exploration of crime-writer Dashiell Hammett's San Francisco (☎ 564-7021).

SPEED LIMITS
Maximum speed limits are indicated on most California roads. Freeway and highway maximums are 55mph; on some busy highways, speed limits may be 50 or 45mph. In city and town centers and in residential areas, the maximum speed is 25mph; on main urban thoroughfares, 30 or 35mph. On roads that pass schools, there is a speed limit of 25mph during school hours. All of these are maximums: you can be charged with reckless driving at lower speeds when driving conditions are poor.

On-the-spot information

PUBLIC HOLIDAYS
January 1; Martin Luther King Day, third Monday in January; President's Day, third Monday in February; Memorial Day, last Monday in May; Independence Day, July 4 (but businesses close on nearest Monday or Friday); Labor Day, first Monday in September; Columbus Day, second Monday in October; Veterans Day, November 11; Thanksgiving, last Thursday in November; December 25.

Banks and almost all businesses are closed on these days, although shops often stay open for sales. Good Friday is a half-day holiday; many offices close on Easter Monday.

TIME ZONES
All of California is within the Pacific Time Zone: 3 hours behind New York, 2 hours behind Chicago and 1 hour behind Denver. The Pacific Time Zone is 8 hours behind Greenwich Mean Time. Daylight Saving Time runs from the first Sunday in April through the last Saturday in October.

BANKS AND FOREIGN EXCHANGE
Normal business hours for banks are Monday-Thursday 10am-3pm and Friday 10am-5pm. An increasing number of banks keep later weekday hours; fewer open on Saturday. Travel service firms typically open Monday-Friday 9am-5pm and Saturday 10am-noon.

Banks can sometimes present a problem if you wish to change foreign currency and travelers checks. Unless you are a regular customer, there may be a hefty service charge.

But there are alternatives. In addition to the **American Express Travel Service Offices** listed under USEFUL ADDRESSES, there are the **Bank of America Foreign Exchange Office** (*Central Terminal, San Francisco International Airport* ☎ *876-7055, open daily 7am-11pm*), **Thomas Cook** (*100 Grant Ave., downtown* ☎ *362-3452, map* **6** *D8, open Monday-Friday 9am-6pm*) and **Foreign Exchange Ltd** (*415 Stockton St., at Union Sq.* ☎ *397-4700, map* **6** *D8, open Monday-Friday 8.30am-5pm, Saturday 9am-1.30pm*).

SHOPPING AND BUSINESS HOURS

Department stores and **clothes and sports equipment stores** generally open between 9 and 10am and close at 5.30 or 6pm. **Late-night shopping**, particularly in the malls, is usually until 9pm on Thursday. The larger **supermarket chains** and **drugstores** are open 24 hours seven days a week. **Coffee shops** and **fast-food restaurants** may open as early as 6am and close as late as midnight; some stay open around the clock. More formal **restaurants** open from about noon-3pm and 6-11pm, with last orders an hour earlier. **Bars and cocktail lounges** do not have to close until 2am.

RUSH HOURS

Morning freeway rush hours begin at 6am, reach a peak between 7 and 8am, then ebb by 9.30am; the evening rush begins by 4pm, peaks by 5pm, and ebbs at major intersections after 7pm.

TELEPHONE SERVICES

San Francisco's area code **415** has now been split, and a new code — **510** — has been assigned to encompass all of Alameda and Contra Costa counties in the East Bay, including the communities of Oakland, Berkeley, Richmond, Martinez, Concord, San Leandro, Hayward, Fremont, Pleasanton and Livermore. Marin County and the peninsula cities keep the **415** code. The area code for the wine country is **707**.

When dialing outside the **415** code area, callers must always dial **1** plus the appropriate area code and seven-digit number. Check the telephone directory or consult a local person before dialing.

Public telephones are numerous and are usually in working order. Pay telephones accept 5¢, 10¢ and 25¢ coins. Local calls cost between 15¢ and 25¢. Long-distance charges are paid as the call progresses, so arm yourself with a heap of coins. Helpful operators will give guidance on how much you need. Long-distance rates reduce sharply between 6pm and 8am and are lowest on Saturday.

In addition to their regular numbers, airlines, car rental firms and hotels often have **no-charge (toll-free) numbers** with an 800 prefix. Numerous hotel, tourist information and other listings in this book have toll-free 800 numbers. Often these are valid only for calls within California; calls outside the state commonly require a different number after the 800 prefix. Before dialing national hotel chains or other nationwide service companies from out-of-state, check the local *Yellow Pages* to verify 800 numbers. Remember to prefix **800** with a **1**.

Emergency information

EMERGENCY SERVICES
San Francisco Police Department (SFPD) ☎911 in
emergencies, ☎553-0123 otherwise.
Fire (including **Rescue**) ☎911 or (415) 861-8020.
Coast Guard ☎556-5500
Emergency hospital/city ambulance ☎911 or (415) 931-3900
Medical Society referrals ☎567-6230
Dental Society referrals ☎421-1435
Suicide Prevention ☎221-1424
Narcotics Anonymous ☎621-8600

OTHER MEDICAL EMERGENCIES
To find a private doctor, consult the Yellow Pages of the telephone
directory under *Physician.* Otherwise, contact the **SF Medical Society**
(☎(415) 567-6230). Dentists are listed under *Dentist.* If in a hotel, ask
the reception desk for help.

LATE-NIGHT PHARMACIES
Walgreen Drugs *(3201 Divisadero, at Lombard* ☎931-6417, *map*
4B5, open 24 hours; 135 Powell St., at Union Sq. ☎391-4433, *map*
6C8, open Monday-Saturday 8am-midnight, Sunday 9am-8pm); **Man-**
darin Pharmacy *(895 Washington St.* ☎989-9292, *map 6C8, free*
delivery, open Monday-Friday 10am-6.30pm, Saturday 10am-6pm);
Merrill's Drug Center *(805 Market St.* ☎781-1669, *map 6D8, open*
Monday-Friday 7am-10pm, Saturday-Sunday 7.30am-8.30pm); **Bot-**
kia Pharmacy *(3189 Mission St.* ☎648-5577, *map 2D4, open daily*
9am-midnight).

HELP LINES (CRISIS LINES)
Some crisis intervention organizations are quasi-official; and many are
private; all, however, are either local or narrowly regional. For help
consult the Yellow Pages under: *Crisis Intervention Service, Drug*
Abuse Information and Treatment Centers; or *Suicide Prevention*
Counselor.
   A useful contact point is **Traveler's Aid:** ☎(415) 781-6738.

AUTOMOBILE ACCIDENTS
- Call the police immediately.
- **On city streets**, call municipal police at emergency number, which is universally **911**. Nonemergency numbers are in local telephone directories. **On all freeways** (even within city limits) and **all highways and roads** outside municipal boundaries, call California Highway Patrol (CHP). **On urban freeways**, roadside phone boothes automatically connect to the nearest CHP office. **Elsewhere ☎911** in emergency.
- If a car is rented, call the number in the rental agreement. (You should carry this, and your license, at all times when driving. Failure to do so can complicate matters.)
- Never admit liability or incriminate yourself.
- Ask eyewitnesses to stay, and take down their names, addresses and statements.
- Exchange names, addresses, car details, driver's license numbers, insurance companies' names and policy code numbers.
- Stay at the scene to give your statement to the police.

CAR BREAKDOWNS
Call one of the following from the nearest telephone.
- The number indicated in the car rental agreement.
- The local office of AAA if you are a member. The AAA is listed as California State Automobile Association (CSAA) in northern California, or Automobile Club of Southern California (ACSC) in southern California.
- The nearest garage with towing service (listed under *Towing-Automotive* in Yellow Pages).

LOST TRAVELERS CHECKS
Notify the local police immediately, then follow the instructions provided with your travelers checks, or contact the issuing company's nearest office. Contact your consulate or American Express if you are stranded without money.

BABY-SITTERS
Temporary Tot Tending ☎355-7377; 871-5790 after 6pm

PUBLIC REST ROOMS

On interstate and US highways, California maintains excellent public rest rooms in roadside miniparks called "rest areas." Many gas stations maintain facilities for their customers. In cities, rest rooms are common-place in shopping malls, department stores, restaurants, fast-food chains and hotels. Public rest rooms are few, and best avoided.

ELECTRIC CURRENT

Electric current is 110-120V 60cycles AC. Conventional household ap-pliances generally have standard two-prong plugs or earthed plugs with an additional half-cylinder prong. Most wall outlets are designed to accept either type of plug. Anyone wanting to use non-US-style plugs should purchase an adaptor before leaving home, although major department stores may sell adaptors in their travel departments.

LAWS AND REGULATIONS

In a society that prides itself on tolerance of minority rights, smokers are fast becoming an almost uniquely oppressed minority group. **Smoking** is prohibited in elevators and buses, theaters and cinemas. Restaurants and public rooms allow it only in specified areas. Many hotels now have non-smoking floors.

Laws prohibit **jaywalking** and **littering** but are unevenly enforced. **Hitchhiking** is also illegal, and although seldom punished it is strongly discouraged on freeways.

Parking violations are not taken lightly, so pay attention to color-coded curbing. **Red** means no stopping or parking, **Yellow** means a maximum half-hour loading time for vehicles with commercial plates, **Blue** is reserved for disabled people, **Green** allows 10 minutes' parking for all vehicles, and **White** gives a 5-minute limit during business hours. Do not park at bus stops or fire hydrants. Violation can incur a fine of up to $20, plus a $100 towing fee and a daily storage charge, and charges rise dramatically if you park in a space reserved for disabled people.

Because of the steep gradients of the city's streets, it is a legal require-ment to leave the wheels of the car facing toward the street when **parking uphill** and toward the curb when **parking downhill**.

See also SPEED LIMITS on page 42.

Persons must be 21 years or older to buy, serve or consume **alcoholic beverages** in California, and proof of age can be required. Liquor may not be purchased, served or consumed in public eating places and bars from 2-6am. The consumption of "controlled substances" (narcotic drugs) is prohibited by law; far more severe laws prohibit their sale.

CUSTOMS AND ETIQUETTE

Although they are almost unfailingly polite, as a rule Californians do not stand on formality. But there are certain conventions. It is custom-ary to shake hands on meeting. Once people have been introduced, first names are used by Californians in all but the most formal circum-stances.

Californians can be erratic about lining up; they form orderly lines outside movie theaters and intercity bus stations, but not for sporting events or for buses in the cities themselves. Courtesy is important: kindnesses done are rewarded with generous thanks, on buses men still give up seats for women, and everyone urges everyone else to "have a good day."

TIPPING
Waiters expect a tip of 15 percent of the bill before tax, but you may want to tip more if service has been especially good, less if it has been poor. Barmen and hairdressers should also receive 15 percent. Doormen and staff who valet park your car will expect $2, bellhops $1 per bag, and rest room attendants (although rarely encountered) $1. When there is no fixed charge for leaving coats and parcels, you should give $1 per item.

DISABLED TRAVELERS
California law requires new hotels, restaurants and other public buildings to be accessible to wheelchairs and to have wheelchair rest rooms. Older hotels and restaurants have converted rooms. Many cities reserve curbside parking for handicapped people, as do major banks, supermarkets and drugstores. Some companies operate buses with motorized platforms.

MAPS AND PUBLICATIONS
As befits a highly literate city with a long newspaper tradition, there is plenty to read in San Francisco. The major city newspapers are the morning *Chronicle* and the evening *Examiner,* especially Friday editions for weekend events, and "Datebook" section from combined Sunday edition for coming week's events.

Also interesting are the free *SF Weekly* and *San Francisco Bay Guardian* for weekly news, arts and entertainment, and the free monthly *City Sports.* Monthly magazines with useful information for tourists are *California* and *San Francisco.*

In addition to all of these, there are newspapers in Chinese, Japanese and other languages, and a profusion of local community newspapers. And the *San Jose Mercury,* probably a better source of international news coverage than either of the two San Francisco papers, is widely available. "What's On" freesheets include *SF Weekly,* offering up-to-date information on the hot spots, with everything from eating out to shopping and the arts.

Newsstands offer a wealth of local, national and international publications. Most hotels provide magazines that can be useful, although full of advertisements. The **San Francisco Convention and Visitors Bureau** (☎*(415) 391-2000)* publishes frequently updated booklets detailing what's on offer.

Guidebooks and maps available in bookstores include: *San Francisco/Access* (Access Press); *Hidden San Francisco* (Ulysses Press); *San Francisco AM/PM; Thomas Brothers Road Atlas and Driver's Guide to California* (Thomas Bros Maps).

Useful addresses

TOURIST INFORMATION
American Express Travel Service   American Express offers a valuable source of information for any traveler in need of help, advice or emergency services, as well as a full range of travel services, currency handling, and tours:

- **Downtown:** 237 Post St. ☎981-5533, map **6**C8
- **Financial district:** 295 California St. ☎788-4367, map **6**C8
- **Financial district:** 455, Market Street ☎512-8250, map **6**C8
- **Fisherman's Wharf:** 2500 Mason St., in the Sheraton Hotel ☎788-3025, map **5**B7

Offices are open Monday-Friday 9am-5pm; Post St. also open Saturday 10am-5pm; Mason St. open 7 days 10am-6pm.

California State Park System   PO Box 2390, Sacramento 95811 ☎(916) 445-6477, for camping reservations forms and list of parks. In San Francisco ☎(415) 556-0560 and (1-800) 444-7275.

US Forest Service 630 Sansome St., San Francisco 94111 ☎(415) 556-0122, map **6**C8, for camping reservation forms and information on national forests.

Redwood Empire Association   One Market Plaza, San Francisco 94104 ☎(415) 543-8334, for information on the coastal region from San Francisco N to the Oregon border.

San Francisco Convention and Visitors Bureau   201 3rd St., Suite 900 ☎(415) 974-6900, map **6**D8; Monday-Friday 9am-5pm; for recorded information any time ☎391-2001 (English), 391-2003 (French), 391-2004 (German), 391-2122 (Spanish), 391-2101 (Japanese).

San Francisco Visitor Information Center   Lower level, Hallidie Plaza, 900 Market St., at Powell St. ☎391-2000, map **6**C8, open Monday-Friday 9am-5pm, Saturday 9am-3pm, Sunday 10am-2pm, longer hours in summer. Multilingual staff.

Travelers Aid Society ☎(415) 781-6738.

AIRLINES
The following list gives local (San Francisco) and toll-free telephone numbers of the major airlines serving San Francisco International Airport.

- **Air Canada** ☎800/776-3000
- **American Airlines** ☎800/433-7300
- **British Airways** ☎800/247-9297
- **Delta Airlines** ☎552-5700 or 800/221-1212
- **Japan Airlines** ☎765-8510 or 800/525-3663
- **Northwest Airlines** ☎800/225-2525
- **United Airlines** ☎397-2100
- **USAIR** ☎956-8636 or 800/428-4322

The following airlines offer flights to San Francisco from various parts of the United Kingdom.

- **American Airlines:** in London ☎081 572 5555, outside London ☎0800 010151; one-stop flights from Gatwick (via Dallas),

Glasgow (via Chicago), Heathrow (via Chicago or New York), Manchester (via Chicago or New York), Stansted (via Chicago).

- **British Airways:** in London ☎081 897 4000, outside London ☎0345 222111; flights nonstop from Heathrow.
- **Continental Airlines:** ☎0293 776464; one-stop flights from Gatwick (via Denver, Houston or Newark).
- **Delta Airlines:** ☎0800 414767, one-stop flights from Gatwick (via Atlanta, Cincinnatti, Detroit or Minneapolis).
- **Northwest Airlines:** ☎0345 747800, if calling from outside the UK ☎0293 565666); one-stop flights from Gatwick (via Boston or Minneapolis) or Glasgow (via Boston).

CONSULATES

Australia   360 Post St. ☎(415) 362-6160
Canada   1 Maritime Plaza ☎(415) 981-2670
Republic of Ireland   681 Market St. ☎(415) 392-4214
Japan   1601 Post St. ☎(415) 921-8000
New Zealand   1 Maritime Plaza ☎(415) 788-7430
United Kingdom   120 Montgomery St. ☎(415) 981-3030

A city has to be a place where you can see old ladies
riding bicycles and older men in limousines. Where the hotels
have doormen and the bellboys can produce a bottle of Scotch
at 3am. Where, if the mood is upon you, you can get blinis
and caviar, fisherman's spaghetti, white figs and prosciutto,
a '45 Mouton Rothschild or a movie in any one of six languages.
A city is where sirens make white streaks of sound in the sky
and fog horns speak in dark grays.
San Francisco is such a city.
(Herb Caen, *San Francisco: City on Golden Hills*)

Planning

When to go

Forget the idealized picture of California, State of perpetual sunshine; that's the Southland. Mark Twain wasn't joking when he said the coldest winter he ever spent was one summer in San Francisco. The chills he experienced were, and are, a trick of the fogs produced by cold ocean waters along the shore N of Santa Barbara. These summer fogs cover a very narrow band, just a few miles wide where there is coastal shelf; perhaps only a few hundred yards wide where hills rise rapidly from the surf. After the fogs lift in August, San Francisco enjoys its warmer, sunnier days, its temperate approximation of summer cooled by ocean breezes.

An imitation of winter comes between November and February, with weather that is rainy rather than really cold. Winter rains do not restrict themselves to the coastal shelf, although there is a steady increase in the amount and frequency of rains from S to N. Broadly speaking, San Francisco has a temperate marine climate: November through February are wet, June through October are dry. In late summer the mercury seldom climbs above 70°F (21°C) and in winter it rarely falls below 40°F (5°C). Spring and fall are the most pleasant seasons.

See also CLIMATE and CLOTHES on page 36.

Calendar of events

See also SPORTS on page 117 and PUBLIC HOLIDAYS on page 42. Some dates vary from year to year, so check ahead.

JANUARY
San Francisco International Boat Show, Moscone Center ☎521-2558. • **Shrine East-West All Star Football Classic and Pageant**, Stanford Stadium, Palo Alto ☎661-0291. • **Chinese Lunar New Year celebration and parade**, Chinatown ☎974-6900.

FEBRUARY
Golden Gate Kennel Club All-breed Dog Show, Cow Palace ☎530-1466. • **Orchids by the Bay**, orchid display, Fort Mason, Marina District ☎332-9100. • **Crab Festival**, Bay Area ☎981-8030.

MARCH

San Francisco International Film Festival, America's oldest film festival, Bay Area movie theaters ☎567-4641. • **St Patrick's Day** celebration and parade, Downtown ☎467-8218. • Annual **Battle of Harmonicas**, Palace of Fine Arts Theater ☎762-2277. • **Bammies (Bay Area Music Awards)**, local talent on display at various locations ☎974-4000. • **National Championship Cat Show**, Cow Palace ☎469-6065. • **Grand National Junior Rodeo and Horse Show**, Cow Palace ☎469-6000. • **Easter Sunrise Service**, Mt. Davidson ☎974-6900.

APRIL

Cherry Blossom Festival and parade, Japantown, Post and Buchanan ☎922-6776. • Annual **Golden Gate International Rugby Tournament** ☎556-0560. • **San Francisco Giants baseball season opens** (through October), Candlestick Park ☎467-8000. • **Yachting season opens**, San Francisco Bay ☎563-6363. • **Bay Meadows Thoroughbred Racing season opens**, San Mateo ☎574-7223.

MAY

Cinco de Mayo celebration and parade, Hispanic festival, Mission District ☎826-1401. **Carnaval**, Mardi Gras revel, Mission District ☎826-1401. • *San Francisco Examiner* **Bay to Breakers race**, annual run from Bay to Ocean ☎777-7770. • **San Francisco Historic Trolley Festival**, Market Street ☎974-6900. • **San Francisco New Performance Festival** of drama, dance, music and opera, at various locations ☎863-1320.

JUNE

Union Street Festival of Arts and Crafts, Union St. ☎346-4446. • Friends of the San Francisco Public Library **Annual Book Sale**, Pier 2, Fort Mason ☎558-2200. • **Carnival**, Mardi-gras style festival/parade with music and dance, Mission District ☎826-1401. • **Lesbian-Gay Freedom Parade** ☎864-3733. • **Kitemakers' Annual Father's Day Kite Festival**, Marina Green ☎956-3181. • San Francisco Symphony **Beethoven Festival**, Davies Symphony Hall and Herbst Theater, Civic Center ☎431-5400. • **Vaudeville Festival**, San Francisco State University ☎338-2467. • New North Beach Fair, Upper Grant Ave. ☎346-4446.

JULY

Fourth of July Celebration and Fireworks, Crissy Field, Presidio ☎556-0560. • **Summer Pops Concerts**, San Francisco Symphony at Civic Auditorium ☎431-5400. • **KQED International Beer Festival**, Concourse Exhibition Center ☎553-2200. • **Stern Grove Midsummer Music Festival**, America's oldest free festival, in a natural amphitheater, Sunset District ☎398-6551. • **San Francisco Marathon** ☎681-2323. • **Midsummer Mozart Festival**, Herbst Theater, Civic Center ☎552-3656.

AUGUST

San Francisco 49ers football season opens (through December), Candlestick Park ☎(408) 562-4949. • **Japantown Summer Festival**, Japantown ☎563-7656. • **San Francisco Hill Stride**, 7-mile walk ☎546-6150. • **San Francisco County Fair**, Flower Show and Arts Festival, County Fair Building, Golden Gate Park ☎558-7962. • **Pacific States Craft Fair**, Fort Mason, Presidio ☎896-5060.

SEPTEMBER

American Indian Trade Fair and Exposition, intertribal pow-wow, arts and crafts, Civic Center Plaza ☎626-8122. • **Ringling Brothers Barnum and Bailey Circus**, Cow Palace ☎469-6000. • **Youth Fair**, carnival, skateboarding, contests, entertainment, Civic Center Plaza ☎557-8758. • **San Francisco Blues Festival**, Great Meadow, Fort Mason ☎826-6837. • **San Francisco Opera Season** opens (through December), Opera House, Civic Center ☎864-3300. • **Bridge-to-Bridge Run**, 8-mile race and 5-kilometer fun-run, Ferry Building ☎995-6800. • **Transamerica Men's Open Tennis Championship**, Cow Palace ☎469-6000.

OCTOBER

Columbus Day Celebrations, Italian community pageant and parade plus Blessing of the Fleet, at North Beach and Fisherman's Wharf ☎434-1492. • Grand National Livestock Exposition, Rodeo and Horse Show, Cow Palace ☎469-6000. • **Halloween and Pumpkin Festival**, Clement St. ☎346-4446, and **Halloween Costume Promenade**, Polk, Castro and Market Sts. • **American Conservatory Theater Season** opens (through May), Geary Theater, Downtown ☎673-6440. • **Castro Street Fair**, Castro District ☎346-2640. • **Jazz in the City Festival**, various locations ☎864-5449.

NOVEMBER

Folk Art Exhibition and Sale, Conference Center, Fort Mason ☎441-6100. • **Annual KQED Wine and Food Festival**, Concourse Exhibition Hall ☎553-2000. • **San Francisco Automobile Show**, Moscone Center, SoMa ☎673-2016. • **Dickens Christmas Fair**, 19thC London re-created in northern California, Fort Mason ☎441-5705. • **Traditional Tree-lighting Ceremony**, Pier 39 ☎981-8030.

DECEMBER

Sing-It-Yourself-Messiah, singalong with the **San Francisco Symphony Chorus**, Davies Symphony Hall, Civic Center ☎979-8098. • **Pickle Family Circus**, Palace of Fine Art Theater, Marina District ☎826-0747. • *Nutcracker,* **San Francisco Ballet's annual performances**, War Memorial Opera House, Civic Center ☎621-3838. • *A Christmas Carol,* seasonal Dickens from the **American Conservatory Theater**, Geary Theater, Union Sq. district ☎673-6440. • **Santa Parade**, Mission St. ☎826-1401. • **Annual Campbell's Soup First Run**, Crissy Field, Presidio ☎387-2178.

Sightseeing

San Francisco's neighborhoods

San Francisco has the manageable, understandable, conventional characteristics that most of us expect of a city; it is user-friendly. Above all, it owes its character to the 1849 Gold Rush, the event that turned a sleepy pueblo into a port city that was not merely cosmopolitan but chameleon-like. Today, Americans think of it as American, Europeans call it America's most European city, and Asians are reminded of Asia.

To know San Francisco in all its guises, it is necessary to explore all its varied neighborhoods. With just 49 square miles, inhabited by 750,000 people, this goal is achievable. But the city proper, perched on its water-lapped peninsula, is not the entire story. San Francisco does not exist in splendid isolation; the Bay Area, including Berkeley and Oakland to the N, and San Jose to the S, begins to rival LA for almost continuous urban sprawl.

However, the more than a dozen neighborhoods identified below are distinct. In addition to the detailed orientation sketches of San Francisco, this section gives pointers for those intending to explore outside the city limits.

THE AVENUES *(map 1)*

The W side of the city is known as The Avenues, after N-S avenues numbered 2-48. Residents often speak more specifically of the **Sunset** (S of Golden Gate Park) and the **Richmond** (N of the Park). A considerable number of the city's treasures are to be found here. **Golden Gate Park**, at 3 miles long by $\frac{1}{2}$ a mile wide one of the greatest urban parks in the US, has forest groves, gardens, playgrounds, lakes, sports fields, and some of the city's finest museums: the M.H. DE YOUNG MEMORIAL MUSEUM and the Asian Art Museum; the Morrison Planetarium and the Steinhart Aquarium at the CALIFORNIA ACADEMY OF SCIENCES. Also in the area: the 270-acre **Lincoln Park** and another worthy art museum, the CALIFORNIA PALACE OF THE LEGION OF HONOR, Ocean Beach, the SAN FRANCISCO ZOOLOGICAL GARDENS and SIGMUND STERN GROVE.

And there is Clement St., with its small shops and restaurants, almost 100 of them within one mile, whose ethnic diversity also signals the gradual changes in what, traditionally, has been largely a residential White middle-class area. Clement St. between 1st and 11th Aves. is known as "**New Chinatown**," and the **Richmond** district today has more Japanese residents than Japantown. More recently, people of Vietnamese, Thai, Khmer and Laotian origin have moved in. They do not yet rival the Eastern Europeans, Irish or Jews in numbers, but they are giving the area a more cosmopolitan complexion. The two most notable buildings are an Orthodox church (the Cathedral of the Holy Virgin, on Geary Blvd. and 26th Ave.) and a Jewish temple (EMANU-EL, on Arguello Blvd. and Lake St.).

The same is true of the **Sunset** district, s of the Park, where the traditional White, middle-class conservatism is being enlivened by new waves of ethnic immigration. The residential architecture is uninspired, but the Sunset is considered an ideal spot in which to raise a family.

CIVIC CENTER *(map 5 D7)*

A mile w of Union Sq. and downtown, the CIVIC CENTER is the heart of San Francisco's political and cultural life. Here, in an eight-block area regarded as the finest grouping of Beaux Arts architecture in the US, are City Hall, the San Francisco Opera House, the Louise M. Davies Symphony Hall, the War Memorial Building, the SAN FRANCISCO PUBLIC LIBRARY and the Civic Auditorium, a huge hall used for basketball, boxing and conventions.

In recent years several fine restaurants attuned to concert-goers' schedules have blossomed in the district. The only drawback for visitors is that the city's burgeoning number of homeless people are also attracted. Panhandlers and muggers can be a problem, especially after dark.

FISHERMAN'S WHARF/NORTHERN WATERFRONT *(map 5 B7)*

Once this was an industrial area with a working port; now it is almost entirely tourist country, containing the altogether predictable seaside entertainments of FISHERMAN'S WHARF and PIER 39 (which attracts almost 10.5 million visitors a year), along with two elegant shopping complexes, The Cannery and Ghirardelli Sq. (once a wool factory, later a chocolate factory), the SAN FRANCISCO MARITIME MUSEUM, and the diverse community center within FORT MASON. For recreation there is Aquatic Park and Municipal Pier.

The Powell St. cable cars end their routes here, and the area is well served by buses. There are fast-food restaurants, less predictable fresh-seafood stalls, and, occasionally, excellent street theater and musicians. It is also the best place from which to pick up sightseeing cruises around the Bay.

GOLDEN GATE/MARINA/PACIFIC HEIGHTS *(map 1 B3-2 B4)*

The area toward the mouth of San Francisco Bay has some of the city's most rewarding scenery and some very pleasant places to relax in. The GOLDEN GATE BRIDGE and FORT POINT are here; so is the monumental PALACE OF FINE ARTS and, inside it, the EXPLORATORIUM. On the harborside, the Marina Green is a popular spot for strollers, kite-flyers, joggers and sunbathers.

The chic shopping district of **Union St.** is on the s side of Lombard St., the major link between downtown and the Golden Gate Bridge. In this exclusive neighborhood resides a well-heeled blend of "old money" and high flyers; they live in the converted Victorian mansions of **Pacific Heights**, resplendent luxury apartments or the Mediterranean-revival houses on the Marina. The cluster of houses known as the "PAINTED LADIES" and beloved of postcard photographers is near Alamo Square, a quiet neighborhood full of spectacular Victorian houses.

GRANT AVENUE/CHINATOWN (map 6 C8)

For many years San Francisco's Chinese-origin inhabitants lived in a veritable city of their own. They were among the city's earliest residents and are now second in numbers in the US only to the New York Chinese. To the N of downtown, the main artery of this city-within-a-city was Grant Ave. from Pine to Broadway.

Of late, the large and growing population of Chinese-Americans and newly immigrated Chinese have burst the old boundaries in all directions, as the more affluent move away from the city center. But some 75,000 still live in Chinatown, and Grant Ave., with its imposing Dragon Gate (built as recently as 1969), remains the heart of their community. It looks, smells and feels like an Asian street, and the residents live in quarters that are often as cramped and spartan as in downtown Hong Kong or Taipei.

Dragon Gate, Chinatown

In truth, the dedication to amusing foreign tourists with restaurants, bars and curio stores is secondary to the self-sustaining life of the community. The cross streets and Stockton St., which runs parallel to Grant St., are more authentically Asian, to the point that English is not much help in some shops. Here, curio shops yield to workaday butchers, fish and grocery stores, and bakeries. Waverly St., a narrow alley parallel to Grant St., is about as authentic as Chinatowns come, with traditional Chinese roofs, and shops selling exotic herbs and dry goods.

Two engaging places, the CHINESE CULTURE CENTER and the CHINESE HISTORICAL SOCIETY, make useful starting points.

THE HILLS (maps 5 B-C7, 6 B8)

San Francisco is a city that is known for its hills; Nob, Telegraph and Russian are the most famous. The Hills are, first and foremost, residential areas, with some notable neighborhood restaurants and fine hotels. There are many dramatic views and, for anyone who is the slightest bit out of condition, a number of even more dramatic climbs.

Russian Hill is named after a cemetery for Russian fur-hunters and traders. A century ago, the neighborhood was vaguely bohemian, and the original Swensen's ice cream parlor is there, on Union St. But nowadays it is primarily "old money" and the upwardly mobile who live there, and on Union St. they sustain what is perhaps the city's most fashionable shopping.

Telegraph Hill has the city's best views, and in recent years, an influx of affluent young residents has provoked a flowering of chic new restaurants. The many interesting features include, on the harbor slopes down from COIT TOWER, the hillside wooden cottages that survived the great 1906 earthquake and fire; they are accessible via rickety wooden walkways and steps.

Nob Hill, derived from "nabob" and characterized by Robert Louis Stevenson as "the Hill of Palaces," has some especially good examples of classic San Francisco architecture. Some of the finest estates were leveled in the earthquake and fire. But, like the rest of the city, the bourgeoisie bounced back, rebuilt, and remain entrenched atop the hills to this day.

Nob Hill also has the GRACE CATHEDRAL, built between the wars and now the largest Gothic building in the western US. Needless to say, many of the city's swankiest restaurants are to be found on the hills.

JAPANTOWN (NIHONMACHI)
(map 5 D6)

Since the 19thC, members of San Francisco's sizeable Japanese population have resided, for the most part, in a compact area stretching three blocks N from Geary Blvd., between Franklin and Fillmore Sts. Only a small proportion of San Francisco's Japanese population are resident here today, but the infrastructure and ambience of Japantown are a magnet for a wider-spread community, and the area remains its spiritual nexus.

The district has a number of distinctly Japanese hotels, shops, nightclubs, restaurants, Buddhist temples, shrines, festivals, movie theaters, traditional massage parlors, and even hardware stores, in and near a three-block-long commercial and cultural center, which forms the s boundary of the neighborhood. The center

Peace Pagoda, Japantown

57

was designed by Professor Yoshiro Taniguchi, an expert on Japanese traditional architecture, with the tall 8thC-style PEACE PAGODA (pictured on previous page) as its centerpiece. Within it are an outstanding Japanese bookstore, a shop that specializes in *koi* carp, and a Japanese theater.

Japantown is spick, span, bustling and delightful by day. However, a note of caution should be sounded. Gangs from the neighboring Western Addition have been known to prowl by night, so vigilance is recommended for after-dark pedestrians.

THE MISSION *(map 2 C4-D4)*
Within this sprawling district centered at the intersection of 24th St. and Mission St. lives most of San Francisco's large population of Hispanics. Mexicans and Mexican-Americans are the largest group, but substantial numbers of Salvadoreans, Chileans and others share the space.

The city's oldest building, MISSION DOLORES (or, more correctly, *Mission San Francisco de Asís,* pictured left), which marks the beginning of European civilization in San Francisco, is here, as is the Mexican Museum. Mission St. has galleries and shops specializing in Hispanic arts and crafts, and a galaxy of good, inexpensive restaurants.

In recent years, the Mission district has been brightened by an increasing number of murals. There were 200 at the last count, some as large as a 3-story building.

However, the Mission is essentially a residential community with a strong sense of Hispanic identity and, as one of the city's less prosperous areas, is not a recommended base for tourists. Visitors are best advised to go there during daylight hours.

MONTGOMERY STREET/FINANCIAL DISTRICT *(map 6 C8-9-D8)*
Montgomery St., sometimes called "Wall Street West," is convenient shorthand for the city's long-established financial district, which is to the E of downtown and is concentrated on but not limited to Montgomery St. between Market and California Sts. On what had been mudflats, the city's banking and financial center grew, like so much else, from the Gold Rush. The hulks of "ghost ships," abandoned by crews infected with gold fever, were used as foundations for building. It was here that A.P. Giannini founded the Bank of Italy, which later became the Bank of America.

As with similar districts worldwide, this is not the liveliest place for after-dark entertainment, except for some lively after-work bars. The splendidly varied architecture of its banks and other financial institutions, and the public art in and around them, are the main attractions. Much of the public art is in the Embarcadero Center, three office towers between Sacramento and Clay Sts., two blocks E of Montgomery. Tucked away in office buildings in the area are three worthy if small museums of history, the BANK OF CALIFORNIA OLD COIN AND GOLD EXHIBIT, the LEVI STRAUSS HISTORY ROOM and the WELLS FARGO HISTORY ROOM.

NORTH BEACH *(map 6 B8-C8)*

Traditionally, **Little Italy** — better known as North Beach — faced Chinatown across Broadway and Columbus Ave. During the past few years, Chinese businesses have edged across the unofficial boundary, and now one-third of the population is Chinese. But the skirts of **Telegraph Hill** remain a bastion of the city's older generation of Italians, as well as the descendants of early Irish, Basque and Mexican families. It is not a beach at all, but it is a rewarding place to go for some fine examples of Edwardian domestic architecture, for its coffee houses, serious bars, bakeries, superb Italian grocery stores and satisfying meals at bargain prices.

The North Beach area has always enjoyed a slightly "alternative" flavor. The infamous Barbary Coast of red-light districts, gambling and "shanghaied" sailors was here. Jack London and Mark Twain lived here, and the bohemian Beat Generation was born here in the 1950s. Echoes remain here and there, most notably in the still-thriving City Lights bookstore, the haunt of Ferlinghetti and Ginsberg, and the timeless Caffe Trieste coffee house. What was the Barbary Coast, s of Broadway between Montgomery St. and Kearny St., is now **Jackson Square**, where some attractive pre-quake buildings survive.

North Beach is one of the city's liveliest quarters for nightclubs, including the sleazier variety whose garish neon and ever-optimistic barkers tend to dominate along the w stretch of Broadway. To be fair, however, they are intermingled with more worthwhile establishments. The centerpiece of the district is WASHINGTON SQUARE, which, with the Romanesque Church of Saints Peter and Paul as its backdrop, is a good place to see North Beach in all its splendid ethnic, linguistic and social diversity.

PRESIDIO *(map 3-4 B3-C4)*

San Francisco began as a Spanish military settlement under the name Yerba Buena. The original Presidio remains an army post, occupying much of the NW corner of the San Francisco peninsula. The Army Museum is within its confines, as are FORT POINT HISTORIC SITE and Sandy Baker Beach, both of which are part of the GOLDEN GATE NATIONAL RECREATION AREA.

UNION SQUARE AND DOWNTOWN *(map 6)*

Hotels, theaters, grand department stores and upscale shops all cluster around Union Sq. in a ten-block area bounded on the s by O'Farrell St., on the N by Sutter St., on the w by Jones St. and on the E by Kearny St. If the city has a center, this is it. The Square itself, around a 90-foot (27m) Corinthian column, is a pleasant oasis of greenery and flowers amid all the conspicuous consumption: a pleasant spot to take the air, feed the pigeons and watch the street parade and the street performers.

The Geary and Curran Theaters, side by side on Geary St. between Mason and Taylor Sts., are the home of the city's repertory company, the American Conservatory Theater, and other touring companies. Otherwise, the district is of interest mainly to shoppers.

OTHER CITY AREAS

In recent years, whole neighborhoods have become monuments to nostalgia. **Cow Hollow** is the old name for the valley W of Van Ness Ave. between Russian Hill and the Presidio. From 1850s farmland when cows grazed and washerwomen scrubbed the Presidio officers' laundry, to sedate residences and modest stores at the turn of the century, Cow Hollow was pulled smartly to the fore by those who saw potential in the clapboard dwellings and converted stables and barns. It is best to reconnoiter on foot this area of flower-filled courtyards, antique stores and handicraft galleries.

The mostly commercial strip of **Market St.**, particularly from Powell St. E to the Embarcadero, is trying to become a grand boulevard. So far hopes exceed performance, and S of Mason St. it degenerates somewhat into an array of budget shops and porno theaters. But, moving N, the street has some large department stores and some impressive new architecture, and there is usually lively street entertainment around the Powell St. CABLE CAR BARN.

The traditionally industrial area called **South of Market** (or **SoMa**) has been redeveloped around the MOSCONE CONVENTION CENTER, built in 1981 and named after the city's assassinated mayor. Taking its lead from New York's artsy SoHo district, its converted warehouses are becoming a focus for restaurants, and nightclubs with names as zany as the entertainment, centered around Folsom and Harrison Sts.

Most of San Francisco's large homosexual population lives on or near two commercial streets, Polk St. between Geary St. and Pacific Ave., and Castro St. S of Market St. to 19th St. or just beyond. Castro St. is the axis for male homosexuals, Valencia for lesbians. As the restored "gingerbread" Victorian properties testify, the Castro gays have done much to gentrify and prettify what was previously a somewhat run-down district. Clubs, bars and nightclubs cater to their tastes.

Not all of San Francisco is always safe for strangers, or even wandering residents. A district best avoided by pedestrians after nightfall is the **Tenderloin**, a triangle bounded by Ellis St. to the N, Market St. to the S and E, and Hyde St. to the W. However, moderately-priced restaurants and markets opened by recent immigrants from Southeast Asia are making it an increasingly attractive area to visit.

The area known as the **Western Addition** has seen particular violence against tourists, primarily because its location near the Civic Center and between downtown and Golden Gate Park leads many unwitting strangers into it. The section bounded by Gough St. to the E, Masonic Ave. to the W, Geary Blvd. to the N and Duboce Ave. to the S should not be risked by visitors on foot, either by day or night. Passengers on municipal buses have also been known to be the subject to violence within this zone.

ENVIRONS OF SAN FRANCISCO

Much of San Francisco's charm comes from adjacent regions that are so different in character and climate that they offer a complete change of pace. Highlights are described in EXCURSIONS and WINES AND WINERIES. Among the major day-trip destinations are MARIN COUNTY and POINT REYES PENINSULA across the Golden Gate to the N, BERKELEY and OAKLAND on the E side of San Francisco Bay, SAN FRANCISCO PENINSULA directly S of the city, the wine country of the SONOMA and NAPA VALLEYS to the N, and SANTA CRUZ to the S.

There is plenty of public transportation to these outlying areas. **Golden Gate Transit** (☎ 332-6600), a bus and ferry system, connects the city with Sausalito, Mill Valley, Point Reyes and some Sonoma cities. **BART** (see PUBLIC TRANSPORTATION, page 38) and **A-C Transit**, a bus system, connect the city with Oakland, Berkeley, and other cities in the East Bay counties of Alameda and Contra Costa. **Caltrain** (☎ 557-8661 or (800) 558-8661) operates commuter trains between the city, the San Francisco Peninsula and Santa Clara Valley. **Sam Trans** (☎ 761-7000), a bus system, connects the city with the San Francisco Peninsula.

For tours to the areas mentioned above, see the list of tour operators on pages 39-40.

Sights and places of interest

San Francisco is a compact city, so most of its important sights are easily accessible or at least visible. In the case of those places too distant to visit on foot, the city has several modes of public transportation that are attractions in themselves. See CABLE CARS for one example.

"The gayest, lightest-hearted, most pleasure-loving city of the Western Continent," was Will Irwin's verdict on San Francisco. Exuberance, vitality and a sense of fun are key aspects of the city's personality. But beneath the froth, there are the components of a substantial cultural background: one of the West Coast's most important collections of modern art, one of the country's finest museums of natural history, and a wealth of eclectic architecture.

San Francisco is built on 42 hills, some of them steep, some of them requiring cars to defy gravity. A number of them are so unlikely as thoroughfares that they have become sights in their own right (see GRADIENTS and CROOKEDEST STREET), and they are all natural observation platforms from which to take in the stunning views for which the city is famed (see VIEWPOINTS).

Many of San Francisco's sights are inexpensive to visit, and many more are totally free (**IOI**). Most have at least one day each month when admission is free, and schemes designed to aid visitor numbers appear each year. It is now possible, for example, to gain discounted admission to 24 visitor attractions if you are the holder of a Muni one, three- or seven-day passport, making San Francisco a very cheap place in which to soak up the sights.

HOW TO USE THIS SECTION
On the following pages, our selection of San Francisco's sights and places of interest is arranged in alphabetical order. **Bold type** highlights points of special interest within an entry. Entries given without addresses and opening times are described more fully elsewhere: check the **cross-references**, which are in SMALL CAPITALS.

Look for the ★ symbol against the most important sights, and the 🏛 symbol for buildings of great architectural interest. Good views ◀€ and places of special interest to children ♣ are also indicated. For a full explanation of symbols, see page 7.

San Francisco's sights A to Z

ALCATRAZ ★
An island one mile offshore from the northern waterfront. Off map 2A4 ◀€ 🖾 for expert guided 2hr tours by National Park Service rangers. Ferries from Pier 43 (Fisherman's Wharf) to the island are expensive. Reservations advised for boats in all seasons, but especially in summer when they may be reserved 2-6 weeks in advance. For information or reservations, Red and White Fleet, Pier 41, San Francisco 94133 ☎546-2833. Ferry crossings take about 20mins. Open 9am-4.30pm.
The formidable concrete hulks of the old federal prison buildings that once held Al Capone, Robert Stroud and other famous felons, echo every day to the footsteps of as many visitors as the tour boats can carry.

Alcatraz rises a craggy and commanding 135 feet out of the forbidding tides of San Francisco Bay. One of the city's most dominating sights, from certain angles the infamous prison has a decidely Mediterranean air. The outcrop on which it was built is oddly lush; wild flowers grow there in riotous profusion. The views of the San Francisco skyline and the Golden Gate are magnificent.

But for a century, Alcatraz was a byword for grim incarceration. Since 1858 it has been a fortification, a military prison, an army disciplinary barracks, and a federal penitentiary run under an administrative code of "total control." In this last, most infamous role, "The Rock" acquired its legendary reputation as a place of no escape. No more than 250 captives at a time occupied its 450 cells, patrolled by as many as 100 staff.

In spite of this, three inmates, Frank Lee Morris and John and Clarence Anglin, managed to dig their way out with sharpened spoons in 1962. Their apparently successful feat (none of them was ever found) was the subject of *Escape from Alcatraz,* the 1979 movie with Clint Eastwood, in which the prison played one of several starring Hollywood roles. *The Birdman of Alcatraz,* the story of Robert Stroud, with Burt Lancaster in the title role, was another.

When the prison closed in 1962, the 12-acre island was claimed as their birthright by a group of Native Americans, who set fire to a number of the buildings. Since 1973 it has been open to the public under the custodianship of the National Park Service. The visitor with a taste for self-imposed claustrophobia will find the main prison block, with its 9-foot by 5-foot cells and "dark holes," where uncooperative prisoners cooled their heels in solitary blackness, still intact.

ANCHOR STEAM BREWERY
1705 Mariposa St. Map 6F9 ☎863-8350 ⚡ (call for times).
This tiny independent brewery employs only 25 people but produces excellent beer that is sought after throughout the United States. You can take a one-hour tour culminating in a sampling of the products.

ANGEL ISLAND STATE PARK
Information ☎435-1915.
The largest island in San Francisco Bay offers a 740-acre haven for hikers, cyclists and picnickers. There are three trails, in addition to camping, barbecue and picnic facilities. Dogs and skateboards are banned.

Once known as the "Ellice Island of the West," — until 1940 it housed immigration and quarantine stations — Angel Island has also been the site of two military installations.

ANSEL ADAMS CENTER
250 4th St. Map 6D8 ☎495-7000 ▣ Open Tues-Sat 11am-6pm.
Five galleries in all are dedicated to creative photography, with changing exhibits on the history of photography. One gallery is devoted to the legacy of Adams himself, who lived from 1902-84. His photographs, in particular those of the Yosemite Valley, are noted as some of the most potent images of the Californian landscape.

ASIAN ART MUSEUM   See M.H. DE YOUNG MEMORIAL MUSEUM.

BALCLUTHA
Pier 43. Map 5A7 ▣ Open 10am-10pm.
A typical iron-hulled, square-rigged ship from the end of the era of sail, the *Balclutha* was built in Scotland in 1886, and was the last of the Cape Horn fleet.

Some below-deck areas look much as they did when the ship sailed the oceans in the 1890s, spending 20 years in the Alaskan salmon trade. Elsewhere, there are displays of memorabilia. See also FORT MASON and SAN FRANCISCO MARITIME NATIONAL HISTORICAL PARK.

BANK OF CALIFORNIA OLD COIN AND GOLD EXHIBIT
400 California St., lower level. Map 6C8 ▣ Open Mon-Thurs 10am-3pm, Fri 10am-5pm. Closed Sat, Sun, bank hols.
In addition to rare coins, the display includes pieces of gold-bearing quartz that show how the precious metal looks to a miner.

CABLE CAR MUSEUM, POWERHOUSE AND CAR BARN
Washington St., at Mason St. ☎474-1887. Map 6C8 ▣ ♣ Open 10am-5pm seven days.

The control center where the 11 miles of wrapped steel cable that carries the city's beloved cable cars is played out and reeled in, is a 3-story, red brick barn.

Exhibits there include three **vintage cable cars**, including inventor Andrew Hallidie's prototype Car No. 8, and scale models of some of the 57 types of cable car that have operated in San Francisco. A **mezzanine gallery** provides a viewpoint on the giant winders that thread the cable, and a glass-enclosed room allows visitors to watch the cable passing through sheaves and onto the streets. There is also a good display of vintage photographs.

CABLE CARS

A cherished part of the city's public transportation system and a national landmark, San Francisco's cable cars offer an exhilarating, and inexpensive (tickets cost $2, or $1 for children) way to see the soaring hills and swooping dales of the city. They were invented in San Francisco before the turn of the century, to haul passengers up and down hills too steep for horse-drawn carriages. A rollicking joyride to the tourist, and a lifeline to the city's commuters, the preservation of these moving museum-pieces has not been without cost.

Mothballed in 1982, when engineers found that 109 years of service had taken an irreparable toll on the cable cars' propulsion system, the network was rebuilt after sympathizers from all over the world sent contributions. Most of the $60 million that was needed came from a combined effort of public and private funding. Residents and commuters were then subjected to two years of appalling traffic disruption as the life-saving surgery was performed; 69 blocks of streets were torn up.

> San Francisco without its cable cars
> would be like a kid without his yo-yo
> (Phil Baker)

The cars themselves, and their control center at Washington and Mason Streets (see CABLE CAR BARN, above) had a facelift while out of service, before making a glorious, bell-clanging comeback in 1984.

The number of lines has dwindled from eight to three: Powell-Mason and Powell-Hyde (the most scenic route) run from Powell St. at Market St. to the northern waterfront. The third line runs along California St. from Market St. to Van Ness Ave.

CALIFORNIA ACADEMY OF SCIENCES

Golden Gate Park, via entrance road from 8th Ave. and Fulton St. ☎221-5100, or 750-7145 for recorded schedule of events. Map 3E3 ▨ ▣ ✷ Open 10am-5pm every day of the year. Free first Wed of each month.

One of the five finest natural history museums in the US, the Academy has eight departments, some of which function on separate schedules, and a changing program of special exhibits. It is set amid the 1,017 acres of GOLDEN GATE PARK.

The **Discovery Room** *(behind Morrison Planetarium ▣ but attend-*

ance limited to 20 at a time, open Tues-Fri 1-4pm; Sat, Sun 11am-3.30pm, closed Mon) was designed for children, who can investigate boxes for everything from spices to seashells and animal skulls.

The **Morrison Planetarium** *(☎ 750-7141 for times ☒ but separate from general admission)* has a domed ceiling screen that is used for star and **Laserium** shows, which are presented in the Planetarium on selected evenings *(☎ 750-7138).*

The most dramatic element of the **Steinhart Aquarium** (★) is its Fish Roundabout, a kind of reverse theater-in-the-round where observers stand in an open central area to watch a 360˚ panorama of all the great Pacific coast sport fish, including sharks, swimming into an induced current in a 100,000-gallon circular tank. A simulated tidepool and coral reef tank are other major attractions.

In all, the aquarium has more than 14,000 aquatic species. For a home-away-from-home experience, watch the fish being fed *(every 2hrs starting at 10.30am);* the penguins receive their chow twice daily.

The **Wattis Hall of Man** displays aspects of vanishing cultures from Eskimos to Australian aborigines. Other halls display stuffed specimens of the world's great animals.

CALIFORNIA PALACE OF THE LEGION OF HONOR 🏛

Lincoln Park, 0.4 miles NW of 34th Ave. and Clement St. entrance to park ☎ 750-3600, or 863-3330 for recorded message. Map 1B2. Administered jointly with the M.H. DE YOUNG MUSEUM. Closed for two-year renovation until spring 1994.
The art and culture of Europe, and particularly France, from medieval tapestries to Post-Impressionism, are the main focus of the collection kept in this magnificent copy of the 18thC Parisian palace where Napoleon chose to house his *Légion d'Honneur.* The California Palace of the Legion of Honor merged with the M.H. DE YOUNG MEMORIAL MUSEUM in 1972 under the heading The Fine Arts Museums of San Francisco.

The museum is currently closed for a two-year period of renovations and seismic upgrading. During the period of closure, some parts of the collection will be toured to other US museums and as far afield, it is expected, as Japan. Other parts of the collection will be displayed in the temporary exhibition spaces at the M.H. DE YOUNG MEMORIAL MUSEUM, so the works by Rodin, El Greco, Manet, Monet, Degas, Seurat and Cézanne will continue to find an audience.

CALIFORNIA PIONEERS MUSEUM

456 McAllister St. ☎861-5278 Map 5D7 ☒ Open Mon-Fri 10am-4pm; closed Aug, holidays ✱
This museum charts the history of the pioneers of California, including the Gold Rush and the birth and growth of San Francisco. It has an interesting collection of 19thC paintings, and a children's gallery with a Wells Fargo **stagecoach** and 19thC costume displays.

CANDLESTICK PARK

On an access road between freeway US-101 and San Francisco Bay at the s city limits. Map 2E5.

This 55,000-seat stadium is the site of home games for the baseball **Giants** *(☎ 467-8000)* and football **49ers** *(☎ 468-2249)*.

CHINATOWN ☆ 🏛

*Map **6**C8. See also* *SAN FRANCISCO'S NEIGHBORHOODS, page 56.*

San Francisco's Chinese community has spread into other areas of the city, but an eight-block length of Grant Ave. is still the cultural and geographical nucleus of the biggest Chinese stronghold E of Taiwan. The oldest Oriental-style building in Chinatown is the three-tiered **Bank of Canton** (pictured on page 30), built in 1909.

"A ward of the city of Canton set down in the most eligible business quarter of the place" was Rudyard Kipling's impression of Chinatown on a visit in the 1880s, and it still rings true. Guangzhou dialect is the first language, carved dragons entwine themselves around the lamp posts, and buildings are exotically adorned with arched eaves, carved cornices and filigreed balconies. The **Chinese New Year** is celebrated in a glorious pageant of cavorting dragons and lions.

Today, Chinatown's shops are crammed with art objects and curios. Restaurants, from award-winning temples of taste to *dim sum* teahouses, line the streets. The **Bank of America** is ornamented with splendid golden dragons.

Chinatown has had a checkered history. "Du Pon Gai," as the area was known in the 19thC (the English name was then Dupont St.), had a reputation for tong wars, opium dens, and sing-song girls. The name of the 18th President of the US was bestowed on the street in the hope of driving it upmarket.

Although Grant Ave. is dotted with food markets, Stockton Street, a block to the W, is an overwhelming 1,000-plus blocks of stalls piled high with ginger root, shark fin, live chickens and glazed duck.

CHINESE CULTURE CENTER

750 Kearny St. (on the 3rd floor of the Holiday Inn-Financial District)
*☎ 986-1822. Map **6**C8 🎫 ✗ Open Tues-Sat 9am-5pm. Closed Sun, Mon.*

Attractions here include galleries of Chinese and Chinese-American art, historic exhibits and cultural exchange exhibits from Asia. The Culture Center also sponsors programs aimed at visitors, including heritage and culinary walking tours of old Chinatown.

CHINESE HISTORICAL SOCIETY

*650 Commercial St. between Kearny and Montgomery ☎ 391-1188. Map **6**C8*
🎫 Open Tues-Sat noon-4pm.

This jewel box of a museum documents the remarkable contributions made by the Chinese to the Gold Rush, the building of America's transcontinental railroads and the development of agriculture in California. Other exhibits show how the Chinese have maintained their traditions in an alien land. Captions are given in English and Chinese.

CIVIC CENTER 🏛

*On Van Ness Ave., between McAllister and Grove Sts. Map **5**D7.*

San Francisco's Civic Center Plaza is one of the most impressive group-
ings of municipal buildings in the US. Dominated by the French Renaissance grandeur of the **City Hall** (pictured on page 29), the Civic
Center was begun immediately after the earthquake and fire of 1906,
designed by architects, Arthur Brown Jr. and John Bakewell Jr.

To the w of City Hall is the **San Francisco War Memorial and
Performing Arts Center**, the second largest performing arts complex
in the US. It houses the **Louise M. Davies Symphony Hall** (see THE
PERFORMING ARTS), the **War Memorial Opera House**, and the **War
Memorial Veterans Building**. The latter contains the SAN FRANCISCO
MUSEUM OF MODERN ART and the **Herbst Theatre**, site of the signing of the
United Nations Charter in 1945.

Other buildings in the complex and in similar classic styles are the
Civic Auditorium, the SAN FRANCISCO PUBLIC LIBRARY and the **State Building**.

COIT TOWER

*At the peak of Telegraph Hill, E end of Lombard St. Map **6B8*** 🖭 ◀€ *Open
10am-4.30pm. Closed Jan 1, Dec 25.*
Built with a $125,000 legacy from Lillie Hitchcock Coit, dedicated to the
purpose of "adding beauty to the city I have always loved," the tower is
one of San Francisco's landmarks. It is also a memorial to the volunteer
firemen of early San Francisco. An elevator takes visitors to the 210-
foot observation platform, to see a 360° panorama of the city. Murals by
25 "Social Realism" artists, depicting *Life in California, 1934,* are displayed in the tower's gallery. See also VIEWPOINTS on page 78.

COW PALACE

*Geneva Ave. and Santos St., Daly City, slightly less than a mile w of Freeway
US-101, directly s of the San Francisco city limits via the Old Bayshore exit. Map
2F4.*
The home of the San Francisco Grand National Rodeo and Livestock
Exposition, the Trans America tennis tournament (see SPORTS) and
other annual and special events (see CALENDAR OF EVENTS) ranging from
conventions to rock concerts.

CROOKEDEST STREET ★

*One block off Lombard St., between Hyde St. and Leavenworth St. Map **5B7*** ◀€
Carving the sort of track a timid skier might make, this street snakes its
way down a steep hill. Throngs drive down it, so expect a wait at the
top.

EXPLORATORIUM ★

In the Palace of Fine Arts, 3601 Lyon St. (off Marina Blvd. via Baker St.)
🕿*561-0360 for recorded information on exhibitions and events. Map **4B5*** 🖭
and valid for six months (🔟🖭 *first Wed of month)* ᕒ ✿ *Open Tues, Thurs-Sun
10am-5pm; Wed 10am-9.30pm. Closed Mon except holidays.*
A huge cavern filled with first-rate lessons in science disguised as fun
and games. Ingenious gadgets let children and adults measure their

own eyes, ears and voices; others deal with broader questions of physics, exploring color, electricity, motion, weather etc. There are 700 exhibits, so be prepared to spend hours here.

FERRY BUILDING
At the foot of Market St. Map 6C9.
Modeled on Seville's Giralda Tower, the Ferry Building is the headquarters of the Port of San Francisco and the San Francisco World Trade Center. The days when 50 million ferryboat commuters passed through it every year are long gone (vanished with the building of the city's two great bridges), but the building is still a landmark, and boats still run from here to Alameda, Oakland, and Marin County.

FILBERT STEPS
Filbert St., on E side of Telegraph Hill between Coit Tower and Sansome St. Map 6B8.
Starting from the top, just off Telegraph Hill Blvd., near Coit Tower, a series of walkways and steps leads down past some of the city's oldest, quaintest houses and prettiest small gardens. Many date from the 1850s. The Steps has been and remains a much sought-after address, and is especially popular with artists, writers and entertainers.

FISHERMAN'S WHARF
◀€ ✿ Map 5A7.
Rows of colorfully painted fishing boats face an inexhaustible number of seafood restaurants at one of the city's most popular tourist attractions. From here you can watch the crab catch being landed between mid-November and June or embark on a sightseeing cruise (see GETTING AROUND, page 40).

Fisherman's Wharf is perhaps the city's prime spot for an irrepressible horde of street jugglers, clowns and musicians, performing in what might look like colorful chaos, but is not. Each performer is required to obey a set of rules demanding that shows contribute to the favorable impression visitors get of the city.

Whatever you think of the al fresco floorshow, the backdrop is superb, with views of the Bay, the GOLDEN GATE BRIDGE, and ALCATRAZ. See also PIER 39.

FORT MASON
Entrance in Marina Blvd. at the foot of Laguna St. Map 5B6 ▦ for some events. Hours vary for each element. For scheduled activities, which include mushroom fairs and trade exhibitions but focus most heavily on plays, music and classes, check with Fort Mason Foundation, Laguna St. and Marina Blvd., San Francisco 94123; Visitor Center in Building A near main entrance, open 9am-5pm ☎441-5705.
Once an embarkation port for US troops headed into the Pacific, Fort Mason now operates as a diverse and lively community center within the GOLDEN GATE NATIONAL RECREATION AREA. Among the elements are: GGNRA headquarters, a youth hostel, an extraordinary vegetarian res-

taurant called **Green's**, several theater companies and four museums:

African-American Historical and Cultural Society *(Building C* ☎ *441-0640* 📷 *requested, open Tues-Sat noon-5pm, closed Sun, Mon)* — art, artifacts and a research library.

Museo Italo-Americano *(Building C* ☎ *673-2200* 📷 *open Wed-Sun noon-5pm, closed Mon, Tues)* — Italian and Italo-American art and artifacts. Its most intriguing displays trace patterns of immigration from Italy and settlement in the US.

Mexican Museum *(Building D* ☎ *441-0404* 📷 *open Wed-Sun noon-5pm, first Wed of month open noon-8pm and* 📷*; closed Mon, Tues)* — Mexican and Mexican-American art and artifacts. The great muralist Diego Rivera's influence is much seen here.

SS *Jeremiah O'Brien* *(Pier 3* ☎ *441-3101, open Mon-Fri 9am-3pm, Sat-Sun 9am-4pm* 📷*)*, part of the SAN FRANCISCO MARITIME NATIONAL HISTORICAL PARK, is the last unaltered Liberty ship afloat. In 1941 American shipyards turned out 2,751 of the vessels, each completed in less than a week. Many sailed from Fort Mason. A footpath leads from the *O'Brien* to the main Maritime Museum building.

FORT POINT 🏛

Directly beneath the San Francisco end of the Golden Gate Bridge (access from Lincoln Blvd. 400 yards N of bridge approach) ☎ *556-1693. Map **3A3*** 📷 ✗ ♿ ♺ *Open 10am-5pm.*

The gloomily handsome brick structure of Fort Winfield Scott was completed in 1861. Decommissioned in 1914, it now provides instructive images of an earlier military life, through its architecture and troop drills (including artillery practice) from its original period. The latter are staged by National Park Service personnel dressed in period uniforms.

The seawall alongside is excellent for fishing and wave-watching, and especially for watching surfers in perilously rocky shoals. The view of the bridge from below is awesome.

GOLDEN GATE BRIDGE ★

*Stretches from San Francisco's N shore across to Marin County. Map **3A3**.*

If one image were to be chosen to symbolize San Francisco, it would be the Golden Gate Bridge, the world's first truly great suspension bridge (between 1937-59 the longest in the world) and an incomparable place from which to see the city skyline.

A near-miracle of engineering, the Golden Gate Bridge spans the mile-wide strait that is the only cleft for nearly 600 miles in the Northern Californian coastal wall. Until this century, it was considered to be unbridgeable, and with very good reason.

The tide rips through the Golden Gate with three times the flow of the Amazon, 14 times that of the Mississippi. Add to this the 60-miles-per-hour currents, the vicious winds that whip around the headland, and the inevitable San Francisco fogs, and the scale of the challenge is clear.

The "curve of soaring steel" masterminded by engineer Joseph B. Strauss opened in May 1937 after a two-decade battle to ignite the public imagination and a four-year building program costing eleven lives and $35 million. Its 746-foot towers were the highest elevations w of the Empire State Building. The two cables that suspend the awesome structure contain 80,000 miles of steel wire.

The most breathtaking view is at the Marin County N end of the bridge. Pedestrians and bicyclists can (and do in throngs) cross at a leisurely pace for no fee. An inexpensive toll must be paid by vehicles, but only those traveling southbound.

GOLDEN GATE NATIONAL RECREATION AREA
Along the city's shoreline, from Fort Funston to Aquatic Park. Map 1B2
☎556-0560 ◀€ *A small visitor center in Fort Mason is open 9am-5pm.*
The GGNRA encompasses all of San Francisco's ocean beaches, and most of the city's waterfront from the Golden Gate E to Aquatic Park, adjoining Fisherman's Wharf. See separate entries for ALCATRAZ, FORT MASON, FORT POINT and SAN FRANCISCO MARITIME NATIONAL HISTORICAL PARK. (For details of beaches, see SPORTS.) The GGNRA also includes much of the Marin County shore from the Golden Gate W and N to Point Reyes National Seashore.

GOLDEN GATE PARK ☆
Bounded by Stanyan St. to the E, the Great Highway to the w, Fulton St. to the N and Lincoln Ave. to the s. Maps 3E1-4E4.
Four blocks wide and more than 40 blocks long, the park contains an outstanding museum of natural history, the CALIFORNIA ACADEMY OF SCIENCES; the city's greatest museum of art, the M.H. DE YOUNG MEMORIAL MUSEUM; the **Strybing Arboretum**; and a whole range of outdoor and indoor sports facilities. Informally, it is a paradise for bicyclists (especially on Sunday, when cars are forbidden in some streets), roller skaters and joggers.

Most of the developed areas are in the easterly third of the park, between Stanyan St. and 10th Ave. These include:

The CALIFORNIA ACADEMY OF SCIENCES (see separate entry).

A **children's playground** *(near Stanyan St. and Waller St. entrance, open during daylight)*, which has a fine merry-go-round (▧) and a children's zoo.

The **Conservatory of Flowers** *(Kennedy Dr., near Arguello Blvd. and Fulton St. entrance* ▣ *open 9am-6pm)*, is a copy of the Kew Gardens conservatory near London. It contains especially fine collections of orchids and other tropical plants, and the flower gardens fronting it are kept in bloom much of the year.

The **Japanese Tea Garden** *(adjoining de Young Museum, near 6th Ave. and Fulton St. entrance* ▧ ✦ *open 8am-5pm)*, dating from 1894.

It comprises fine gardens and carp ponds (complete with photogenic moon bridge), surrounding an open-air teahouse. Spectacular during cherry-blossom time in March.

The **Music Concourse** (*in a shallow depression between de Young Museum and California Academy of Sciences*), the site of free concerts in summer, on Sunday.

Shakespeare's Garden (*w of the Academy of Sciences Buildings*), containing labeled specimens of every plant mentioned in the works of William Shakespeare.

Stow Lake (*directly w of the Japanese Tea Garden, also accessible from Kennedy Dr. or South Dr. by a clearly signed loop road*), with rowboats and canoes for rent, for leisurely trips around Strawberry Island.

Strybing Arboretum (*on South Dr., near the 9th Ave. and Lincoln Ave. entrance* 🖃 ✗ *open Mon-Fri 8am-4.30pm; Sat, Sun, hols 10am-5pm*) contains a collection of plants from every part of the globe. In it is the **San Francisco County Fair Building** used for horticultural shows and other events (*for schedules* ☎ *558-3622*).

The **Tennis Center** (*off Kennedy Dr., opposite Conservatory of Flowers*), has 21 hard courts open to the public daily during daylight. (See SPORTS for information on playing.)

In the more open, western parts of the park are a paddock with a small herd of buffalo, a polo field, an equestrian field, fly-casting pools, a par-3 golf green, and a perfectly restored **Dutch windmill**. Unfortunately, the park is not a safe place to be in after dark, except for those attending an event at one of the museums, when crowds offer a certain amount of protection.

GRACE CATHEDRAL 🏛

At the top of Nob Hill, at California and Taylor Sts. Map 5C7 ⇐

Seat of the Episcopal Bishop of California, the cathedral is an impressive example of Neo-Gothic architecture, begun in 1910 and not finished until after World War II.

An undisguised concrete exterior gives the cathedral its air of enduring strength. Its treasures include an **altar** from 11thC France, a 16thC carved wooden Flemish **reredos**, stained-glass **windows** by Connick, and a **carillon** of 44 bells cast in Croydon, England.

GRADIENTS

San Francisco has 42 hills, ten of which are most frequently used to thrill the vertiginous visitor. To sample the sensation of running down a gradient of 20 percent or more, or to give the brakes of your car an unrepeatable test, head for Russian and Nob Hills, and Pacific, Dolores and Buena Vista, where all ten are located.

The steepest streets, according to the San Francisco Bureau of Engineering, are: **Filbert** between Leavenworth and Hyde, and **22nd** between Church and Vicksburg, at an awesome 31.5 percent; **Jones** between Union and Filbert, 29 percent; **Duboce** between Buena Vista and Alpine, 27.9 percent; **Jones** between Green and Union, and **Webster** between

Vallejo and Broadway, both 26 percent; **Duboce** between Divisadero and Alpine; **Duboce** between Castro and Divisadero, both 25 percent; **Jones** between Pine and California, 24.8 percent; and **Fillmore** between Vallejo and Broadway, 24 percent.

> When you get tired of walking around in San Francisco,
> you can always lean against it.
> (Anon)

The city's finest free white-knuckle ride must, however, be to travel in a car as it careers down one-way Filbert Street (31.5 percent) then pitches up intersecting Jones Street (29 percent), somehow managing not to somersault.

Whatever you do, you should not wear new leather-soled shoes, which have an effect on the near-perpendicular concrete like that of skis on snow. See also CROOKEDEST STREET.

HAAS-LILIENTHAL HOUSE 🏛
2007 Franklin St. ☎441-3004. Map 5C7 ▨ ✗ Open Wed noon-4pm; Sun 11am-5pm. Closed Mon, Tues, Thurs-Sat.
This is an immaculately maintained Victorian building in the Queen Anne style, dating from 1886. The museum, which is the headquarters of the Foundation for San Francisco's Architectural Heritage, is the only fully furnished Victorian house in the city to be open to the public.

The house is also the starting point for excellent walking tours of the grand homes of Russian Hill and around the Pacific Heights neighborhoods, and tours are arranged regularly on Sundays. Summer walks on Saturdays (🔟) are another option.

HEART OF THE CITY FARMERS MARKET
United Nations Plaza, Larkin and Fulton Sts. Map 5D7. Open Sun, Wed 8am-5pm.
Up to 90 stalls selling fresh produce, preserves, honeys, nuts, olives, herbs, flowers etc.

JACKSON SQUARE 🏛
Formed by Jackson, Montgomery, Gold and Sansome Sts. Map 6C8.
Not really a "square" at all, but a rectangular block of distinguished 19thC buildings that survived the 1906 earthquake. After slipping into disrepair, the block underwent painstaking restoration from the early 1950s. The Square is now a Historic District, with 17 of the 3-story brick houses designated as landmarks. Most are occupied by antique dealers, art galleries and gift stores, or offices of interior design companies, but are well worth viewing, even from the outside.

JAPAN CENTER 🏛
Post and Buchanan. Map 5D6.
Stretching for three blocks, and a focal point of the Japantown area (see SAN FRANCISCO'S NEIGHBORHOODS, page 57), this cultural and commercial complex has shops, hotels, theaters, *sushi* bars and restaurants.

Designed by Professor Yoshiro Taniguchi, an expert on Japanese traditional architecture, the center has the astonishing, five-tiered **Peace Pagoda** (illustrated on page 57) as its centerpiece, a gift from the Japanese people.

LEVI STRAUSS HISTORY ROOM
2 Embarcadero Center (Sacramento at Front St.). Map 6C9 🔯 *Open Mon-Fri 10am-4pm. Closed Sat, Sun, major hols.*
This traces with wit and style the history of jeans (the first ones were brown, not blue) from the 1870s to the present day.

MISSION SAN FRANCISCO DE ASÍS (Mission Dolores) 🏛
Dolores St., at 16th St. Map 5F6 🔯 *Open 10am-4pm. Closed Thanksgiving.*
Its formal name was and is as given, but it is nearly always called **Mission Dolores**. Founded in 1776, the year of American independence, this was the sixth of 21 Franciscan missions. It moved to its present site in 1782 and is believed to be the oldest structure in the city. Now dwarfed by the adjoining **Mission Dolores Basilica**, this old mission chapel is the least changed of any of the original missions. Moorish, Mission and Corinthian styles are combined in its adobe structure. See illustration on page 58.
The garden cemetery is a roll call of San Francisco pioneers.

MORRISON PLANETARIUM See CALIFORNIA ACADEMY OF SCIENCES.

MOSCONE CENTER
Howard St., between 3rd and 4th Sts. Map 6D8 ☎ *974-4000* ◄€
The Moscone Center is the first stage of the Yerba Buena development, a billion-dollar scheme aimed at further revitalizing the SoMa district. Recently doubled in size after a three-year expansion project, it now offers 143,362 square feet of meeting space and 442,000 square feet of exhibit space.
Work continues on the Yerba Buena development, in the hands of the city's Redevelopment Agency. Plans include the Esplanade Gardens, which will be on top of the Moscone Center and the adjacent Center for the Arts complex. Scheduled for completion in fall, 1993, the complex will incorporate a 750-seat visual arts facility.

MURALS OF THE MISSION
Between Mission, 20th, Potrero and Precita Ave. Map 2D4 🕴 *every first and third Sat leaves from Precita Eyes Mural Center, 348 Precita Ave., map 2D4* ☎ *285-2287.*
Enlivening walls and doors of the Mission district are more than 200 murals, some big, some small, some political, some religious, some global, some parochial, all wonderfully vivid. Some are painted by single artists, while others are the collaborative efforts of artists and members of the community.
The first community mural was painted in 1973, but the whole living museum grew out of the 1960s. Around 40 percent of the muralists come

from the Hispanic community, and the Hispanic heritage is a strong motif in the paintings. The site of the first mural was **Balmy Alley**. Today it displays 28 murals by the Placa group, which includes artists of international status.

By car, **24th St.** offers the chance to view some of the larger murals. On foot, walk ten blocks along 24th St. between Mission and York Sts. Inexpensive guided tours are preceded by a slide show and historical talk.

MUSEUM OF THE CITY OF SAN FRANCISCO
The Cannery, Third floor, 2801 Leavenworth St. (at Fisherman's Wharf)
☎ *928-0289. Map 5B7* ▣ *Open Wed-Sun 11am-4pm. Closed Mon, Tues.*
A significant exhibition of historical items — photographs, maps, paintings and artefacts, many of them never previously on show elsewhere. Items include the eight-ton head from the statue of the Goddess of Progress, which once adorned the dome of the old City Hall, before its destruction in the 1906 earthquake.

OLD SAN FRANCISCO MINT
88 5th St. (downtown between Market and Mission Sts.) ☎ *744-6830. Map 6D8*
▣ ✗ *Open Mon-Fri 10am-4pm. Closed Sat, Sun, major hols.*
Considered an outstanding example of Federal Classical Revival architecture, this 1874 stone building is now a federal museum devoted mainly to money. Among its exhibits are privately minted coins and a **pyramid of gold** valued at approximately $1 million.

"PAINTED LADIES" 血
Steiner St., between Fulton and Hayes Sts. Map 5E6.
The six matching Victorian houses set against the backdrop of the modern cityscape are a "must shoot" for visiting photographers. The best angle is from the edge of a neighboring park, Alamo Sq.

PALACE OF FINE ARTS 血
Baker St. and Lyon St., in the Marina. Map 4B5.
In less than a decade from the devastation of 1906, San Francisco had resurrected itself. In 1915 it celebrated its rebirth, and the opening of the Panama Canal, with the Panama-Pacific International Exposition. The Palace of Fine Arts was its centerpiece.

The Palace is a Greco-romanesque rotunda with Corinthian colonnades. Designed by famed local architect Bernard Maybeck, it was made originally as a temporary structure of plaster on light framing, but has been rebuilt in concrete. Appearance aside, it is notable as the home of the EXPLORATORIUM and the San Francisco Film Festival.

The Palace was restored in 1967 at a cost of $8 million, and a generation later, a public "Light up the Palace" campaign raised the money to keep it permanently illuminated. Set against its reflecting pool, it is a major attraction for photographers.

PEACE PAGODA   See JAPAN CENTER.

PIER 39

Beach and Embarcadero Sts. (on the Bay, two blocks E of Fisherman's Wharf)
☎ *981-8030. Map 6A8* ⬥ ⬥ ⬥ ⬥ ⬥ *Pier* 🔲 *but some attractions* ▨ *Open daily from 10.30am.*

There are plenty of man-made diversions at Pier 39, but the biggest crowd-puller lately has been the 200-or-so male sea lions who have installed themselves on **K-Dock**. The sea lions come and go, so their presence isn't guaranteed. But if they are in residence, the show they put on is among the best in town.

Otherwise, Pier 39, the country's third most popular attraction (after the Florida Walt Disney World and Disneyland) with an annual 10.5 million visitors, is mainly about specialty shops, restaurants, games arcades, a carousel, talented street performers, and Bay views.

A recent addition is **Underwater World**. Visitors take a "dry walk under the sea" down a wide transparent tunnel through a 700,000-gallon tank. On view are 2,000 examples of aquatic life, including fish, sharks, rays and sea turtles.

ST MARY'S CATHEDRAL OF THE ASSUMPTION 🏛

Gough St., at Geary Blvd. Map 5D6. Open Mon-Fri 7am-5pm; Sat, Sun 7am-6.30pm, except during special Masses.

This replacement for the earlier, traditional cathedral of the Catholic Diocese of San Francisco, following its destruction by fire in 1962, was controversial throughout its construction because of its radical style. Completed in 1970, under the guidance of architects Pietro Belluschi and Pier Luigi Nervi, it rises to a height of 190 feet on concrete pylons.

Officially described as a hyperbolic paraboloid, it resembles a washing-machine agitator from the outside, but its soaring, cruciform interior is more awesome.

The cathedral's **pipe organ** is a grand sculpture as well as a musical instrument.

St Mary's Cathedral

SAN FRANCISCO ART INSTITUTE

800 Chestnut St. (near Jones St.), on Russian Hill above Fisherman's Wharf
☎ *771-7020. Map 5B7* 🔲 ⬥ *Walter McBean Gallery open Tues-Sat 10am-5pm, Thurs 10am-8pm; Diego Gallery open Mon-Fri 10am-5pm.*

This college of fine arts maintains two public galleries showing contemporary works. One boasts a **mural** by Diego Rivera.

The buildings that house the galleries — one of which is Spanish colonial, the other ultramodern — are of interest both for themselves and for the views they offer across the city.

SAN FRANCISCO FIRE DEPARTMENT MUSEUM
655 Presidio Ave. (between Pine and Bush Sts.) ☎*558-3891. Map 4D5* 🖸 *ʀ*
Open Thurs-Sun 1-4pm. Closed Mon-Wed.
Among fascinating displays of the history of local firefighting, there are relics from the great earthquake and fire of 1906.

SAN FRANCISCO MARITIME NATIONAL HISTORICAL PARK
Map 5B7.
The various elements of the museum are all controlled by the National Park Service, as part of the GOLDEN GATE NATIONAL RECREATION AREA. Together they explain much of San Francisco's complex maritime history, through a pleasing mixture of grand and humble vessels.

At the **Hyde Street Pier** *(at the foot of Hyde St., directly w of Fisherman's Wharf* ☎*556-6435* 🖾 *ʀ open 10am-5pm)* are moored the old San Francisco-Oakland car ferry *Eureka,* the lumber schooner *C.A. Thayer* (a common 19thC vessel), the scow *Alma* (a hay-hauler in the bay) and — a quaint stranger — the side-wheel **Thames River tugboat** *Eppelton Hall* . Other ships in the museum fleet are the BALCLUTHA, SS *Jeremiah O'Brien* (see FORT MASON) and the World War II submarine USS *Pampanito,* which is berthed at Pier 45.

The **Maritime Museum** building *(Beach St., at the foot of Polk St.* ☎*556-8177* 🖸 *open 10am-5pm)* houses models, artifacts, photographs and other memorabilia of local maritime history. Some of the most telling exhibits relate to the Gold Rush era. Linking the museum building and Hyde Street Pier physically is **Aquatic Park**, a patch of lawn and garden, a beach, and, hidden away in trees near the base of Municipal Pier, some big-league bocce courts. **Municipal Pier**, accessible from Aquatic Park or the end of Van Ness Ave., is a breakwater and heavily used fishing pier.

SAN FRANCISCO MUSEUM OF MODERN ART
Veterans Memorial Building, McAllister St., at Van Ness Ave. in the Civic Center
☎*863-8800. Map 5D7* 🖾 *(but* 🖸 *1st Tues of month)* *ʀ* ▮ *Open Tues-Wed, Fri 10am-5pm; Thurs 10am-9pm; Sat, Sun 11am-5pm. Closed Mon, major hols.*
Permanent collections include most familiar modern names, including Picasso, Matisse and Kandinsky, but changing exhibitions are a major part of the museum's program.

Opened in 1935, this was the first West Coast Museum to devote itself exclusively to 20thC art. Collections include paintings, sculpture, drawings, photography, architecture and design objects, as well as media and video works. Among SFMOMA's paintings are major works of the American Abstract Impressionist school, including Pollock, Still, Diebenkorn and Guston. Special attention is paid to Bay Area artists; an adjoining gallery rents out and sells contemporary works, and there is an excellent bookstore.

The permanent photographic collection, including works by Ansel

Adams, Edward Weston and 1930s European surrealists, is worth a visit, as are many of the changing exhibitions. There is also a useful Fine Arts Library that is open to the public.

SAN FRANCISCO PUBLIC LIBRARY
Larkin St. and McAllister St. (Civic Center) ☎558-3949. Map 5D7. Open Tues-Thurs 10am-9pm, Mon, Fri-Sat 10am-6pm, Sun 1-5pm.
The library's outstanding special holdings are the History of the Printed Book, the Richard Harrison Collection of Calligraphy and Lettering, the George M. Fox Collection of Early Children's Books, the Schmulowitz Collection of Wit and Humor, and Norman H. Strouse's collection on the Panama Canal. The San Francisco History Room contains photographs, maps and other memorabilia.

SAN FRANCISCO ZOOLOGICAL GARDENS
Sloat Blvd., near 45th Ave. in the sw corner of the city ☎753-7083 (recorded message). Map 1D2 ▨ but ▨ to under 12s, and to all on first Wed of month. ✗ ▯ ✿ Open 10am-5pm every day of year.
Primates, especially gorillas, are the big attraction at San Francisco's zoo. The privileged creatures live in the **Primate Discovery Center**, a $7 million home for 16 rare and endangered species, and **Gorilla World**, which, at an acre, is said to be the world's largest enclosed gorilla habitat, with eight separate viewing areas for humans. All of the great animals are represented, many in enclosures with such names as **Koala Crossing** and **Penguin Island**. You can even watch the big cats have their lunch *(feeding daily (except Mon) at 2pm)*.

Some enclosures are naturalistic; others are smaller. An elephant train saves walking.

A connected **children's zoo** *(▨ open 10am-5pm, weather permitting)* has animals that can be petted, and gentle rides.

SIGMUND STERN GROVE
Sloat Blvd., at 19th Ave. in the Sunset. Map 1D2.
A beautiful, natural amphitheater hidden in a little valley below street level. Here, on summer Sundays, you can while away the time, or bring a picnic, to listen to free afternoon concerts.

STEINHART AQUARIUM   See CALIFORNIA ACADEMY OF SCIENCES.

TEMPLE EMANU-EL 🏛
Arguello Blvd., at Lake St. Map 4D4.
The cultural and religious center of Reform Judaism in San Francisco. The architect, Arthur Brown Jr., also designed City Hall (see CIVIC CENTER and ARCHITECTURE), and the contrast between these two massively domed buildings is a tribute to Brown's versatility.

TIEN HOU TEMPLE 🏛
125 Waverly Pl., 4th Floor, w of Grant Ave. at Clay St. Map 6C8. Open daily 10am-4pm.

This CHINATOWN Temple was dedicated to Tien Hou, the Queen of Heaven, soon after the earliest Chinese immigrants arrived safely in San Francisco in 1852.

TRANSAMERICA PYRAMID 🏛

600 Montgomery St., at Columbus Ave. Map 6C8.
The tallest structure on the San Francisco skyline, the sharp pyramid, 853 feet (260m) tall, was not greeted with universal rejoicing when built in 1972. Some San Franciscans wryly observe that the Los Angeles architects William Pereira and Associates designed it.... Still, it is a remarkable landmark that one cannot fail to see. It is illustrated in ARCHITECTURE on page 32.

TWIN PEAKS

Via Twin Peaks Blvd. Map 1D3 ◀€
Nothing to do with the bizarre TV soap, but a scenic drive leads to the 910-foot (227m) summit. On a clear day or night, there is a breathtaking 360° panoramic view of the city.

VIEWPOINTS ◀€

In a city with 42 hills, there is no shortage of vantage points from which to take in San Francisco's exhilarating skyline. These are some of the finest.

From the ritzy residential crest of **Nob Hill**, most easily reached by cable car, you can look down on the Bay Bridge, cradled between the towers of the Financial District on one side and the pagoda roofs of Chinatown on the other. Nearby **Russian Hill** offers a sweeping panorama of the Golden Gate and the Bay. At the NE corner of the city, **Telegraph Hill** overlooks the N and E Bay. One of the most spectacular hilltop vantage points is TWIN PEAKS. San Francisco looks especially uplifting from the water: board a ferry or drive to **Treasure Island**, or take in the view of liberty from the confinement of ALCATRAZ.

Inspiring views can also be had from in and around a number of buildings in the city, such as the COIT TOWER and the CALIFORNIA PALACE OF THE LEGION OF HONOR. The view from the pedestrian walkway on the GOLDEN GATE BRIDGE is breathtaking, while that from the **Marin headlands**, on the other side of the bridge, is hair-raising.

WASHINGTON SQUARE

Columbus Ave., at Union St. Map 6B8.
This is not a "square" at all and has nothing to do with Washington, which makes North Beach, which is not a beach, the perfect home for it. Washington Square is one of the city's best spots for an informal picnic lunch; perhaps some *prosciutto* and *mozzarella* from one of the many nearby delicatessens. Even the statue in Washington Square is not what you would expect, for it is Benjamin Franklin that watches the crowds in the Italian Piazza, from his pedestal.

It is also good place to sit and watch the world go by, or bask in the sun beneath the graceful spires of Saints Peter and Paul.

WELLS FARGO HISTORY ROOM
420 Montgomery St., between California St. and Sacramento St. ☎396-2619. Map 6C8 ▣ ✦ Open Mon-Fri 9am-5pm. Closed Sat, Sun, bank holidays.
Dominated by a stagecoach that proudly identifies itself as the Wells Fargo Overland Stage, this museum occupies two levels of the Wells Fargo Bank headquarters. It depicts the American West from the founding of Wells Fargo at the time of the Gold Rush to the early 1900s. Covering the theme of California, 1849-1906, the museum contains memorabilia of legendary stagecoach drivers and robbers, along with gold nuggets, miners' equipment, guns and badges.

M.H. DE YOUNG MEMORIAL MUSEUM ★
Golden Gate Park (two blocks s of park entrance at 8th Ave. and Fulton St.) ☎750-3600 or 863-3330 for recorded message. Map 3E3 ▣ (but ▣ first Wed of each month) ✖ ✗ ▣ Open Wed-Sun 10am-5pm (closed Mon, Tues), Asian Art Museum (☎668-8921), open Wed-Sun 10am-5pm (closed Mon).
Opened in 1895 with funds earned from the California Midwinter International Exposition (San Francisco's World's Fair), the de Young was named in honor of the publisher of the *San Francisco Chronicle,* one of the Exposition's leading lights. Most of what went on display had been acquired from the exposition. A roaring success from the start, the museum levied no admission charges.

De Young immediately began a program of acquisitions, adding paintings and sculpture, arms and armor, porcelain and objects from the South Pacific and American Indian cultures. From this eclectic collection was formed the backbone of what is today one of the West Coast's leading cultural institutions.

Important objects in the collection of ancient art and art of Africa, Oceania and the Americas came into the collection in the early days, much of the latter collected by the first curator of the museum, Charles P. Wilcomb. One of de Young's early acquisitions, a painting by John Vanderlyn entitled *Marius Amidst the Ruins of Carthage,* was the foundation for the collection of American art.

American art has been a constant focus of acquisition and exhibition programs in both the de Young Museum and the CALIFORNIA PALACE OF THE LEGION OF HONOR from their foundation, and especially since their 1972 merger to become The Fine Arts Museums of San Francisco. However, it was the gift of Mr and Mrs John D. Rockefeller III's outstanding private collection of American paintings and works on paper, in 1979, that really brought the stature and importance of San Francisco's holdings to public attention nationwide.

Today the de Young's American paintings are recognized as one of the country's finest survey collections of American art — a comprehensive overview of cultural ambition and accomplishment from 1670 through the 20thC.

In 1989, the de Young enhanced its status when it unveiled the first phase of a $1 million reorganization of its entire collection.

Exhibits date from ancient times through the 19thC and are drawn from Europe, America, Africa and Oceania. Of the Great Masters, specific

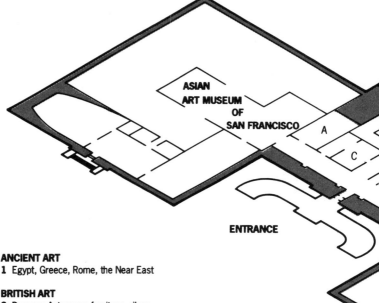

ENTRANCE

ANCIENT ART
1 Egypt, Greece, Rome, the Near East

BRITISH ART
3 Regency Anteroom; furniture, silver
4 George III dining room, Adam-style
5 Paintings by Gainsborough, Reynolds,
Lawrence
Rococo-style furniture

GLASS GALLERY
25 16thC drinking vessels
Franz W and Sylvia Sichel collection

AFRICA, OCEANIA & THE AMERICAS
42-43 Traditional arts of Africa, Oceania,
and the Americas

SPECIAL FUNCTION ROOMS
20 Hearst Art Education Classroom
21 Visitors' Orientation
23 Board Room

TEXTILES GALLERY
22 Theme exhibitions — permanent
collection

SPECIAL EXHIBITIONS
22, 36, 37, 39 Theme exhibitions —
permanent collection
28-31, 41, 44 Special and traveling
exhibitions

AMERICAN ART
(listed in chronological order)
7 17th–18thC: Colonial Decorative Arts;
Paintings by John Smibert, John Singleton
Copley
9 18thC: Silver by Paul Revere; Paintings
by Charles Wilson Peale, Henry Benbridge
8 Late 18th–early 19thC: Paintings by John
Vanderlyn, Benjamin West;
Federal period furniture
6 Federal parlor (1805)
10A Dufour wallpaper; Samuel Gragg chairs
10 Early 19thC: Paintings by Gilbert Stuart,
Thomas Sully; Furniture and decorative arts
11 19thC Sculpture: Works by Hiram
Powers, William Wetmore Story
12 19thC: Shaker and Folk Art
13 Mid 19thC: Landscape paintings by
Albert Bierstadt, Frederic Church;
Belter furniture
13A Documents from American Art
Archives
17 Mid 19thC: Genre paintings by George
Caleb Bingham, Eastman Johnson

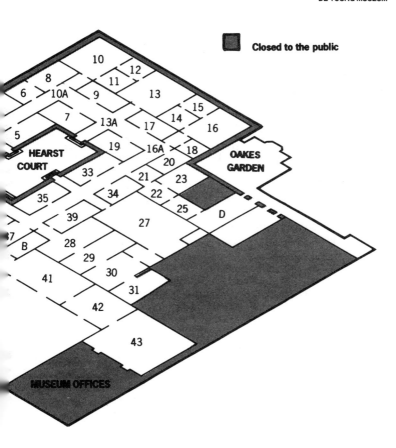

Closed to the public

19 Late 19thC: Genre paintings by Thomas Eakins, Thomas Anschutz
16A Late 19thC: Paintings by George Inness, George Fuller
18 *Trompe l'Oeil* and Still-life Painting. Works by William Michael Harnett, John Frederick Peto
16 Impressionists and Expatriates: Paintings by Mary Cassatt, John Singer Sergeant, James McNeill Whistler
15 Artists and the West: Paintings by Ralph Blakelock, Thomas Moran; Sculpture by Frederic Remington
14 Late 19th–early 20thC Sculpture. Works by Arthur Putnam, Augustus Saint-Gaudens

33 Late 19thC: California Art. Paintings by Thomas Hill, William Keith; furniture
34 Arts and Crafts Movement: Stickley furniture; ceramics; paintings by Arthur Matthews
35 Early 20thC: Paintings by Robert Henri, George Bellows
27 20thC: Paintings by Marsden Hartley, Charles Demuth, Edwin Dickinson, Grant Wood; sculpture by Gaston Lachaise

A Women   B Men
C Bookshop   D Café de Young

galleries show El Greco, Rubens and his contemporaries, the age of Rembrandt, and Gainsborough and British art. There is also an important textile collection.

The galleries are arranged by period, genre, theme and discipline: American Art of the Federal Period, American Folk Art and Shaker material, American *trompe l'oeil* and still-life paintings, and so on. Ancient art runs from the 3rdC BC, with relics from Egypt, Greece, Rome and Assyria. Oceanian and African exhibits include Pacific Island carvings, pre-Columbian jade and gold, Mexican murals and African sculpture. The floorplan on the previous pages helps you to follow the collections either by category or in chronological order of their creation.

The 15 galleries that formed part of the initial wave of refurbishment feature one of the country's finest collections of American art from colonial times to the 20thC. They cover paintings throughout the period, with especially strong examples of landscape, realism and *trompe l'oeil*, sculpture, folk art, documents and photographs, as well as wood carving, silver and glass work.

Among the many notable paintings are *The Mason Children* (1670), Frederic Church's monumental 19thC landscape *Rainy Season in the Tropics,* George Caleb Bingham's *Boatmen on the Missouri,* Eastman Johnson's *Pension Claim Agent,* Thomas Anshutz' *The Ironworkers' Noontime,* James McNeill Whistler's *The Gold Scab,* Maxfield Parrish's *The Pied Piper,* and a strong collection of Surrealist works by Yves Tanguy, Kay Sage and Charles Howard.

Sculpture includes the work of 19thC artists such as Herbert Powers and William Wetmore Story, Augustus Saint-Gaudens and Arthur Putnum. The 20thC is represented by artists such as Herbert Haseltine, Boris Lovet-Lorski and Isamu Noguchi. Other objects seldom seen before are furniture designs by Frank Lloyd Wright and lamps by Louis Comfort Tiffany.

The **Asian Art Museum of San Francisco** (★ ✖️), housed in a separate wing of the de Young, is built around the legendary Avery Brundage Collection. The Chicago millionaire agreed to donate his huge collection of Asian art to San Francisco on the condition that the city built a museum to house it. It opened in 1966 and now features 12,000 objects from 40 countries. It is the largest museum outside Asia devoted exclusively to Asian art.

Among the notable exhibits are the oldest known dated Chinese Buddha image (AD338) and the largest collection of Japanese *netsuke* and *inro* in the US. The first floor is devoted to China, with exhibits including Shang and Zhou bronzes and neolithic painted pottery, plus Ming and Qing objects and jade. The upper floor covers Japan, Korea, India and the rest of Asia as far as the Middle and Near East.

Refurbished galleries, with special earthquake safeguards, include the 2nd-floor Indian gallery, which features sculptures, miniatures, paintings and Mughal jade carvings. As well as the permanent collections, there are lectures and frequent and changing guest exhibits; and there are further improvements in the pipeline.

The de Young is jointly administered with the CALIFORNIA PALACE OF THE

LEGION OF HONOR. This building, a copy of an 18thC Napoleonic Parisian palace, has for some years housed an extensive collection of mainly French works, ranging from medieval tapestries to 20thC Post-Impressionist paintings.

It was closed in spring 1992 for a period of 2 years, for refurbishment and seismic upgrading. During its closure, some parts of the collection will tour, to other US museums and beyond, while other exhibits will be displayed in the de Young's temporary exhibition spaces.

Cities are like gentlemen, they are born, not made.
You are either a city or you are not. Size has nothing
to do with it.... San Francisco was a city
from the very first time
it had a dozen settlers.
(Will Rogers)

Where to stay

Making your choice

From glamorous old grand hotels and newer luxury establishments to handsome little Victorian bed-and-breakfast inns and inexpensive motels, San Francisco lodgings cater to all tastes and budgets. This is only to be expected, perhaps, of a city with a long history of playing host to travelers and one which has more recently busied itself with conventions and tourists. With some 30,000 rooms on hand, catering to visitors is the city's biggest single money-earner, and much thought and effort goes into making their stay pleasant and memorable.

At the top end of the market, geographically as well as figuratively, are Nob Hill's **Fairmont Hotel & Tower** and **Mark Hopkins Inter-Continental**. Around Union Sq., the **Westin St Francis** and **Four Seasons/Clift** share the 5-star billing. Many fine and/or good-value examples of the genre feature on the following pages: look for the 🏨 symbol following the hotel name.

However, the great landmark hotels are not alone in providing luxury. The alternatives are small downtown hotels and less well-known inns in refurbished mansions, many distinguished by an almost European intimacy and ambience, plus others with service and decor that owe more to Asian traditions. Good, reasonably priced examples are the **Prescott Hotel** and its sisters in the **Kimco Group**, both included in this chapter.

VALUE FOR MONEY
Then there are plainer downtown hotels, and motor inns and motels, the latter suitable for visitors requiring parking space in a city where it is either hard to find or expensive, and usually both. The **Fisherman's Wharf** area has a cluster of larger motor inns, but the greatest concentration of medium-size and small motels ranges from **Van Ness Ave.**, westward along **Lombard St.** toward the **Golden Gate Bridge**. And every quarter has at least one motel.

The best, or best-value, of these affordable alternatives to the grand hotels find their way into our main listings, backed up by selective lists of **Holiday Inns** and **motels** toward the end of this chapter.

INNS AND B & B
San Francisco has quantities of inns, ranging from 8 to 30 rooms, in luxuriously restored early-day mansions and small hotels. They are scattered about the city in such neighborhoods as Alamo Square, the

Civic Center, Cow Hollow/Union Street, Haight-Ashbury, Marina District, Nob Hill, North Beach, Pacific Heights and Union Square/Downtown. Prices range from expensive to very expensive. For a $1 fee, **Bed & Breakfast Innkeepers of Northern California** *(PO Box 766, Calistoga, CA 94515)* will send a brochure listing San Francisco members.

B & B and small-hotel information is also available from **Bed & Breakfast International** *(PO Box 282910, San Francisco, CA 94128* ☎ *696-1690 or (800) 872-4500)* and, more expensive and upscale, **Four Sisters Inns** *(PO Box 3073, Monterey, CA 93942).*

USEFUL TO KNOW

If you have difficulty in finding a room, contact **San Francisco Reservations** *(22 2nd St., 4th Floor* ☎ *227-1500, map 6 D9),* a free centralized service covering more than 200 city hotels, motels and breakfast inns and offering discount rates, the **Convention and Visitors Bureau** (see USEFUL INFORMATION for contact details) or the **San Francisco Hotel Association** *(323 Geary St., Rm 611* ☎ *392-7860, map 5 D7)*

Hotel reservations are advised and, although there are a few exceptions, most hotels require a reservation deposit. An 11-percent hotel tax is added to quoted room rates.

See HOW TO USE THIS BOOK on page 7 for the full list of symbols.

HOTELS CLASSIFIED BY AREA

CIVIC CENTER
Holiday Inn-Civic Center ▥
Inn at the Opera ▥ to ▥
FISHERMAN'S WHARF/NORTHERN WATERFRONT
Holiday Inn-Fisherman's Wharf
▥ to ▥
Howard Johnson's Motor Lodge
at Fisherman's Wharf ▥
Ramada Hotel-Fisherman's Wharf ▥
Rancho Lombard ▥
Tuscan Inn ▥ to ▥
THE HILLS
The Cow Hollow Motor Inn ▥
Fairmont Hotel & Tower ▥ 🏛
Holiday Inn-Golden Gateway ▥
The Huntington ▥ to ▥ 🏛
Mark Hopkins Inter-Continental
▥ to ▥ 🏛
Ritz Carlton ▥ to ▥ 🏛
Stanford Court ▥ 🏛
JAPANTOWN
Best Western Miyako Inn ▥
Miyako ▥
MISSION
Beck's Motor Lodge ▥
MONTGOMERY STREET
Hyatt Regency ▥

SOMA
ANA San Francisco ▥ to ▥
Sheraton Palace ▥ 🏛
TENDERLOIN
Phoenix Inn ▥
UNION SQUARE AND DOWNTOWN
Beresford ▥
Campton Place ▥ 🏛
Chancellor ▥ to ▥
Diva ▥
Four Seasons/Clift ▥ 🏛
Galleria Park ▥ to ▥
Holiday Inn-Financial District
▥ to ▥
Holiday Inn-Union Square ▥
Hotel California ▥
Grand Hyatt ▥
Inn at Union Sq. ▥ to ▥
Juliana ▥ to ▥
Mandarin Oriental ▥ 🏛
Monticello Inn ▥ to ▥
Parc Fifty Five ▥
Prescott ▥
The Raphael ▥ to ▥
Savoy ▥
Sir Francis Drake ▥
Villa Florence ▥ to ▥
Westin St Francis ▥ to ▥ 🏛

ANA SAN FRANCISCO

50 3rd St., San Francisco 94103
☎*974-6400 or (800) 223-9918*
☒*543-8268. Map 6D8* ▥ *to* ▦ *675
rms* ▦ ▣ ▤ ⬛ ⬛ ▦ ⬛ ⬛ ✸ 𝄞 ⬅ ☐ ♞ ☀ ♈ ⊟

Location: In SoMa, just off Market St.
Formerly Le Meridien, the French-managed hotel looks far better from inside than it does from without. One modern tower hotel among many, it distinguishes itself from the others with excellent public rooms, thoughtfully designed private rooms and suites with stylish furnishings and decor, first-rate service, and breathtaking panoramic views of the Bay Bridge and downtown from floor-to-ceiling windows on upper floors.

BERESFORD

635 Sutter St., San Francisco 94102
☎*673-9900. Map 6C8* ▥ *114 rms* ⬛
▤ ⬛ ⬛ ▦ ✸ ☐ ⬛ ♈

Location: Two blocks w of Union Sq. A sense of well-being pervades this old hotel. It has good-sized rooms furnished with plain but tasteful old furniture. Bathrooms are a little time-worn, but impeccably clean. (**Beresford Arms**, the sister establishment a block to the s, has 90 similar rooms, many with kitchens.) The Beresford's **White Horse Tavern** is a replica of the original in Edinburgh.

BEST WESTERN MIYAKO INN

1800 Sutter St., San Francisco 94115
☎*921-4000. Map 5D6* ▥ *125 rms* ▦
⬛ ▦ ▤ ⬛ ⬛ ⬛ ⬛ ☐ ⬛

Location: Near Japan Center, a mile w of Union Sq. To meet the tastes of Japanese guests, many rooms have steam baths. Reservation deposit required.

CAMPTON PLACE ⬛

340 Stockton St., San Francisco 94108
☎*781-5555. Map 6D8* ▦ *126 rms* ⬛
▦ ▤ ⬛ ⬛ ▦ ✸ 𝄞 ☐ ⬛ ♞ ♈ ⊟

Location: Union Sq. An old building refurbished into a luxury hotel with near-residential comforts. Its restaurant became a legend overnight.

CHANCELLOR

433 Powell St., San Francisco 94102
☎*362-2004. Map 6C8* ▥ *to* ▦ *140
rms* ⬛ ▤ ⬛ ⬛ ▦ ✸ ☐ ⬛ ♞ ♈

Location: Half block N of Union Sq. A comfortable, well-staffed, quiet old hotel. A few of its cheerfully decorated rooms are small, but all are kept fresh and immaculately clean.

DIVA

440 Geary St., San Francisco 94102
☎*885-0200. Map 6D8* ▥ *125 rms* ⬛
⬛ ▦ ✸ 𝄞 ☐ ⬛ ♞

Location: Two blocks w of Union Sq. Brushed metal, glass, VCRs, and other high-tech surfaces and gadgets are its hallmarks.

FAIRMONT HOTEL & TOWER ⬛ �🏛

950 Mason St., San Francisco 94106
☎*772-5000. Map 6C8* ▦ *596 rms* ⬛
⬛ ▤ ⬛ ⬛ ▦ ✸ 𝄞 ☐ ⬛ ♞ ⬅ ☀
♈ ♉ ❀ ⊟

Location: At the top of Nob Hill. The original turn-of-the-century lobby, with its towering marble columns and staircases, is a grand place for people-watching. Big-name entertainers stay at the Fairmont; politicians and other celebrities favor it as well. There is a choice between luxuriously spacious rooms in the old building and more up-to-date comforts in the 24-story tower added in 1962. Don't take the outside elevator if you fear heights: there is an indoor elevator.

FOUR SEASONS/CLIFT ⬛

495 Geary St., San Francisco 94102
☎*775-4700 or (800) 828-1188. Map 6D8*
▦ *329 rms* ⬛ ▤ ⬛ ⬛ ▦ ✸ 𝄞 ☐
⬛ ☀ ♈ ♉ ⊟

Location: Two blocks w of Union Sq. Known simply as The Clift until its acquisition a few years ago by a Canadian company, the hotel was for years almost an overseas club for well-heeled Britons. Its clientele has grown more international, but its traditional, pale-hued elegance survived a recent renovation intact, and its staff performs all the old functions of grand luxury hotels with undiminished skill. A bar and restaurant, the **Redwood Room**, is a splendid demonstration of finely finished redwood. The **French Room** is among the city's most esteemed restaurants.

GRAND HYATT
345 Stockton St., San Francisco 94108
☎398-1234. Map **6D8** ⅢⅢ 693 rms ▦
▣⇒▦▣▣▦❉♨◻◪▼♪
Location: On Union Sq. A tower hotel built in 1972, it has conventionally comfortable rooms of generous size by the standards of its era. The decor and furnishings add some touches of luxury.

HOLIDAY INNS   See page 90.

HOTEL CALIFORNIA
405 Taylor St., San Francisco 94102
☎885-2500 or (800) 622-0961. Map **6D8**
ⅢⅢ 242 rms ▬⇒▦▣▣▦❉♨◻
◪♪▼
Location: Two blocks w of Union Sq. Less spartan by miles than its prices suggest.

THE HUNTINGTON ▣
1075 California St., San Francisco 94108
☎474-5400. ⅢⅢ to ⅢⅢ 143 rms ▣⇒▦▣▦❉◻◪♛▼♪
▤
Location: At the top of Nob Hill. This small hotel in the grand tradition is almost a club for local society because of its restaurants: the lobby-level **Big Four** (for good-value lunches and an after-work bar) and the downstairs **L'Étoile**. The rooms are quietly luxurious. The staff is impeccable. There is even an elevator operator.

HYATT REGENCY
5 Embarcadero Center, San Francisco 94111 ☎788-1234. Map **6C9** ⅢⅢ 806 rms ▦▬⇒▣▣▦❉♨◻◪♨♛
▼♪♈▤
Location: In the Montgomery St. area, at the foot of California St. near Market St. This hotel has one of those Hyatt trademark lobbies — a soaring atrium with giant welded-steel sculpture and a reflecting pool visible from the door of virtually every room. Afternoon tea

dances and Sunday brunches enliven interior views still further. Rooms are functional and modern.

INN AT THE OPERA
333 Fulton St., San Francisco 94102
☎863-8400 ◫861-0821. Map **5D7** ⅢⅢ to ⅢⅢ 48 units ▬▦▣⇒❉♨◻◪
♛▼♪▤
Location: Near the Civic Center, one block w of Van Ness. A friendly, cozy, understated hotel at the heart of the city's mainstream performing arts venues, the Inn is understandably popular with visiting artists. Culture vultures will love the location; for others a complimentary limousine service runs to the financial district. The room furnishings are more European than Californian and usefully include a microwave oven in each room. Continental breakfast is complimentary.

INN AT UNION SQUARE
440 Post St., San Francisco 94102
☎397-3510. Map **6C8** ⅢⅢ to ⅢⅢ 27 rms
▣▣▦▣❉◻◪♛▤
Location: Four doors w of Union Sq. An instant success with celebrities and business travelers, the inn has a tiny lobby on each of its six floors where guests have continental breakfast, tea and hors d'oeuvres. Large rooms are elegant, with Georgian furnishings, yet lightened with whimsy: most beds have gaily designed half-canopies, and the high ones have brass footstools. The staff is hospitable.

MANDARIN ORIENTAL ▣
222 Sansome St., San Francisco 94104
☎885-0999 ◫433-0289. Map **6C8** ⅢⅢ 160 units ▦▬▣⇒▣▣▦▦♨
❲♛❉◻◪♨▼♪▤
Location: In the financial district. Offspring of the superb Asia-based hotel group, the Mandarin Oriental has some hard acts to follow. The location, in the top 11 floors of the 48-story twin-tower First Interstate Center Building, certainly helps, and old Asia hands have few complaints. The hotel aims primarily at the sophisticated business traveler, with a hi-tech business center,

HOTELS A TO Z

express elevator, three telephones and computer modem hookup per room. But spectacular views (from the 48th floor *directly at* the Transamerica Pyramid, for example), tasteful furnishings and a good restaurant give it a broader appeal.

MARK HOPKINS
INTER-CONTINENTAL 🏨
999 California St., San Francisco 94108
☎392-3434. Map 6C8 ▥ to ▥ 406 rms ▣ ▤ ▦ ▣ ▦ ▦ ▣ ▮ ▣ □ ▱ ♠ ≪ ≙ ♈ ♉ ♈ ▣

Location: At the top of Nob Hill. Every Hollywood movie set in the Pacific in World War II had its obligatory scene shot in The Top of the Mark. Today San Francisco's skyline looks quite different, but the great bar still sets the tone for the hotel, which remains as traditional as a grand tradition should. The skilled hotel staff dispels any feeling of hurried bustle.

MIYAKO
1625 Post St., San Francisco 94115
☎922-3200. Map 5D6 ▥ 208 rms ▦ ▣ ▤ ▦ ▣ ▦ ▦ ▮ □ ▱ ▵ ≪ ♈ ♉ ▣

Location: At Japan Center, a mile w of Union Sq. In a modern 14-story building, the hotel caters to a Japanese clientele with Japanese-influenced decor in the rooms, and authentic Japanese decor and furnishings in the suites, many of which have saunas. Japanese guests dominate, but are far from alone.

PARC FIFTY FIVE
55 Cyril Magnin St., San Francisco 94102
☎392-8000 or (800) 228-9898. Map 6D8 ▥ 1,005 rms ▦ ▣ ▤ ▦ ▣ ▦ ▣ ▮ ▵ □ ▱ ♠ ≪ ≙ ♈ ▣

Location: Near Market and Powell. The largest modern tower hotel in the city underwent a name change in mid-1989. Previously it was the Ramada Renaissance. Its decor remains stylish, its staff excellent.

PHOENIX INN
601 Eddy St. San Francisco 94109 ☎776-1380. Map 5D7 ▥ 44 rms ▰ ▤ ▦ ▣

▣ ▦ ▵ ≋ ≋ □ ▱ ♈
Location: Two blocks E of Van Ness Ave. Don't let the Tenderloin location put you off: the Phoenix is a gem. Service is friendly; the rooms, all overlooking the large central courtyard garden, are spacious, comfortable and decorated with modern art; there's complimentary breakfast from the lobby; and the parking lot is free. A special feature is the in-house video system showing movies set in San Francisco, e.g., *The Maltese Falcon.* Integral to the Phoenix is **Miss Pearl's Jam House** (☎775-JAMS). This is a moderately priced Caribbean restaurant that has a trendy clientele and offers live music Thursday through Saturday.

PRESCOTT
545 Post St., San Francisco 94102
☎563-0303 ▣563-6831. Map 6D8 ▥ 174 units ▦ ▰ ▤ ▦ ▣ ▦ ▦ ▵ ♈ ≙ ▰ ▮ □ ▱ ♠ ♈ ▣

Location: One block w of Union Sq. Opened in 1989, this "boutique" hotel is the downtown flagship of the Kimco Group (see page 90), whose aspiration to achieve European-style levels of luxury and excellence reaches its apogee in the pampered Club Level, located on the refurbished top four floors of the old Press Club. Attached to the hotel is the city's best new restaurant, Wolfgang Puck's **Postrio** (see WHERE TO EAT), for which Prescott guests enjoy preferential reservations.

THE RAPHAEL
386 Geary St., San Francisco 94102
☎986-2000 or (800) 821-5343. Map 6D8 ▥ to ▥ 151 rms ▦ ▰ ▤ ▦ ▣ ▦ ▮ □ ▱ ♈ ▣

Location: One block w of Union Sq. Extensively remodeled within the past few years, The Raphael is extremely comfortable, verging on luxurious. All rooms are cheerfully light and comfortably modern. Bathrooms are particularly spacious. Some rooms on the upper floors of this 14-story building are quite large, and those away from the street are quiet. Multilingual desk staff are helpful.

RITZ CARLTON

600 Stockton St., San Francisco 94133
☎296-7465. Map 6C8 ▥ to ▥ 336
units ⇦ ▦ ⇛ AE ◉ ◐ ▨ ঊ ≈ ⚇
⚌ ‡ ☐ ◲ 🎄 🏛 ☗ ☜ ▣

Location: Three blocks N of Union Sq.
Opened in 1991 hard on the heels of the
new Ritz Carlton in Marina del Rey.
Clearly, the location is less dramatic
than that of its southern cousin, but
everything else, whether service, furnishings or restaurants, promises an
equally high standard. Choose from
"Club" or "Butler" level; the latter provides personalized service. The refurbished Nob Hill building, previously
Metropolitan Life, is a registered historic
landmark.

SAVOY

580 Geary St., San Francisco 94102
☎Ⓕ441-2700. Map 5D7 ▥ 83 units ▣
▦ ⇛ AE ◉ ◐ ঊ ⚌ ‡ ☐ ◲ ▣
Location: Three blocks w of Union Sq.
Reopened in 1990 after a major renovation, the Savoy style is best described as
"French Provincial." All the usual comforts are here at remarkably competitive
prices, plus the **Brasserie Savoy**,
which is already rated one of the best
seafood restaurants in town.

SHERATON PALACE 🏛

2 New Montgomery St., San Francisco
94105 ☎392-8600 or (800) 325-3535.
Map 6D8 ▥ 550 rms ▣ ⇛ AE ◉ ◐
▨ ‡ ☐ ◲ ঊ ⚌ ☗ ▣
*Location: In SoMa, four blocks E of
Union Sq.* Mark Twain was dazzled by
the lobby clock in the days when the
hotel had a carriage entrance, both long
since gone. Guest rooms in the impressive old pile of bricks still show
signs of the grand era, and an $85-mil-
lion facelift completed in 1991 has given
the place a new gloss. The outstanding
treasure in the hotel has occupied the
old carriage entrance since 1909: the
Garden Court, a magnificent atrium
with leaded glass canopy, crystal chandeliers and Italian marble columns.

SIR FRANCIS DRAKE

450 Powell St., San Francisco 94102
☎392-7755. Map 6C8 ▥ 415 rms ▣
⇛ AE ◉ ◐ ▨ ‡ ☐ ◲ 🎄 ⚌ ☗ ▣
Location: One block N of Union Sq. The
towering lobby is as big as a railroad
station, and not much warmer, but
guest rooms in this aging hotel are con-
servative in furnishing and decor, and
most are spacious. The Sir Francis is
easy to spot: in a somewhat off-center
tribute to the name, doormen wear
Beefeater uniforms.

STANFORD COURT 🏛

905 California St., San Francisco 94108
☎989-3500. Map 6C8 ▥ 402 rms ▦
▣ ⇛ AE ◉ ◐ ▨ ☖ ‡ ☐ ◲ ⚌ ☗
▣
Location: At the top of Nob Hill. Converted from an apartment building into
a hotel in 1972, Stanford Court is the
standard by which San Francisco's luxury hotels are measured. Rooms are
spacious. In addition to telephones in
the bathrooms and similar practical
amenities, decor and furnishings are of
a style and quality hard to find in private
homes. Cosseting by skilled staff helps
make the price a bargain. **Fournou's
Ovens** French restaurant adds luster
(see WHERE TO EAT).

WESTIN ST FRANCIS 🏛 🏛

335 Powell St., San Francisco 94119
☎397-7000 or (800) 228-3000. Map 6D8
▥ to ▥ 1,200 rms ▦ ▣ ⇛ AE ◉
◐ ▨ ‡ ☐ ◲ ⁕ ⚌ ☗ ☜ ☊ ♥ ▣
Location: Overlooking Union Sq. The
staggering number of rooms is split between 600 in the handsome original
stone building, rebuilt directly after the
great earthquake and fire of 1906, and
600 in a soaring 32-story tower behind
it. The new rooms are luxurious and
modern. The best of those in the old
structure, refurbished in 1980, are pala-
tial. The main lobby and an adjoining
wine bar, **The Compass Rose**, are ex-
quisitely finished in traditional styles. In
the new tower, a disco called **OZ** is
phantasmagoric in ways that only modern materials could achieve. **Victor's**, a
tower-top restaurant that is reached on
vertiginous outdoor elevators, has one
of the best chefs in the city.

HOLIDAY INNS

Like their cousins the world over, they are all conventional, modern towers, save for the 5-story hotel at Fisherman's Wharf, which rambles. The choice includes:

Holiday Inn-Civic Center ☎626-6103 ▥ map **5**D7, at Market St.
Holiday Inn-Financial District ☎433-6600 ▥ to ▥ map **6**C8, one block E of Chinatown, at N boundary of Financial District
Holiday Inn-Fisherman's Wharf ☎771-9000 ▥ to ▥ map **5**C7, three blocks S of Fisherman's Wharf
Holiday Inn-Golden Gateway ☎441-4000 ▥ map **5**C7, $\frac{3}{4}$ mile N of Civic Center
Holiday Inn-Union Square ☎398-8900 ▥ map **6**C8, at Sutter and Powell St.

KIMCO HOTELS

The corporate goal of the Kimco Group is to provide European-style luxury and service. Its lodgings are all small, stylish, moderately priced hotels, and each has a signature restaurant attached. Besides the flagship PRESCOTT (described above), other Kimco Hotels (all ▥ to ▥) in San Francisco include:

- **Galleria Park**, 191 Sutter St. ☎781-3060, map **6**C8
- **Juliana**, 590 Bush St. ☎392-2540, map **6**C8
- **Monticello Inn**, 127 Ellis St. ☎392-8800, map **6**D8
- **Tuscan Inn**, 425 Northpoint St., Fisherman's Wharf ☎561-1100, map **6**B8
- **Villa Florence**, 225 Powell St ☎397-7700, map **6**C8

MOTELS

- Among the myriad choices, **The Cow Hollow Motor Inn** *(2190 Lombard St., San Francisco 94123, map 5 B6* ☎*921-5800* ▥ *60 rms)* is a comfortable motor inn.
- **Howard Johnson's Motor Lodge at Fisherman's Wharf** *(580 Beach St., San Francisco 94133* ☎ *775-3800, map 5 B7* ▥ *128 rms)* and **Ramada Hotel-Fisherman's Wharf** *(590 Bay St., San Francisco 94133* ☎ *885-4700 or (800) 228-2828, map 5 B7* ▥ *231 rms)* are both conventional modern motor inns.
- Standard motels include **Beck's Motor Lodge** *(2222 Market St., San Francisco 94114* ☎ *621-8212, map 5 E6* ▥ *56 rms)* and **Rancho Lombard** *(1501 Lombard St., San Francisco 94123* ☎ *474-3030, map 5 B6* ▥ *34 rms)*.

Eating and drinking

Dining out

From its earliest days, San Francisco has welcomed expatriates from every country with a cuisine worth considering, and some without, and has fed them all to their satisfaction. Although the contemporary city offers every degree of luxury and a striking variety of national and ethnic cookery, the pure San Francisco-style restaurant has its roots in the pioneer ethic, which believes that money spent on decor cannot be spent in the kitchen.

Thus plain tables, plain walls, bare wood floors and aging waiters in black are the hallmarks of **Jack's**, **Sam's Grill** and **Tadich Grill**, true originals that have begun to spawn a new generation of similar restaurants where the main difference is that the waiters are younger and wear blue aprons instead of black. Even such in-vogue places as **Chez Panisse** (see BERKELEY in EXCURSIONS), with a near-legendary culinary reputation, would strike a Spartan as bare. Yet these may be the very places to find some of the best food in San Francisco.

LOCAL CUISINE

In a city with 3,300 restaurants and so many cultural cross-currents, pinning down a local cuisine defies both imagination and logic. Old, famed faithfuls, which originated here in the city's earliest days, come to mind: *cioppino* (a seafood casserole), hangtown fry (oysters dipped in egg and flour and fried, often with bacon), sourdough bread, fortune cookies and Irish coffee. Numbers of stylish restaurants now list Gold Rush recipes alongside the *chèvre* and turkey *scallopini.* The old San Francisco restaurants pay expert attention to the grilling of fresh fish, but may add anything from a Slavic to a French touch — or, more likely these days, a dash of home-grown Californian originality.

ETHNIC DIVERSITY

Traditional French cookery is widely available in the city; there is an excellent choice of Chinese places, some of the best only recently transplanted from Hong Kong; and Italian restaurants with both Northern and Southern specialties are plentiful. Solid communities of Armenians, Basques, Russians, Greeks, Japanese, Mexicans and Central Americans, and a newer wave of Vietnamese, Thais and Khmers, maintain echoes of home, mainly faithful, some innovative. They range from elegant to downhome, with prices to match.

WHERE TO LOOK

Most of the city's famous restaurants lie within the quarter bounded by **Market St.** to the s, **Van Ness Ave.** to the w and **the Bay** on the other sides. However, for adventurous eaters, some of the most intriguing restaurants hide away in neighborhood shopping streets.

As ever, the best of them are always busy; eating out counts among San Francisco's most popular recreations. Either make a reservation, or expect to wait for a table.

In the following pages, the ⬦ symbol following a restaurant's name identifies it as a luxury establishment, and the ✿ symbol indicates that in our opinion it provides particularly good value in its class. Symbols and price categories are explained in HOW TO USE THIS BOOK on page 7.

RESTAURANTS CLASSIFIED BY AREA

THE AVENUES
Alejandro's ▥ ✿
Angkor Wat ▥
Khan Toke Thai House
　▥ to ▥
Yet Wah ▥ to ▥
CIVIC CENTER
Club 690 ▥
Hayes Street Grill ▥
Stars ▥ to ▥
FISHERMAN'S WHARF/
NORTHERN WATERFRONT
Mandarin ▥ ⬦
Paprikas Fono ▥
Scoma's ▥ to ▥ ✿
GRANT AVENUE/CHINATOWN
Empress of China ▥ to ▥
Imperial Palace ▥ to ▥
THE HILLS
Acquerello ▥
Fournou's Ovens ▥ to ▥ ⬦
JAPANTOWN/MARINA/
GOLDEN GATE/PRESIDIO/
PACIFIC HEIGHTS/RICHMOND
Scott's Seafood Grill ▥
Straits Cafe ▥ to ▥
MONTGOMERY STREET
Blue Fox ▥ to ▥ ⬦
Harbor Village ▥ to ▥
Iron Horse ▥ to ▥
Jack's ▥ to ▥
Sam's Grill ▥ to ▥

Tadich Grill ▥ to ▥
Tommy Toy's ▥ to ▥ ⬦
Waterfront ▥ to ▥
NORTH BEACH
Alfred's ▥ to ▥
Caffe Sport ▥ to ▥
Ernie's ▥ ⬦
Fior d'Italia ▥ to ▥
Fog City Diner ▥ to ▥ ✿
Helmand ▥ to ▥
Hunan ▥
Square One ▥ to ▥
Vanessi's ▥
Washington Square Bar
　& Grill ▥
SOMA
Le Piano Zinc ▥ to ▥
TENDERLOIN
California Culinary
　Academy ▥
Thai Binh Duong ▢ to ▥
UNION SQUARE AND DOWNTOWN
Campton Place ▥ ⬦
Le Central ▥ to ▥
Corona Bar & Grill ▥ to ▥
Donatello ▥ ⬦
Fleur de Lys ▥ to ▥
Harris' ▥
Masa's ▥ ⬦
Postrio ▥ to ▥
Lascaux ▥ to ▥
Trader Vic's ▥ to ▥ ⬦

Restaurants A to Z

ACQUERELLO
1722 Sacramento St. ☎567-5432. Map
5C7 ⅢⅢ ■← ⊂⊐ ⊞ ⊞ Open Tues-Sat
6-10.30pm.
North Italian *nuova cucina* in cozy and
elegant surroundings. There's an impressive list of Californian and Italian
wines and, once a month, dishes and
wines from a noted restaurant in Italy
are featured. *Specialties: Antipasti
misti, spinach gnocchi.*

ALEJANDRO'S ♠
1840 Clement St. ☎668-1184. Map 3D3
ⅢⅢ ⊂⊐ ❦ ⊞ ⊞ Open Sun-Thurs 5-11pm;
Fri-Sat 5pm-midnight.
A hit with pundits and patrons for its
paellas and *tapas*, Alejandro's — sometimes Alejandro's Sociedad Gastron-
omica — is where the city's Central and
South American chefs gather to com-
pare notes. The Peruvian owner-chef
has an affinity with Mexican and Spanish cuisines as well as his own. The
eclectic results are spectacular. Reservations are vital. *Specialties: Conejo in
salsa de mani (rabbit in peanut sauce),
sopa 7 mares-parihuela, and, above
all, paella.*

ALFRED'S
886 Broadway ☎781-7058. Map 6C8 ⅢⅢ
to ⅢⅢ ⊂⊐ ■← ⊞ ⊞ ⊞ ⊞ Open Mon-Fri
11.30am-2pm, 5.30-11pm; Sat 5.30-11pm;
Sun 5.30-10.30pm.
Alfred's is both an Italian restaurant and
a great steakhouse. By firmly established consensus, its mesquite char-
coal-grilled steaks are the best in town,
but the rack of lamb and *osso bucco*
(lunch only) ought not to be overlooked. The decor is a faintly dated San
Francisco plush — red banquettes, red
wallpaper, big chandeliers, waiters in
tuxedos — but relieved by a big glass
case full of aging beef. *Specialties: Anti-
pasto; porterhouse and Delmonico
steaks.*

AMELIO'S
1630 Powell St. ☎397-4339. Map 6C8
ⅢⅢ to ⅢⅢ ⊂⊐ ■← Open 6-10pm.

This one-time speakeasy and Italian
restaurant turned French is an enduring
favorite with well-to-do locals. *Specialties: Fish baked in a crust, plume de
veau.*

ANGKOR WAT
4217 Geary Blvd. ☎221-7887. Map 3D3
ⅢⅢ ⊂⊐ ❦ ⋔ ⊞ ⊞ ⊞ Open Tues-Sat
5-10.30pm; Sun 5-10pm.
The swankier of two restaurants run by
French-trained chef/owner Keau Ty,
who brought San Francisco its first taste
of Khmer cuisine. The decor recalls the
ancient Khmer monument, and excellent food is enhanced by traditional
music and dance. *Specialties: Broiled
chicken, beef with lemon soup.*

BLUE FOX △
659 Merchant St. ☎981-1177. Map 6C8
ⅢⅢ to ⅢⅢ ⊂⊐ ■← ⊶ by valet ⊞ ⊚ ⊞
⊞ Open Mon-Sat 6-11pm.
The rooms have a formal elegance —
paneling, old oil paintings, crystal chandeliers — that continues to bring
people back year after year for anniver-
sary dinners. A veteran staff and a con-
servative continental menu keep the
celebrants content. Reservations are advised, and jacket and tie are required.
*Specialties: Gamberi alla livornese,
mousseline de poisson, frogs' legs.*

CAFFE SPORT
574 Green St. ☎981-1251. Map 6B8 ⅢⅢ
to ⅢⅢ ⊂⊐ ⊞ ⊞ Open Tues-Sat noon-2pm,
6.30-11pm.
It takes real concentration to notice that
the garlicky food is good in this Neapolitan kitsch palace and general tower
of babble. Reservations are required,
although they do not guarantee exactly
when you will eat, or with whom. The
waiter may overrule a diner's choice,
and will be right. *Specialties: Pasta alla
vongole, scampi al'Antonio, calamari.*

CALIFORNIA CULINARY ACADEMY
625 Polk St. ☎771-3500. Map 5D7 ⅢⅢ
⊂⊐ ■← ⨍ ⊞ ⊚ ⊞ ⊞ Open Mon-Fri:
lunchtime seatings noon, 12.30pm; dinner

seatings 6pm, 6.45pm, 7.30pm. *Academy shop open Mon-Fri 8.30am-6pm.*

Tutored by European-trained chefs, students of the West Coast's best cooking school prepare and serve classic French cuisine with some Californian touches. The food is first-rate and reasonably priced, and service is friendly. Reservations, well ahead, are essential for the main dining room and are recommended for the lighter brasserie lunches served on the balcony. There is a small coffee shop/bakery/culinary shop/bookstore next door. Tours by reservation Monday-Friday at 3pm.

CAMPTON PLACE ☖
340 Stockton St. ☎*781-5155. Map 6D8* ▦ ▭ ▧ ▣ ▩ ▤ *Open 8am-10pm.*

In the hotel of the same name (see WHERE TO STAY), an altogether original chef presents an altogether original menu drawn from old American resources. Astonishing renewals of old familiars include — *Specialties: Grilled quail, spring lobster, blue corn cakes.*

LE CENTRAL
453 Bush St. ☎*391-2233. Map 6C8* ▥ *to* ▦ ▭ ▾ ▣ ▩ ▤ *Open Mon-Fri 11.45am-10.15pm; Sat 6-10.15pm.*

A bustling brasserie has the city's longest-cooking *cassoulet* among other entries on a properly simple and tasty menu. A firm lunchtime favorite with some of the city's movers and shakers. Reservations are advised. *Specialties: Boudin noir, cassoulet.*

CLUB 690
690 Van Ness Ave. ☎*255-6900. Map 5D7* ▦ ▭ ▣ ▩ ▤ *Open Mon-Fri 11.30am-2.30pm; Mon-Thurs 5.30-10pm; Sat 5-10.30pm; Sun brunch 11am-2.30pm.*

Following the big success of STARS (see below), Jeremiah Tower's latest venture has quickly attracted a large following among local and visting foodies. The cuisine is innovative Californian, heavily influenced by Southeast Asian and Caribbean spices and methods.

CORONA BAR & GRILL
88 Cyril Magnin St. ☎*392-5500. Map 6D8* ▥ *to* ▦ ▭ ▾ ▣ ▣ ▩ ▤ *Open Mon-Sat 11.30am-11pm.*

Persuasive evidence here that Mexican food can be much more than tacos and refried beans. The *Cucina Mexicana* on offer is altogether more upscale, with plenty of fresh seafood and regional specialties. The bar serves snacks and light meals throughout the day.

DONATELLO ☖
501 Post St. ☎*441-7182. Map 6C8* ▦ ▭ ▾ ▣ ▣ ▩ ▤ *Open 11.30am-2.30pm, 6-10.30pm.*

The Donatello uses marble and silk to achieve a light, refined, original appearance in each of two long, narrow rooms. The northern Italian menu follows suit, giving San Francisco by far its most elegantly prepared and served Italian cuisine. *Specialties: Lo scrigno di Venere, quaglie farcite alla Bolognese.*

EMPRESS OF CHINA
838 Grant Ave. ☎*434-1345. Map 6C8* ▥ *to* ▦ ◀ ▭ ▬ ▾ ▣ ▣ ▩ *Open Mon-Sat 11.30am-3pm, 5-11pm; Sun 12.30-11pm.*

The food is good, but it is the luxurious decor, attentive service and good view that set this restaurant a little apart from several other Grant Ave. institutions. Pleasant bar. *Specialties: Flaming young quail, Szechuan spiced beef.*

ERNIE'S ☖
847 Montgomery St. ☎*397-5969. Map 6C8* ▦ ▭ ▬ ▾ ▣ ▣ ▩ ▤ *Open 6.30-10.30pm.*

The decor at Ernie's could outglitter and outplush San Francisco's most famous Gold Rush bordellos. Jackets and ties are required at this award-winning landmark, as are reservations, sometimes several days in advance.

FIOR D'ITALIA
621 Union St. ☎*986-1886. Map 6B8* ▥ *to* ▦ ▭ ▬ ▾ ▣ ▣ ▩ ▤ *Open 11am-11pm.*

The great winemaker Louis M. Martini was a regular customer of the original Fior d'Italia, because he liked to be surrounded by a discriminating clientele. At its present address, and with plusher decor, it remains a quiet, comfortable restaurant for those who appreciate northern Italian food and excellent wine. *Specialties: Veal Stelvio, chicken Mascotte, zabaglione Montecarlo.*

FLEUR DE LYS
777 Sutter St. ☎673-7779. *Map 6C8* ▥ *to* ▥ ▭ ▣ ☱ ⬤ *by valet* ▥ ▣ ▣ ▣ *Open Tues-Sun 6-11pm.*
Fleur de Lys is an entirely happy place to have dinner, unless your billfold is slender. The principal decoration is a vast expanse of red and green floral fabric draped to form, more or less, a tent inside the room. The food is traditional French, with an occasional Algerian nuance, well prepared and skillfully served. *Specialties: Moules marinière, coq au vin, duckling with figs.*

FOG CITY DINER ✿
1300 Battery St. ☎982-2000. *Map 6B8* ▥ *to* ▥ ▭ ▣ ▣
In this architectural tribute to a 1950s diner, the menu offers full meals, but also a sort of American equivalent to *dim sum* — small plates that can be ordered by the half-dozen. The crowd is half the fun. Reservations are mandatory. *Specialties: Crab cakes, Buffalo chicken wings, black bean chili.*

FOURNOU'S OVENS ⬙
905 California St. ☎989-1910. *Map 6C8* ▥ *to* ▥ ▭ ☱ ⬤ *by valet* ▥ ▣ ▣ ▣ *Open Mon-Fri 11.30am-2.30pm, 6.30-10.30pm; Sat-Sun 6.30-10.30pm.*
In the Stanford Court hotel (see WHERE TO STAY), the restaurant descends from a bar to a conservatory overlooking Powell St. and the cable cars, then through several terraces to a bank of tile-fronted ovens from which it draws its name. Although the decor remains tastefully plain from top to bottom, there is no more elegant dining room in the city. The menu is tried-and-true French, and without a failure. *Specialties: Rack of lamb aux aromates, James Beard's duckling with kumquat sauce.*

HARBOR VILLAGE
4 Embarcadero Center, Lobby Level ☎781-8833. *Map 6C9* ▥ *to* ▥ ⬟ ▭ ☱ ▥ ▣ ▣ ▣ *Open Mon-Fri 11am-9.30pm; Sat-Sun 10.30am-9.30pm.*
First-rate Cantonese cuisine and seafood, orchestrated by award-winning Hong Kong masterchef Hui Pui Wing, in smart surroundings with fine views across the harbor. Lunchtime *dim sum* is the best in town, so you may wait for a table on weekends. Private banquets ranging in price from around $30 to $2,000 per person can be pre-booked. *Specialties: Minced pigeon, steamed crab with ginger and garlic.*

HARRIS'
2100 Van Ness Ave. ☎673-1888. *Map 5C7* ▥ ▭ ☱ ▥ ▣ ▣ *Open Mon-Fri 11.30am-11pm.*
Dark, handsome wood paneling and uniformed waiters lend elegance, and the menu provides fish and other diversions (especially at lunch); but at heart this is a steak house, and a good one. *Specialties: Dry-aged steak, prime rib.*

HAYES STREET GRILL
324 Hayes St. ☎863-5545. *Map 5D7* ▥ ▭ ☱ ▣ ▣ *Open Mon-Thurs 11.30am-10pm; Fri 11.30am-11pm, Sat 6-10pm.*
Tucked behind the San Francisco Opera House, this restaurant follows the fine San Francisco tradition of bare wood floors, unadorned walls and bentwood chairs as a properly informal environment for serious attention to grilled fish; but here the touch is French rather than Slav. A choice of fresh fish (halibut, sole, sea bass, angler, shark, trout) is cooked to taste, and served with any of several fine sauces (*beurre blanc*, sorrel butter, caper sauce Grenobloise). *Specialties: Grilled fish, Monterey Bay prawns in season.*

THE HELMAND
430 Broadway ☎362-0641. *Map 6C8* ▭ *to* ▥ ▭ *Open Mon-Fri 11.30am-3pm; Mon-Thurs 6-10pm; Fri-Sat 6-11pm.*
An Afghan restaurant that has won many local admirers. The health-conscious particularly enjoy the various yo-

gurt-based dishes. Helmand is very popular, so reservations are recommended. *Specialty: Grilled kebabs.*

HUNAN
924 Sansome St. ☎*956-7727. Map 6C8* ▯▯ ▭ ▾ ▧ ▦ ▨ *Open Mon-Fri 11.30am-9.30pm.*
Hot, spicy, trendy North Chinese cookery is what you can expect here. The place looks like a decorated gymnasium, but for connoisseurs of fiery peppers, decor is beside the point. Knowledgable locals take their meals in the relatively intimate bar. *Specialty: Spicy chicken salad.*

IMPERIAL PALACE
919 Grant Ave. ☎*982-4440. Map 6C8* ▯▯ *to* ▯▯ ▭ ▾ ▧ ▣ ▦ ▨ *Open Sun-Thurs 11.30am-1pm; Fri-Sat 11.30am-2am.*
One of Chinatown's enduring grand bastions of Cantonese-style cookery has left it to others to chase after the recent fashion for North Chinese dishes. The room is so softly lit that museum-quality art objects make their presence felt only slowly. Even the bar is subdued to the point of serenity. Jacket and tie advised; reservations required. *Specialties: Minced squab Imperial, barbecued lamb with Chinese zucchini, lobster Imperial.*

IRON HORSE
19 Maiden Lane ☎*362-8133. Map 6D8* ▯▯ *to* ▯▯ ▭ ▰ ▰ ▾ ▧ ▣ ▦ ▨ *Open Mon-Sat 11.30am-4pm, 5.30-10.30pm. Closed Sun.*
Conveniently located, and elegant without being over-formal, the Iron Horse is a good Italian/continental restaurant and has one of the busiest after-work bars in town. Reservations are advised. *Specialties: Medallion of veal Ruggero, chicken sauté Mascotte.*

JACK'S
615 Sacramento St. ☎*986-9854. Map 6C8* ▯▯ *to* ▯▯ ▭ ▾ *Open Mon-Sat 11.30am-9.30pm; Sun 4.30-9.30pm.*
Opened in 1864, this is the quintessential San Francisco-style restaurant, complete with white tiled floors, plain wood chairs, bare walls and utilitarian lighting. The waiters are more permanent than the fixtures, and the clientele is even more permanent than the waiters. To the complete satisfaction of regulars and waiters alike, Jack's menu is just as durable in all its quirky bounty. Jacket and tie required; reservations advised. *Specialties: Sorrel soup, English mutton chops, fillet of sole Marguery.*

KHAN TOKE THAI HOUSE
5937 Geary Blvd. ☎*668-6654. Map 3D2* ▯▯ *to* ▯▯ ▭ ▰ ▾ ▧ ▦ ▨ *Open 5-11pm.*
Widely regarded as among the best of the city's huge number of Thai restaurants. Choice of Thai-style dining, either reclining on cushions at low tables, or upright Western-style. Either way, waitresses wear traditional dress, and there's classical Thai dancing on Sunday. On top of this, the food is reasonably authentic, although less fiery than old Bangkok hands may wish. Tell the staff if you want it hotter. *Specialties: BBQ chicken, chicken coconut soup, curry.*

LASCAUX
250 Sutter St. ☎*391-1555. Map 6C8* ▯▯ *to* ▯▯ ▰ ▭ ▾ ▰ ▣ ▦ ▨ *Open Mon-Fri 11am-3pm; Mon-Sat 5-10pm.*
The vaulted cellar setting, the cozy fireplace, the sizzling rotisserie, the cool jazz combine to make Lascaux splendidly atmospheric. The food is Mediterranean provincial and California inventive, with spit-roasted meats providing the signature dishes. Altogether a peculiarly San Franciscan experience.

MANDARIN △
Ghirardelli Sq. ☎*673-8812. Map 5B7* ▯▯ ◀ ▭ ▰ ▰ ▧ ▣ ▦ ▨ *Open Mon-Fri noon-11pm; Sat-Sun 12.30-11.30pm.*
Cecilia Chiang pioneered fashionable North Chinese cookery in San Francisco, and her breathtakingly opulent restaurant at the top of the Woolen Mill building remains a treasure. The food is always fine, sometimes stunning. Service is impeccable, and the decor and

grand views of the Bay count for almost as much. *Specialties: Minced squab in lettuce leaves, smoked tea duck (one day's notice), beggar chicken.*

MASA'S ⌂
648 Bush St. ☎989-7154. Map 6C8 ▥ ⌷ ▆ ⇒ ⋐ ⋎ ⚇ ◉ ▣ ▦ *Open Tues-Sat 6-9.30pm.*
The late founder, Masa Kobayashi, was one of the first to marry Japanese presentation with French ingredients and techniques. His successors continue the tradition of producing dishes too beautiful to touch and too delicious not to. The room is a luxury in itself. Reservations are mandatory. The menu moves with the seasons.

NAM YUEN
740 Washington St. ☎781-5636. Map 6C8 ▥ ⌷ ▆ ⋎ ◉ ▦ *Open Tues-Sat 11.30am-11pm.*
This pleasantly understated restaurant has for some time enjoyed an unofficial reputation for having trained many of the best-regarded Cantonese chefs in town. True or not, it is still an excellent middle ground between grand Chinese restaurants and those with formica-topped tables where the Chinese truck drivers eat. Reservations are accepted. *Specialty: War won ton.*

PAPRIKAS FONO
900 North Point St. ☎441-1223. Map 5B7 ▥ ⌷ ▆ ◉ ▦ *Open Mon-Thurs 11am-11pm; Fri-Sat 11am-11.30pm; Sun 11am-10.30pm.*
Laszlo and Paulette Fono, the ingenious pair who invented The Magic Pan crepe cooker, run a Hungarian restaurant on one of the upper levels of Ghirardelli Sq. Reservations are advised. The *palacintas* that made them famous are on the menu, plus a broad range of their native dishes. *Specialties: Chicken paprika, veal paprika, gulyas with fried langos.*

LE PIANO ZINC
708 14th St. ☎431-5266. Map 5E6 ▥ to ▥ ⌷ ▆ ⚇ ◉ ▦ *Open Tues-Sun 6pm-midnight.*

This chic brasserie-style restaurant continues to attract homesick resident and visiting Parisians. Classic French cuisine, plus jazz piano on a white baby grand, and singers. Reservations are recommended. *Specialties: Game, breast of duck with peaches.*

POSTRIO
Prescott Hotel, 545 Post St. ☎776-7825. Map 6D8 ▥ to ▥ ⇒ ⌷ ⋎ ⚇ ◉ ▣ ▦ *Open daily 7-10am, 11.30am-2pm, 5.30-10pm.*
Another major success for Wolfgang Puck (of Los Angeles' Spago and Chinois on Main fame), this time trioed with chefs Anne and David Gingrass, Postrio offers four different menus at breakfast, the bar, lunch and dinner, with seasonal changes. As ever, the cuisine, Californian with Asian borrowings, is superb. Even the breakfast menu offers novel winning combinations. How about duck and pistachio sausage, or smoked salmon and sturgeon on brioche? The spacious high-ceilinged dining areas, designed by Pat Kuleto on three different levels, are as inventive, amusing and cheerful as the food. A garden patio area is available for private parties. People-watching, the lively bar area and an open-plan kitchen with wood-burning ovens provide an absorbing complimentary floor show. Reservations are essential for dinner and advisable for lunch. *Specialties: Duck sausage and shiitake mushroom pizza; smoked lobster club sandwich; roasted salmon with an almond black pepper crust; Chinese duck with spicy mango sauce.*

PREGO
2000 Union St. at Buchanan. ☎563-3305. Map 5C6 ▥ *Open 11.30am-midnight.*
A sophisticated spot with a lively bar, wood-burning pizza oven, good Italian food and friendly service. Expect to wait for a table even with a reservation. *Specialties: Tortelloni di Magro al Burro, Trittico di Gnocchi, Pizza.*

SAM'S GRILL
374 Bush St. ☎421-0594. Map 6C8 ▥

to ▥ ⌐ ◨ ▦ *Open Mon-Fri 11am-10.30pm. Closed major hols.*
Another of the old San Francisco no-frills, good fish restaurants, with bare floors and veteran waiters that used to abound downtown but have dwindled to a precious few. This one even has a row of curtained booths for secluded gluttony. Arrive before 11.30am for lunch or wait until after 2pm. A long menu has the faintest Italian flavor. *Specialties: Charcoal-broiled fillet of petrale, clams Elizabeth, deviled crab à la Sam.*

SCOMA'S ❤

Pier 47 ☎ *771-4383. Map 5B7* ▥ *to* ▥ ⌐ ▱ ◉ ◨ ▦ *Open 11.30am-11.30pm.*
Tucked into a corner of Fisherman's Wharf, behind the row of buildings fronting Jefferson St., Scoma's offers traditional San Francisco-Italian fish cookery in abundance. The restaurant does not accept reservations, but always deals with its customary mixed mob of locals and tourists efficiently and with good humor. *Specialties: Cioppino alla pescatore, sautéed calamari and scampi.*

SCOTT'S SEAFOOD GRILL

2400 Lombard St. ☎ *563-8988. Map 4B5* ▥ ⌐ ⅋ ▱ ◉ ▦ *Open 11am-11pm.*
One of the new generation of San Francisco fish houses, Scott's is comfortable but looks as frill-free as uncurtained windows and bare wood floors can make it. The cooks grill fresh fish in full view of the diners. Scott's does not accept reservations. Be ready to wait, and wait, and, on weekends, wait some more. (A branch downtown at Embarcadero 3 serves similar fare in slightly flashier, more modern surroundings.) *Specialties: Blue-point oysters on ice, Pacific salmon with hollandaise, fisherman's stew.*

SQUARE ONE

190 Pacific at Front St. ☎ *788-1110. Map 6C8* ▥ *to* ▥ ⌐ ➡ ➡ ◉ ▦ *Open Mon-Fri 11.30am-2pm; Mon-Sat 6-10pm.*
Owner-chef Joyce Goldstein has plowed a lot of new ground since grad-uating from Chez Panisse and shows no sign of slowing down in her search for yet another heartily flavorful bread, soup, casserole, stew, whatever. The atmosphere in a bright, modern room is always energetic. The menu changes daily.

STARS

150 Redwood Alley ☎ *861-7827. Map 5D7* ▥ *to* ▥ ▱ ◉ ◨ ▦ *Open Mon-Fri 11.30am-2.30pm; nightly 5.30-10 or 11pm.*
Jeremiah Tower had a strong hand in the early days of Chez Panisse and an equally strong hand in developing res-taurants of like temperament. This one is his own, and his inventiveness has not flagged. Great for lunch or after-the-show. The menu changes regularly, but always has fish, pasta and grilled meats as anchors.

STRAITS CAFÉ

3300 Geary Blvd. ☎ *668-1783. Map 4D4* ▥ *to* ▥ ▱ ◉ ◨ ▦ *Open Sun-Thurs 11.30am-10pm; Fri-Sat 11.30am-11pm.*
Singapore cuisine brings together the best of a number of worlds; several Chinese regions, Indonesia, Malaysia, the Indian subcontinent all feature. The Straits Café claims to be more than a family restaurant, but the Singaporean dishes here are as good as you'll find outside Southeast Asia. *Specialties: Chili crab, satay, curried beef.*

TADICH GRILL

240 California St. ☎ *391-2373. Map 6C8* ▥ *to* ▥ ⌐ ⅋ *Open Mon-Sat 11.30am-10.30pm. Closed major hols.*
The full name of this old San Francisco eating house is Tadich's Original Cold Day Restaurant. It doesn't make much sense, but has stuck with the place through at least two moves, as has an atmosphere full of comfort and free of frills. A no-reservations policy means a long wait for booths or small tables, but the long counter usually has vacant places available soon if not immedi-ately. Most of the clientele comes here to have fresh fish grilled by veteran cooks to the magnificent standards of Adriatic Slavs; but casseroles cannot be

overlooked. *Specialties: Snapper, sand dabs, crab, prawns à la Monza.*

THAI BINH DUONG (PACIFIC RESTAURANT)
607 Larkin St. Map 5D7 □ *to* □□ □□
Open Mon-Sun 8.30am-8pm.
A neighborhood Vietnamese restaurant with a pleasant no-frills decor and a predominantly Asian clientele, who know a thing or two about Vietnamese food. The staples are well done and inexpensive. *Specialties: Beef noodle soup, imperial rolls.*

TOMMY TOY'S △
655 Montgomery St. ☎397-4888. *Map 6C8* ▥ *to* ▥ □□ ▤ ♈ ▣ ▣ ▣ ▣ *Open Mon-Fri 11.30am-3pm; daily 6-9.30pm.*
California has been in the vanguard of using Asian techniques and ingredients to re-invent European cooking. At Tommy Toy's the exchange is in the opposite direction. The result is *nouvelle cuisine Chinoise* in opulent surroundings. The dishes and the presentation are refined, with the emphasis on Szechuan and Cantonese specialties. Reservations are recommended.

TRADER VIC'S △
20 Cosmo Pl. ☎776-2232. *Map 5C7* ▥ *to* ▥ □□ ▤ ♈ ▰ *by valet* ▣ ▣ ▣ ▣ *Open Mon-Fri 11.30am-2.30pm, 5pm-midnight; Sat-Sun 5pm-midnight.*
Polynesia is only one influence in a richly varied menu served with flourishes by the European and Asian staff. The decor is whimsically tropical in the main room, but severely nautical in the Captain's Cabin, a gathering place for San Francisco society, especially after the theater. Reservations are required. Men must wear jacket and tie; trouser suits for women are tolerated. In the bar, the unwary will learn the perils of tropical rum drinks. *Specialties: Baked crab (Dec-Feb), Indonesian lamb, salmon in red caviar sauce.*

VANESSI'S
498 Broadway ☎421-0890. *Map 6C8* ▥ □□ ▣ ▣ ▣ ▣ *Open Mon-Sat 11.30am-1am; Sun 4.30pm-midnight.*

In this ever-thrumming hive of eaters and drinkers, cooks working behind a long counter are one of the great long-running shows in town. Flames do not move half as fast. Reservations are advised but guarantee little. San Francisco is full of places famous for Joe's Special, but this is the best place for these cousins to fritattas, made with minced meat, spinach and eggs. Good grilled meats too. *Specialties: Ravioli, calamari (fried or sautéed in tomato sauce), zabaglione, abalone.*

WASHINGTON SQUARE BAR & GRILL
1707 Powell St. ☎982-8123. *Map 6B8* ▥ □□ ▤ ♈ ♫ ▰ *by valet* ▣ ▣ ▣ *Open Mon-Sat 11.30am-2.30pm, 6-11pm; Sun 10am-3pm, 6-11pm.*
A haven for local newspaper people and other writers and for jazz piano players, who may be interested in good Italian food or may be there just to drink real whiskey in preference to vodka and other timid stuff. The menu has some set pieces and some daily specials, but the inclination is always toward fish, veal and pasta. Brunch dishes keep an Italian flavor, too. Everything is good, and much is imaginative. Reservations are advised. *Specialties: Fisherman's salad, fried calamari with anchovy sauce.*

WATERFRONT
Pier 7, The Embarcadero ☎391-2696. *Map 6C9* ▥ *to* ▥ ◀€ □□ ▰ *by valet* ▣ ▣ ▣ ▣ *Open Mon-Fri 11.30am-2.30pm, 5-10.30pm; Sat-Sun 11am-3pm, 5-10.30pm.*
This, one of the younger generation of fish houses, leans toward understated decor (although not as far as **Tadich's** or **Sam's Grill**), and grilling or sautéing rather than frying in batter. Tables are on several levels inside a glass wall, with views of city fireboats and the Bay beyond. Many locals — and visitors — think SF's best brunch is served here. *Specialties: Grilled fish, seafood salads.*

YET WAH
2140 Clement St. ☎387-8040. *Map 3D2* ▥ *to* ▥ □□ ▤ ♈ ▣ ▣ ▣ ▣ *Open 11.30am-11.30pm.*

Yet Wah is a small, family-owned chain, which maintains consistently high standards. But the dining room in this outrageous purple building on Clement St. is emphatically the flagship. The decor is gilt and crimson, but softened by plants in an atrium and by pleasantly dim lighting. Reservations are accepted. A menu with as many as 200 items has most North Chinese dishes that will be familiar to most Americans. Every dish is prepared to order. *Specialties: Potstickers, mushu pork, hot pepper prawns*.

Eating on a budget

Some favorites, if you're traveling with a large family....

INEXPENSIVE NORTH BEACH ITALIAN
Basta Pasta   1268 Grant Ave. ☎434-2248, map **6**C8, a great favorite with children
Gold Spike   527 Columbus Ave. ☎986-9747, map **5**B7
New Pisa   550 Green St. ☎362-4726, map **6**B8
La Pantera   1234 Grant Ave. ☎392-0170, map **6**C8
The US Restaurant   431 Columbus Ave. ☎362-6251, map **6**C8

INEXPENSIVE CHINATOWN
Asia Garden   772 Pacific Ave. ☎398-5112, map **6**C8, for *dim sum*
Hang Ah   1 Pagoda Pl., off Sacramento St., near Stockton St. ☎982-5686, map **6**C8
Sam Wo   813 Washington St. ☎982-0596, map **6**C8, a full menu
Thai Stick   698 Post St. ☎928-7730, map **6**C8, for home-style Thai food without MSG

INEXPENSIVE MISSION DISTRICT CENTRAL AMERICAN
Frutilandia   3007 24th St. map **2**D4, for Cuban beef and black beans
Las Guitarras   3274 24th St. ☎824-1027, map **2**D4
Roosevelt Tamale Parlor   2817 24th St. ☎648-9899, map **2**D4
El Trebol   3324 24th St. ☎285-6298, map **2**D4, for *pupusas* and other Salvadoran specialties

SOUP, SALADS AND SANDWICHES
Clown Alley   42 Columbus Ave. ☎421-2540, map **6**C8, for hot dogs and burgers that can be eaten there or taken out
Hamburger Mary's   1582 Folsom St. ☎626-1985, map **6**E8, said by many to serve the best burgers in town: breakfast, lunch, dinner, bar, all in a funky atmosphere
Perry's   1944 Union St. ☎922-9022, map **5**C6, offering sandwiches and more, in conjunction with a great bar
Salamagundi's   442 Geary St. ☎441-0894, map **5**D7, for especially fine soups

KOSHER DELICATESSEN
David's   474 Geary St. ☎771-1600, map **5**D7

BREAKFAST
Sear's Fine Foods   439 Powell St. ☎986-1160, map **6**C8, where there's always a long line, usually out of the door

Ice cream parlors

Finally, San Francisco is a city in love with ice cream. We end, therefore, with a list of the city's favorite ice cream parlors.

Bud's   1300 Castro St., map **2**C4
Double Rainbow   1653 Polk St., map **5**C7, and 3933 24th St., map **2**D4
Gaston's Ice Cream of San Francisco   3277 Sacramento St., map **4**C5
Gelato   2211 Filbert St., map **4**C5, and 201 Parnassus Ave., map **4**F4
Joe's   5351 Geary Blvd., map **3**D1
St Francis Ice Cream Parlor   2001 24th St., map **2**D4
Swenson's   Hyde St. at Union St., map **5**B7, the original of a vast chain
Uncle Gaylord's   55 Vermont St., 721 Irving St., map **3**F3, and 1900 Market St., map **5**E7

Entertainments

San Francisco by night

San Francisco paid a price for inaugurating topless, and later bottom-less, dancing. For a number of years the city's reputation for nightlife rested primarily on near-naked jiggling and an ever lively rock music scene. An earlier reputation for cabaret, comedy, folk, jazz and show music seemed to dwindle away under the weight of these two. No longer: diversity has made a comeback, with the comedy/cabaret scene especially vibrant. These days it is the burlesque that looks tired.

Many of the trendiest new hot-spots are to be found in the fast reviving SoMa district. What follows is just a brief taste of what's on offer. Consult *Datebook*, the supplement of *The San Francisco Chronicle*, as well as the free-sheets *Calendar* magazine, *SF Weekly* and *The San Francisco Bay Guardian* for detailed week-by-week information on acts and times.

Most nightclubs sell tickets at the door. The bigger the name, the wiser it is to reserve in advance. Some clubs work through ticket agencies, especially **BASS** (☎ *(510) 762-2277)* ; many sell advance tickets direct.

BARS/COCKTAILS/CAFÉS
Here are just a few places where you might wind up to wind down....

ACT IV LOUNGE
Inn at the Opera, 333 Fulton St.
☎*863-8400. Map 5D7* ➧ ⇛ ⚲ ♪ *nightly 5pm-midnight.*
Crackling fireplace, tasteful decor and easy-listening piano playing make this ideal for a romantic evening, or for drinks before or after a performance at one of the many nearby arts venues.

BLUE LIGHT CAFÉ
1979 Union St. ☎*922-5510. Map 5C6* ⚲
Nightly 4pm-1am.
1970s musician Boz Scaggs' place at-tracts an affable yuppie crowd with good recorded music, tasty southwest-ern snacks and excellent cocktails.

BRAINWASH
1122 Folsom St. ☎*841-FOOD. Map 6E8*
▨ ⚲ ♪ *Daily 7.30am-11pm.*
Another radical West Coast break-through in the perpetual battle against real-life tedium; a café-laundromat fea-turing live music on Tuesdays and Wed-

nesdays, occasional comedy plus food and refreshments. Laundry day will never seem the same again.

BUENA VISTA
2765 Hyde St. ☎*474-5044. Map 5B7* ◀€
⚲ *Mon-Sat 9am-2am, Sun 8am-2am.*
They claim to have introduced Irish Coffee to the US. True or not, the bar is famous for it. Usually it's crowded, with great views of the Bay.

CAFFE TRIESTE
601 Vallejo St. ☎*392-6739. Map 5C7* ⇛
♪ *early till late.*
Favorite of beatnik poets, writers, artists and intellectuals. The Giotta family, who run the place, stage sing-songs on weekends.

PERRY'S
1944 Union St. ☎*922-9022. Map 5C6* ⇛
until midnight ⚲ *Daily 9am-2am.*
The city's best-known young and fashionable singles bar.

REDWOOD ROOM
495 Geary St. ☎775-4700. Map 5D7 ♈
♫ *nightly 4.30pm-1am.*
Wood-paneled Art Deco elegance;
soothing piano music; dress formal.

SAN FRANCISCO BREWING COMPANY
155 Columbus Ave. ☎434-3344. Map
6C8 ⇌ ♈ ♫ *Mon-Thurs 11.30am-*
midnight, Fri 11.30am-1.30am, Sat
3pm-midnight, Sun noon-midnight.
Excellent beers made on the spot, a
friendly atmosphere and plenty of history. The bar and its period interior date
from 1907. The location was once the
waterfront Barbary Coast, celebrated
for its anything-went exuberance.

TOP OF THE MARK
Mark Hopkins Hotel, California St. at Mason
☎392-3434. Map 6C8 ➟ ⟪ ♈ ♫ *nightly*
4pm-2am.
The 360° view from the legendary 19th
floor is as spectacular as when it opened in 1939 — maybe more so. The
decor is refined, dress formal. However, there's no need to dress up for
drinks — and the view is available any
time of day or evening.

TOSCA CAFÉ
242 Columbus Ave. ☎986-9651. Map
6C8 ♟ ♈ *Nightly 7pm-2am.*
Another North Beach institution,
Tosca's is cordial, crowded and noisy.
Check out the opera-playing jukebox
and the speciality cappuccino coffee.
Movie fans might spot director Francis
Ford Coppola, who is a regular; his
office is across the street.

VESUVIO CAFÉ
255 Columbus Ave. ☎362-3370. Map
6B8 ♟ ♈ *Daily 6am-2am.*
A landmark North Beach bar and haven
for Beat Generation poets and artists.
Little changed, it is still popular with the
SF artistic and literary crowd.

CABARET AND COMEDY

From the big, brash cabaret reviews via middle-of-the-road coziness to
the wicked intimacy of the alternative comedy scene — there is plenty
to keep you happy in San Francisco.

BEACH BLANKET BABYLON GOES TO...
(new destinations from time to time)
Club Fugazi, 678 Green St. ☎421-4222.
Map 6B8 ▨ *Nightly at 8pm.*
A long-running (18 years and no sign of
a break), locally topical revue with
enough fantastic tall hats and funny
dances to appeal to out-of-towners almost as much as San Franciscans. Reservations are definitely recommended.

CITY CABARET
401 Mason St., near Union Sq.
☎441-7787. Map 6C8 ▣ *(or* ▨ *for* ♫ *)*
Chameleon-like City Cabaret has music,
cabaret or improvisational comedy, depending on who or what is hot news.

COBB'S COMEDY PUB
2069 Chestnut St. ☎563-5157. Map 5B6
▣ *but drink minimum charge. Revue*
Sun-Thurs at 9pm, Fri-Sat at 9pm and 11pm.
In the unlikely environs of the Marina,
Cobb's books a fairly set roster of local
comedians most nights, but spices up
its program with an occasional nation-
ally-known out-of-towner.

HOLY CITY ZOO
408 Clement St., ☎386-4242. Map 3D3
▨ *to* ▨ *plus two-drink minimum for revue;*
daily 8.30pm, Fri-Sat also at 11pm.
Robin Williams is a graduate of this tiny
club where novice stand-up comics en-
courage audience participation.

THE OTHER CAFÉ
100 Carl St. (off Cole St. in the Haight-
Ashbury) ☎681-0748. Map 4F4. Tickets
from BASS ▨ *for revue, nightly from 9pm.*
Local comedians try out. Food available.

PLUSH ROOM
940 Sutter St., in the York Hotel
☎885-6800. Map 5C7 ▨ *plus 2-drink*
minimum for ♫ *Sun, Tues-Thurs at 8.30pm*
and 10.30pm.
Just when it seemed like all the solid old

cabaret performers had run out of anywhere to go other than the Venetian Room... along came the Plush Room.

PUNCH LINE
444 Battery St. ☎*474-3810. Map* **6C8** 🔳

DANCING/NIGHTCLUBS

Whether you're hip or whether you're staid, there are no excuses for not taking the floor.

CESAR'S LATIN PALACE
3140 Mission St. ☎*648-6611. Map* **2D4** 🔳 *but no minimum for* 🎵 *and* 🎤 *Wed-Sat 8pm-6am.*
All-star salsa band plus ⬤ between sets, and tango on Sun.

CLUB DV8
540 Howard St. ☎*777-1419. Map* **6D8** 🔳 🎵 ⬤ 🎵 🎤 *Wed-Thurs 9pm-3am, Fri-Sat 9pm-4am.*
Part of the hip SoMa scene; live entertainment and disco in a large post-industrial space favoured by the young and outrageous.

FIREHOUSE-7
3160 16th St., ☎*621-1617. Map* **5F7** 🔳 🎤 ⬤ 🎵 🎤 *late till later.*
Mostly dancing to rock, punk, reggae, heavy metal etc., with some live performances. The clientele is cool, so wear your shades.

I-BEAM
1748 Haight St. ☎*668-6006. Map* **4E4** 🔳 🎤 ⬤ 🎵 🎤 🔳 *Nightly 9pm-2am.*

JAZZ

Jazz is the great "all-American" musical product. As you would expect, you'll find jazz styles to suit your mood, all around the city.

GREAT AMERICAN MUSIC HALL
859 O'Farrell St. (near Larkin)
☎*885-0750. Map* **5D7** 🔳 *to* 🔳 🎵 *show times variable. Revue sometimes.*
In a splendidly rococo room, the Great American Music Hall offers rock, folk and sometimes comedians, but is best known for being the number-one place in town for big band jazz sounds. Food is also available.

to 🔳 *plus two-drink minimum for revue Wed-Sun 9pm, 11pm. Closed Mon-Tues.*
An intimate bar and club that books established comedians and rising locals Wednesday through Saturday; anybody can take a crack on Sunday.

Rock and New Wave both live and recorded by local and visiting upcoming bands. Impressive lights and lasers.

LAST DAY SALOON
406 Clement St. ☎*387-6343. Map* **3D3** 🔳 🔳 *for* 🎵 *and* 🎤 *Tues-Sun from 9pm.*
Amid photographs of the 1906 earthquake and its aftermath, dancing on a big floor to bands of every kind from classic rock to Country and Western and Rhythm and Blues.

LE MONTMARTRE
2125 Lombard St. ☎*563-4618. Map* **5B6** 🔳 *to* 🔳 *for* 🎵 *and* 🎤 *nightly 9.30pm-2am.*
Styled after Parisian nightclubs, this club books Brazilian and continental bands that appeal to European visitors.

THE OASIS
11th St., at Folsom ☎*621-8119. Map* **5E7** 🔳 🔳 🎤 ⬤ 🎵 🎵 🎤
Upscale dance club with top-40 disco and live bands playing jazz, R&B, rock etc. Dancing over the pool under the stars or indoors. "Egyptian" decor.

KIMBALL'S
300 Grove St., near Civic Center
☎*861-5555. Map* **5D7** 🔳 *but two-drink minimum for* 🎵 *Wed-Sat from 8.30pm.*
Kimball's is the city's front-line, full-time jazz club. Most of the players are local, or out-of-towners on the way up, but some of the great names and faces from the days of bop onward get on the stand here when they are in town.

PIER 23
Embarcadero ☎362-5125. Map *6B8*
🔳 for ♪ Wed-Thurs 9pm-1am, Fri-Sat
9pm-2am, Sun 4-9pm.

A bastion of house-band Dixie (except for jam sessions on Sunday). It is decorated in the style of a waterfront saloon, which it also is. Food also.

ROCK, COUNTRY, FOLK
From punk — to bluegrass — to good old rock'n'roll....

MABUHAY GARDENS
443 Broadway ☎956-3315. Map *6C8* 🔳
plus one-drink minimum. Revue nightly from
9.30pm ♥ from 11pm.
Filippino restaurant by day, and punk
theater/rock palace by night.

WOLFGANG'S
901 Columbus Ave., in North Beach
☎474-2995. Map *6B8* 🔳 but 2-drink
minimum for ♪ or revue at 8pm and 10pm.
This place belonged to the late pioneering 1960s rock promoter Bill Graham. It still has good sound systems, good

PAUL'S SALOON
3521 Scott St. ☎922-2456. Map *4B5* 🔳
but minimum of one drink (beer/wine only)
during each set ♪ (nightly from 9pm).
This is the one, true home of bluegrass.
Even your aged aunt would feel at ease.

sightlines, and tasteful acts of almost any sort, but mostly rock and jazz. Occasionally comedy, and other unexpected things.

Dinner is served before or between shows.

The performing arts

The city is oriented more to music and dance than to theater, but all three scenes are fairly lively, and audiences are as hungry for the experimental and avant garde as for time-honored classics. Most music and ballet is at the Civic Center, and most theater is Downtown.

For current performances, consult the "The Pink Pages" *Datebook* section of the *San Francisco Chronicle*. Ticketing agencies include **BASS** (☎ *762-2277*) and **STBS** (*Stockton St., between Post St. and Geary St.* ☎*433-STBS, map 6D8*), which sells same-day tickets for half-price Tues-Sat noon-7.30pm (cash only).

BALLET

The **American Ballet Theater** (*War Memorial Opera House, Van Ness Ave. and Grove St.* ☎*864-6696, map 5D7*) holds its spring season from February-March. Also at the War Memorial Opera House, the **San Francisco Ballet** (☎*(510) 762-BASS)* is resident for its spring season and July festival. The company had reached its 59th season in 1991.

The **New Performance Gallery** (*3153 17th St.* ☎*863-9834, map 5F7)* stages modern and contemporary dance by various companies, including the **San Francisco Jazz Dance Company** (☎*898-4113)*.

CINEMA

The city has some 50 movie theaters; a great majority of first-run houses showing American, European and Australian films are in residential neighborhoods, especially on Geary Blvd. and Clement St. in the Richmond, on Union St. and Fillmore St. in or near Pacific

Heights, and on Van Ness Ave. N of Civic Center.

The Financial District and Northern Waterfront have a sparse scattering. Downtown has only one regular first-run house. Chinatown has a small number of theaters featuring movies from Hong Kong and Taiwan.

MUSIC

The San Francisco Symphony *(Louise Davies Symphony Hall, Van Ness Ave. and Grove St.* ☎ *431-5400, map 5 D7)* has a September-May season. Major orchestras and recitalists on tour also play at Davies Hall. **San Francisco Opera** *(* ☎ *864-3330)* is at the War Memorial Opera House for its September-December season and June-July festival.

The city has a near-limitless supply of chamber music societies and recitalists. Check the local press for details of current programs.

THEATER

The **American Conservatory Theater** (A.C.T.) is a nationally known repertory company offering a wide range of performances, from comedy to popular classics. The company performs in the **Stage Door Theater** *(420 Mason St. at Geary* ☎ *749-2228)* and the **Theatre on the Square** *(450 Post St. Downtown)*. The **Curran Theater** *(445 Geary St., near Mason* ☎ *673-4400, map 6 C8)*, with 1,000 seats, is used by touring companies. So is the 1,200-seat **Golden Gate Theater** *(25 Taylor St., at Market St.* ☎ *775-8800, map 6 C8)*, by touring companies performing mostly musicals, and the 2,500-seat **Orpheum Theater** *(1192 Market St., near Civic Center* ☎ *473-3800, map 5 D7)*.

The **One-Act Theater Company of San Francisco** *(430 Mason St., near Geary St.* ☎ *421-5355, map 6 D8)*, a local repertory company, presents classic and contemporary one-act plays in a 99-seat theater.

The **Magic Theater** *(Building D, Fort Mason Center, Laguna St., at Marina Blvd.* ☎ *441-8822, map 5 B6)* shows new and contemporary plays by new writers, all year round in two 99-seat theaters.

Indoor and outdoor activities

San Francisco offers varied outdoor recreation. Tennis and golf head the list of specific sports, but running is enormously popular, and health clubs are plentiful. Because of sea fogs and cold ocean waters, the beaches are better for strolling and fishing than for swimming.

BEACHES

San Francisco's principal beach, **Ocean Beach** *(map 1 C-E1)*, stretches for 4 miles from the W end of Geary Blvd. S to the city limits and beyond and is used along its whole length by walkers and joggers, although it is not, in the main, safe for swimming. At the N end, waves are good for surfing. Along the bluffs directly S of SAN FRANCISCO ZOO, perfect upwelling breezes draw large numbers of hang gliders. The

Great Highway runs directly behind the shore along its full length.

A smaller, more secluded Golden Gate National Recreation Area beach, **Baker** *(map3 C2),* stretches away s from the Golden Gate Bridge. Popular with surf fishermen and strollers, and in fair weather with picnickers, it can be reached by a clearly marked road turning w off Lincoln Blvd. However, waves and currents here are too rough for safe swimming. **Aquatic Park**, at the foot of Hyde St., has a sandy beach and sheltered but chilly waters. **China Beach** *(28th Ave. and Sea Cliff)* is one of the few sandy pockets where swimming is also possible. During the summer months, lifeguards are on duty there.

BICYCLING

Only super-fit enthusiasts should think of braving the city's hills. But there are two marked scenic **cycle routes** leading through the city. One winds through GOLDEN GATE PARK to Lake Merced. The other runs from the s of the city N across the Golden Gate Bridge to Marin County.

Bicycles can be rented from shops on Stanyan St. and Geary Blvd.

BILLIARDS

Pool is now the third most popular participatory sport, after basketball and bowling. It is not surprising, then, to find that a number of upscale pool halls have opened. **The Great Entertainer** *(975 Bryant Street, SoMa* ☎ *861-8833)* is the largest on the West Coast. **Chalker's Billiards Club** *(5900 Hollis St., Emeryville* ☎ *(510) 658-5821),* which is the Bay area's premier club and just 10 minutes from downtown across the Bay Bridge, has the atmosphere of a private club.

The Q Club *(61 Golden Gate Ave., downtown* ☎ *252-9643)* has elegant Belle Epoque decor and 37 beautifully restored antique tables.

BOATING/SAILING/WINDSURFING

Probably the best views of San Francisco are to be had while skimming across the Bay. There are a number of companies that exist to fulfill this need, and boats and sailing vessels of all sizes can be rented, with or without a skipper. There are numerous tour companies offering offshore views of the city skyline, ALCATRAZ, Angel Island and so on.

Contact **Pacific Marine Yacht Charters** *(50 Francisco St., Suite 120* ☎ *788-9100),* sailing out of Pier 39, for personal attention and gourmet cuisine, or **Rendezvous Charters** *(Pier 40, South Beach Harbor* ☎ *543-7333)* for excursions on the 78-foot square-rigged schooner *Rendezvous.* **San Francisco School of Windsurfing** *(1 Harding Road* ☎ *750-0412)* gives personalized lessons to first-timers and experienced windsurfers.

FISHING

San Francisco has ample **pier** and **deep-sea fishing**. The former is done mainly from Municipal Pier at the foot of Van Ness Ave., the FORT MASON piers, accessible from Marina Blvd. and Laguna St., and the seawall adjoining FORT POINT, accessible from Lincoln Blvd. on the bay side of the Golden Gate Bridge. Bait is available near Municipal Pier

(Muny Bait Shop, 3098 Polk St. at Bay St ☎*673-9815, map* **5** *B7);* tackle can be rented at the shop.

Many party boats operate from Fisherman's Wharf. Consult the *Yellow Pages* telephone book under the heading Fishing Parties.

Contact the **Department of Fish and Game** *(1416 9th St., 12th Floor, Sacramento 95814* ☎ *(916) 445-3306)* for information on fishing and hunting license requirements, seasons, and game limits.

GOLF

There are several 9- and 18-hole courses in and around the city. **Lincoln Park Golf Course** *(Clement St. at 34th Ave* ☎ *221-9911, map* **1** *C2),* 5,081 yards, par 68, is rated 64.3; it has some holes overlooking the Golden Gate. Harding Park *(off Skyline Blvd. and SR-35 on Harding Rd* ☎*664-4690, map* **1** *E2)* has two courses: the easier **Fleming course** *(* ☎*661-1865)* has 9 holes (2,316 yards, par 32) and the **Harding Park Course** proper (6,637 yards, par 72, rated 70.8), which occupy a peninsula thrusting into Lake Merced.

The **Golden Gate Park Course** *(47th Ave. and Fulton St.* ☎ *751-8987)* is another 9-hole course (1,357 yards, par 27). **Sharp Park Golf Course** *(on SR-1 at Sharp Rd., Pacifica* ☎*359-3380),* 6,398 yards, par 72, rated 70, is a tricky, flat, oceanside 18-hole course just s of the city.

Instruction, plus a number of golfing services such as guides and equipment rental, are available from **Golf Guides** *(3145 Geary Blvd., Suite 520,* ☎ *751-2108)* or **San Francisco Golf Services** *(533 Airport Blvd., Suite 400* ☎ *348-8931).*

JOGGING AND FITNESS

For the complete range of fitness facilities, you can do no better than to pay a visit to the **Plaza Athletic Club** *(350 Third St., SoMa* ☎*543-8466).* This clean, uncrowded facility has weights, treadmills, stairmasters, and lifecycles, as well as a heated outdoor pool. Beneath the freeway at Drumm and Clay Sts., **Marina Green** *(Marina Blvd., from Buchanan St. W),* has a 2.5-mile track for joggers, and a fitness course alongside it. GOLDEN GATE PARK, too, has many paths for joggers.

For a speedy recovery from the rigors of exercise, take the plunge and visit the nationally famous spa and *shiatsu* massage center **Kabuki Hot Spring** *(1750 Geary Blvd. Japantown* ☎*922-6000),* where you can be acquainted with the pleasures of the traditional Japanese bath and massage, from licensed practitioners. By appointment only.

TENNIS

The largest facility is a center with 21 hard courts in GOLDEN GATE PARK *(off Kennedy Dr., opposite the Conservatory of Flowers).* Reservations are required on weekends *(* ☎ *753-7101),* or reserve at the tennis shop. There is a small fee for hourly play. For locations of the 100 other hard courts in the municipal park system, contact the **San Francisco Recreation and Parks Department** *(* ☎ *753-7101).* These are all free of charge, and are available on a first-come-first-served basis.

Shopping
by Nell Bernstein and Joel Simon

Where to go

The array of department stores, fine jewelers, European boutiques and specialty shops that surround Union Square has made San Francisco one of America's premier shopping cities, rivaling New York, Chicago and Los Angeles.

But it is San Francisco's diverse neighborhoods that set the city apart from its more populous competitors. While in many American cities Main Street has been replaced by the mall, San Francisco has preserved its neighborhood shopping streets, where locally owned businesses give each area its distinctive character and flavor.

Whether browsing bookstores in North Beach, searching for souvenirs in Chinatown, bargain-hunting South of Market, or perusing the boutiques along Union St., shopping in San Francisco is not just about finding what you're looking for. It's also about enjoying yourself in the process.

Take a midday break to admire the panoramic vista of the Bay from atop Russian Hill. Drop in for a cappuccino at one of the dozens of neighborhood cafés, from **Cafe Trieste** in North Beach to **South Park Cafe** South of Market.

And remember to wear good walking shoes and bring along a sweater in case the fog rolls in. Shopping in San Francisco is an outdoor sport.

UNION SQUARE

Union Square Park, so named because a pro-Union rally was held here during the Civil War, is San Francisco's most prestigious shopping address. Surrounding the park are such luminaries of the department store world as **Macy's**, **Saks Fifth Avenue**, **Neiman Marcus** and **I. Magnin**. And **FAO Schwarz**, a virtual department store for children, is just off the square on Stockton St.

The best names in European design are also well represented. **Chanel** and **Cartier** have stores on Maiden Lane, a two-block alley off Stockton St. The alley, once the heart of the city's red-light district, acquired its current name after the 1906 earthquake and fire destroyed the bordellos. Local merchants renamed the alley Maiden Lane in an effort to change its character and reputation.

Follow the cable car tracks down Powell St. to reach the **San Francisco Shopping Centre**, at Market and 5th Sts. Opened in 1988, the mall has been widely praised for its architectural innovations. Curved escalators, specially designed by Mitsubishi of Japan, spiral around a skylit atrium. The first four stories are full of shops, and the top five are occupied by upscale department store **Nordstrom**. Next door is **Emporium Capwell**, another department store.

CHINATOWN
San Francisco is at once a cosmopolitan international city and a coalition of distinct communities. This dual heritage can be appreciated by visiting Chinatown, which begins just a few blocks from Union Square. Step through the red-tiled gateway adorned with lions and dragons at the corner of Grant and Bush Sts., and chrome and glass give way to brick and shingle, Gucci shoes to ginseng teas. Born as a ghetto for Chinese laborers who came at the turn of the century to work on the railroad, Chinatown has been constantly renewed by new waves of immigrants.

For shoppers, the eight-block stretch along Grant Ave. from Bush to Broadway is lined with dozens of stores selling jewelry, largely low-quality silks, and mass-produced Chinese vases, as well as trinkets and souvenirs. **City of Shanghai** *(519 Grant Ave.)* sells silks, jade and Asian furniture of a higher quality.

For dabblers in Chinese medicinal herbs, there are numerous herb stores (called "trading companies") along Washington St. off Grant. Try **Great China Art Company**, **Tran's Trading Co.** or **Superior Trading Co.** For tea, go to **Ten Ren's Tea and Ginseng Emporium** *(949 Grant Ave.)*, which boasts a blow-up photograph of President Bush enjoying a cup of tea. **The Wok Shop** *(804 Grant Ave.)* sells Chinese cooking utensils. *(All Chinatown stores are located on map 6 C8.)*

SOUTH OF MARKET (SoMa)
As in New York's SoHo, SoMa's brick warehouses and large factory buildings were taken over by artists after the factories left town. The artists in turn spawned clubs, galleries and trendy restaurants, revitalizing the neighborhood. For shoppers, SoMa offers factory outlets, where local clothing manufacturers sell slightly defective goods for a fraction of what they would cost downtown.

UNION STREET
The cows that used to graze here when it was farmland on the edge of the city have moved on to greener pastures, but the area is still referred to as Cow Hollow. Victorians have been turned into restaurants, art galleries, boutiques, jewelry and interior design stores. Old stables now house antique stores. Today, Union St. runs through the heart of one of San Francisco's most exclusive neighborhoods.

THE OTHER NEIGHBORHOODS
There are numerous other neighborhood shopping streets scattered throughout the city. **Haight St.**, where the summer of love was played out 25 years ago, is a great place to browse for records and books or look for vintage clothing. **Fisherman's Wharf** is a popular tourist destination and a good place to pick up souvenirs and San Francisco

specialties. Near the Civic Center, **Hayes Valley** is an up-and-coming neighborhood, with galleries, unusual furniture stores and assorted bric-a-brac. **24th St.** in Noe Valley has some nice clothing stores.

Stores in Japantown sell hand-made kimonos, pillows, screens, futons and other Japanese items. Stop in for an invigorating steam bath and massage at the **Kabuki Hot Springs**, a Japanese spa. Be sure to call ahead: because the hot and cold baths are communal, facilities are open to men and women on alternate days.

What to look for

In the following pages, map references are given for all streets within the area covered by our maps.

ANTIQUES

Founded as a Spanish mission in 1776, San Francisco was a small backwater until the 1849 gold rush suddenly brought the city tremendous prosperity. The new elite built mansions furnished with the best that Europe had to offer. This legacy, combined with the city's historic ties to Asia, makes San Francisco a great place to both European and Asian antiques.

- First stop for antique aficionados is **Jackson Square** *(map 6 C8)*. In this historic neighborhood, San Francisco's first downtown, 21 different antique stores offer everything from fine English and Continental furniture to silver and tapestries, as well as Asian art and furniture.
- If you don't find what you want there, try the **Great American Collective** *(1736 Lombard St. at Laguna, map 5 B6)*, where 31 dealers are represented.
- There are a number of good antique stores on **Union St.** Try **Old and New Estates** *(2181-A Union St., map 5 C6)* for vintage jewelry and **Sanuk** *(1810 Union St., map 5 C6)* for Asian art.

ART GALLERIES

San Francisco's hilly streets were the inspiration for Richard Diebenkorn's cityscapes, and many galleries continue to highlight local artists. At the downtown galleries you can also find works from some of the best-known 20thC artists. Among major examples are the following:

- **Harcourts Gallery** *(460 Bush St., map 6 C8)*, which exhibits Picasso, Chagall, Motherwell and Rauschenberg
- **Kabutoya Galleries** *(454 Sutter St., map 6 C8)* for Japanese art
- **Kertesz Fine Art Gallery** *(521 Sutter St., map 6 D8)*
- **Eleonore Austerer Gallery** *(540 Sutter St., map 6 C8)*
- **Cobra Fine Art** *(580 Sutter St., map 6 C8)*

Several fine galleries are located on Maiden Lane. All on the same block are:

111

- **Maiden Lane Galleries** *(111 Maiden Lane, map 6 D8)*
- **Conacher Galleries** *(134 Maiden Lane, map 6 D8)*
- **The Circle Gallery** *(140 Maiden Lane, map 6 D8)*, designed by Frank Lloyd Wright
- **Hanson Galleries** *(153 Maiden Lane, map 6 D8)*

Neighborhood galleries include the **Lois Ehrenfeld Gallery** in Cow Hollow *(1782 Union St., map 5 C6)* for Himalayan and Indian Art. **Spectrum Gallery** *(511 Harrison St., map 6 D9)* and **Artspace** *(1286 and 1329 Folsom St., map 6 E8 and 5 E7)* are two major South of Market galleries. Also visit the gallery at the **San Francisco Art Institute** *(800 Chestnut St., map 5 B7)*, where Diebenkorn once studied.

BOOKS AND RECORDS
San Francisco's foggy weather is probably the explanation for the large number of book and record stores. There is something about heavy mist that makes a long night of reading and music particularly inviting.

- **City Lights** *(261 Columbus Ave., map 6 C8)*, founded during the Beatnik era, is still favored by poets and others who dress in black.
- Downtown, try **Albatross Books** *(166 Eddy St., map 6 D8)*, **Hunter's Books** *(151 Powell St., map 6 D8)* or **Brentano's** in San Francisco Shopping Center *(Market St. at 5th St., map 6 D8)*.
- **McDonald's Books** *(48 Turk St., map 6 D8)* is huge but dark and disorganized.
- Established as an answer to the dingy, dirty haunts favored by the beatniks, **A Clean Well Lighted Place for Books** *(601 Van Ness Ave., map 5 D7)* is exactly that.
- **Green Apple** *(506 Clement St., map 3 D3)* is the best of the neighborhood bookstores.
- Haight St. has some good stores selling used books, as well as some of the city's best used-record stores. They include **Reckless Records** *(1401 Haight St., map 4 E5)*, **Rough Trade** *(1529 Haight St., map 4 E5)* and **Recycled Records** *(1377 Haight St., map 4 E5)*.
- **Tower Records** in North Beach *(2525 Jones St. at Columbus and Bay, map 5 B7)* has a great selection of new records and CDs.
- There are also a number of record and bookstores along **24th St.** in Noe Valley.

CAMERAS AND PHOTOGRAPHIC EQUIPMENT
San Francisco was home to such pioneers of modern photography as Ansel Adams and Brett Weston, and still supports a thriving community of aficionados.

- Camera buffs should visit **Adolph Gasser** *(181 Second St., map 6 D9)*, for everything from film to new and used cameras.
- Around the corner is **Photographer's Supply** *(576 Folsom St., map 6 D9)*, for discounted film, camera supplies and processing. They do not sell cameras.
- Downtown, **Brooks Camera** has two locations: a main store at 45 Kearny St., and a smaller one at 243 Montgomery St. *(both map 6 C8)*.

- Up the street is **Discount Cameras** at 33 Kearny St. *(map 6 C8)*, which has a very good supply of used equipment.
- There are a number of other stores on Kearny. But it may be as well to stay clear of the discount camera stores along Market St.

DEPARTMENT STORES
Most of San Francisco's department stores are clustered around Union Square.
- The largest and best known is **Macy's** *(101 Stockton St. at O'Farrell St., map 6 D8)*. Men's clothes are in another building on Stockton St.
- Next door to Macy's is **I. Magnin** *(233 Geary St., map 6 D8)*. The silver-foiled Cosmetic Hall on the main floor is a special treat.
- **Neiman-Marcus** *(150 Stockton St., map 6 D8)* is famous for its glass rotunda, which was rebuilt from the City of Paris Department store of 1908.
- The upscale **Nordstrom** occupies the top five floors of the San Francisco Shopping Centre *(Market and 5th Sts., map 6 D8)*.
- **Emporium Capwell** is next door *(835 Market St., map 6 D8)*.
- San Francisco's most unique department store is **Gump's** *(250 Post St., map 6 C8)*, which has three floors of gallery-quality antique furniture and contemporary furniture, fine china and silver, Asian art and jade, and unusual gifts. Gump's was once described as "the Metropolitan Museum with cash registers." If you're in San Francisco around Christmas, be sure to check out Gump's famous window display.

FASHION AND FASHION ACCESSORIES
For clothes shoppers, San Francisco offers the best European and American names, as well as a variety of stores that reflect the city's own, less conventional sense of fashion.

Clothes for women:

- **Jessica McClintock** *(353 Sutter St., map 6 C8)* and **Laura Ashley** *(253 Post St., map 6 C8, and 1827 Union St., map 5 B6)* sell tasteful, high-quality dresses unswayed by the current fashion.
- **The Chanel Boutique** *(155 Maiden Lane, map 6 D8)*, on the other hand, is strictly this year's model.
- **Banana Republic** *(256 Grant Ave., map 6 C8, and 2253 Polk St., map 5 C7)* sells rugged-style clothes inspired by safari fashion.
- **The Forgotten Woman** *(550 Sutter St., map 6 C8)* has larger-size fashion, from sizes 14 to 24.
- **Jaeger International** *(272 Post St., map 6 C8)* specializes in cashmere.
- **Benetton** *(865 Market St., map 6 D8)* has its usual colorful collection of comfortable sportswear.
- **Rolo** *(1301 Howard St., map 5 E7, and 450 Castro St.)* sells hip fashions to a younger crowd, as does **Esprit** *(900 Minnesota St.)*. **Joshua Simon** *(3915 24th St., map 2 D4)* has a nice selection of washable silk clothing.

- Along Union St. there are numerous boutiques, and it goes without saying that all of the downtown department stores have a large selection of women's clothing.

Clothes for men:

- Men, too, should visit the department stores and **Banana Republic**, **Rolo** and **Benetton**, all of which carry both men's and women's fashions.
- Men's specialty stores include the **Armani Exchange**, next door to Macy's *(map 6D8)*.
- **C & R Clothiers** *(201 Sacramento St., map 6C8, and 785 Market St., map 6D8)* has a wide variety of discounted men's suits.
- **Alfred Dunhill** of London *(290 Post St., map 6C8)* and **Bullocks and Jones** *(340 Post St., map 6C8)* cater with some dignity to the traditionalists.
- Hipsters should check out the myriad high-fashion stores in the **San Francisco Shopping Centre**.
- **Rochester Big and Tall** *(Mission and Third Sts., map 6D8)* has brand-name fashion for larger men.
- **Eddie Bauer** *(220 Post St., map 6C8)* is where to go for original outdoor clothing.

Clothes for children:

- **Heffalump** *(1694 Union St.)*, **Familiar** *(1828 Union St.)*, **Mudpie** *(1699 Union St.)* and **Ragamuffin** *(3044 Fillmore St.)*, all in Cow Hollow *(and all map 5 C6)*, have innovative, entertaining children's fashion.

Discount outlets

Throughout San Francisco's warehouse district there are discount outlets where many name-brand makers sell merchandise that is slightly damaged or defective, at significant savings. Be sure to examine each item carefully before buying.

- The **ACA Joe** outlet *(915 Front St., map 6B8)* sells comfortable cotton sportswear.
- **Esprit Direct** *(499 Illinois St. at 16th St.)* sells active sportswear for women and children.
- The **Burlington Coat** factory *(899 Howard St., map 6D8)* offers clothing for men, women and children, as well as furs, linens and shoes.
- **Gunne Sax Outlet** *(35 Stanford St. off Brannan St., map 6D9)* has old-fashioned party dresses.
- **Rainbeau Bodywear** *(300 Fourth St., map 6D9)* has dance and exercise clothes.
- **Simply Cotton** *(610 Third St., map 6D9)* sells cotton sportswear.
- **Déjà Vu Paris** *(400 Brannan St., map 6D9)* offers high-fashion imports at discounted prices.
- **The Coat Factory Outlet** *(1350 Folsom St., map 5E7)* has wools, rainwear, furs and leather.

Jewelry

Most of the best-known names in jewelry have stores downtown.

*   **Tiffany and Co.** *(350 Post St., map 6D8)* has jewelry, watches, silver, china and crystal, as well as diamonds and other precious gems.
*   **Carrera Y Carrera** of Madrid is in the San Francisco Shopping Center at Market and 5th Sts. *(map 6D8)*.
*   **Cartier** is at 231 Post St. *(map 6D8)*.
*   Around the corner is the **Aurum Gallery–The Ring Shop** *(116 Maiden Lane, map 6D8)*, which has won awards for its imaginative designs.
*   **Union St.** also has smaller, locally-owned jewelry stores.

Leather goods

For high-fashion leather, stick to downtown.

*   **Bottega Veneta** *(108 Geary St., map 6D8)* has handmade Italian handbags, small leather goods and luggage.
*   **North Beach Leather** *(190 Geary St. at Stockton St., map 6D8)* has specially designed Italian-made jackets and clothes in bright colors.
*   **The Coach Store** *(164 Grant Ave., map 6D8)* has simple, functional bags, briefcases and wallets.
*   **Gucci** *(200 Stockton St., map 6D8)* is world-famous for handbags, luggage, shoes and accessories.
*   **Rawhide of California** *(224 O'Farrell St., map 6D8)* sells upscale cowboy fashion including hats and jackets. **Golden Bear Sportswear** *(200 Potrero Ave. at 15th St.)* has suede and leather for men and women at discounted prices.

FOOD AND DRINK

*   San Francisco is famous for its sourdough bread, which is standard fare at many restaurants. If you want to take some home, visit any one of the **Boudin Bakery** shops; there's one in Macy's.
*   In fact, both **Macy's** *(101 Stockton, map 6D8)* and **Emporium Capwell** *(835 Market St., map 6D8)* have food markets in the basement, offering a wide variety of local specialties.
*   If you crave for sweets, duck into **Ghiradelli Premium Chocolates** at Ghiradelli Square *(map 5B7)*.
*   Need a quick pick me up? Cafés abound, but perhaps the best coffee beans to take home can be found at **Peet's** *(2156 Chestnut St., map 4B5)* or **Spinelli's** *(3966 24th St.)* in Noe Valley.

SPORTS AND CAMPING

San Francisco's proximity to Yosemite National Park and other natural wonders has spawned a number of fine camping stores.

*   **The North Face** *(180 Post St., map 6C8)* has everything you'll need for camping, backpacking, rock climbing or looking good around the campfire.

- **Kaplan's Surplus and Sporting Goods** *(1055 Market St., map 6 D8)* sells discounted camping equipment.
- Practitioners of more traditional sports can find shoes, racquets, balls and the like at **Copeland's Sports** *(901 Market St., map 6 D8)* and **Herman's World of Sporting Goods** *(737 Market St., map 6 D8).*

TOYS

- If **FAO Schwarz** *(48 Stockton St., map 6 D8)* did not incessantly play their theme song *Welcome to my World of Toys* through the loudspeakers, the store would be the perfect place for kids of all ages. As it is, children under 12 seem oblivious to the song as they run wild among three stories of toys, including giant stuffed animals and elaborate automated displays.
- If you don't find it at FAO Schwarz, try **Wound About** *(Pier 39, Space J-1, map 6 B8),* where they have a large assortment of wind-up toys; **Basic Brown Bear** *(444 De Haro St.),* where you can take a tour to see how their stuffed animals are made; or **Play** *(The Cannery, 2801 Leavenworth St., map 5 B7),* where you'll find toys from around the world, as well as a large selection of kites.

Ideas for children

San Francisco and the neighboring areas offer visiting children hundreds of opportunities to exhaust their pent-up energies in instructive play. Full details of most of the things mentioned here can be found either through the INDEX or in their individual SIGHTS A TO Z entries.

ANIMAL PARKS/ZOOS/AQUARIUMS/WILDLIFE REFUGES

In California, as in much of the rest of the world, increasing emphasis is being placed on designing zoos that put animals into the best possible reconstructions of their native habitats. Within easy reach of San Francisco, kids can have a number of real-life encounters with wild animals and fish.

- Coyote Point Museum (see San Mateo, SAN FRANCISCO PENINSULA)
- GOLDEN GATE PARK — children's zoo
- Marine World Africa USA (see SAN FRANCISCO PENINSULA)
- Monterey Bay Aquarium (see MONTEREY PENINSULA)
- PIER 39 — K-Dock and Underwater World
- SAN FRANCISCO ZOOLOGICAL GARDENS
- Steinhart Aquarium (see CALIF. ACADEMY OF SCIENCES)
- Wattis Hall of Man (see CALIF. ACADEMY OF SCIENCES)

BEACHES

California's open ocean beaches seldom allow parents with small children to relax, primarily because of heavy surf. Some ocean and many bay beaches are ideal for tots and youngsters, although these tend to be s of San Francisco. See also SPORTS on page 106, and for the list of best Californian sandy beaches, see map on page 20.

THE OLD WEST

California grew up with Indian wars, the Gold Rush and other such Hollywood myths. Some lively souvenirs of the real thing still exist.

- CALIFORNIA PIONEERS MUSEUM — the Gold Rush; stagecoach.
- FORT POINT — early American soldiers.
- LEVI STRAUSS HISTORY ROOM — blue/brown jeans.
- Ponderosa Ranch (see LAKE TAHOE) — the old movie set comes to life.
- WELLS FARGO HISTORY ROOM — stagecoach and memorabilia.

SCIENCE MUSEUMS

In today's high-technology society, touchable science exhibits for children rank near the top of approved playgrounds with parents and youngsters alike.

- Discovery Room (see CALIF. ACADEMY OF SCIENCES) — the natural world.

117

- EXPLORATORIUM — science hands-on.
- Lawrence Hall of Science (see BERKELEY) — computers hands-on.
- MORRISON PLANETARIUM and LASERIUM
- Tech Museum of Innovation (see SAN JOSE)

THEME AND AMUSEMENT PARKS

Since Walt Disney first blended thrill rides into more appealing and instructive environments than the carnival or fairground, theme parks have blossomed, notably in California. These are the major ones, if you have time to travel.

- Disneyland (Orange County, Los Angeles)
- GREAT AMERICA (Santa Clara, 45 miles s of San Francisco)
- Knott's Berry Farm (Orange County, Los Angeles)
- PIER 39 (San Francisco)
- Six Flags Magic Mountain (Valencia, near Los Angeles)

TRANSPORTATION MUSEUMS

Although contemporary California lives by automobile and airplane, it has museums in celebration of railroads and sailing ships as well as its current favorites.

- CABLE CAR MUSEUM, POWERHOUSE AND CAR BARN
- San Francisco Maritime Museum (see SAN FRANCISCO MARITIME NATIONAL AND HISTORICAL PARK) — the Sea and the Gold Rush

"EXPERIENCES"

A child loves new experiences and physical thrills. The steep hills themselves may be unfamiliar. See GRADIENTS for a list of the steepest, and CROOKEDEST STREET too. Always popular with older children are those breathtaking views from the tops of high places. See VIEWPOINTS for a list of ideas.

The CABLE CARS prove to be one of the most popular rides, and to see the city by cable car is very cheap.

A trip to ALCATRAZ might give the kids what you hope will be their only ever trip behind bars.

A little farther out of town, the sheer scale of the redwoods may defy belief. And the OLD FAITHFUL GEYSER in the upper Napa Valley is one of only three such geysers in the world.

ENTERTAINMENT

For pure, unadulterated pleasure, nothing can beat the clowns, musicians and jugglers that entertain the crowds so ably at FISHERMAN'S WHARF.

WHAT'S MORE...

- See SHOPPING on pages 114 and 116 for clothes and toy stores.
- See EATING ON A BUDGET and ICE CREAM PARLORS on pages 100-101.
- See the map of California on pages 20-21, which locates major sights and amusement parks, warm water beaches, memorable structures, seashore parks and natural sights.

Excursions

Environs of San Francisco

San Francisco is such a manageable city, especially for walkers, that it is tempting to stay put and confine yourself to enjoying its variegated delights. By all means explore the compact city to the full, but resist the temptation not to venture farther afield. There are fascinating towns and spectacular scenery in abundance within easy striking distance.

BERKELEY
Map 7E3. From San Francisco, ε across the San Francisco-Oakland Bay Bridge, then N on I-80 to University Ave. exit. Served regularly from San Francisco and Oakland by BART (☎(510) 788-2278 from San Francisco or (510) 465-2278 from Oakland) and A-C Transit (☎(510) 653-3535).
Berkeley is the home of the original University of California campus, and California's self-elected social laboratory. In some respects, its moods can swing with the day, while in others the city remains steadfastly true to itself. In any season, Berkeley shows every sign of a highly educated and politically active citizenry. It has superior museums within the university. There are splendid views back across the bay to San Francisco and the Golden Gate.

However, to discover the temper that has made Berkeley famous, it is necessary to wander aimlessly on UC's campus and in the streets near it, especially on Bancroft Way and Telegraph Ave. Start at **Cody's Bookstore** *(2454 Telegraph Ave.)*.

A visit to Berkeley can also include neighboring OAKLAND.

SIGHTS AND PLACES OF INTEREST
BERKELEY MARINA
A man-made peninsula thrusting W into San Francisco Bay from the foot of University Ave., the Marina has a 3,000-foot (924m) public fishing pier (with bait and tackle store, catering to both pier and party boat fishermen), sailboat rentals, yacht moorings, picnic parks, a hotel and several restaurants, all with unimpeded views of San Francisco's skyline and the Golden Gate.
BERKELEY MUNICIPAL ROSE GARDEN
At Euclid Ave. and Bayview Pl., the park contains 4,000 rose varieties. Open daily during daylight hours.
TILDEN REGIONAL PARK
On Grizzly Peak Blvd. in the steep hills behind UC's campus, Tilden is one of several large parks in the East Bay Regional Parks System. It has a relentlessly rolling

championship golf course (6,301 yards, par 70, rated 69.6), a splendid carousel, picnic lawns and paths for walking.

UNIVERSITY OF CALIFORNIA CAMPUS
At the E end of University Ave. between Hearst Ave. and Bancroft Way.

One of America's largest and most prestigious universities, UC-Berkeley offers a veritable cornucopia of worthy sights and events. A few examples indicate the possibilities.

The **Lawrence Hall of Science** *(on Centennial Dr., just downhill from its intersection with scenic Grizzly Peak Blvd.* ◼ *open 10am-4.30pm, Thurs till 9pm)*, a child's paradise of science displays, lays the emphasis on computers and physics. Check at the information desk for special daily programs.

The **University Art Museum** *(Bancroft Way near College Ave.* ◼ *open Wed-Sun 11am-5pm; closed Mon, Tues, major hols)* is particularly known for its collection of Hans Hofmann paintings. Also housed here is the **Pacific Film Archive**, which regularly shows classic movies. A sculpture garden adjoins the museum building, which is a sculptural statement in itself. Just across the street, in Kroeber Hall, is the **Loewy Museum of Anthropology** *(* ◼ *open Mon-Fri 10am-4pm; Sat-Sun noon-4pm)*, where major collections of North, Central and South American artifacts can be seen.

The **Botanical Garden** *(along Strawberry Creek between the football stadium and Lawrence Hall of Science, open 9am-5pm)* contains rare plants gathered into ecological communities.

Maps for self-guiding campus tours may be obtained at the **Student Union Building** *(Bancroft Way, opposite the end of Telegraph Ave.)*. Guided tours depart from this building Monday-Friday at 1pm. Parking in the area is difficult.

⊨ CHEZ PANISSE ✿
1517 Shattuck Ave., Berkeley 94709 ☎*(510) 548-5525* ▥ ◼ ⊨ *Downstairs open Tues-Sat 6-10pm, upstairs Mon-Sat 11.30am-midnight.*

Some consider this to be California's best restaurant. The decor throughout is simple in the extreme, but the small main dining room is the stage for a perpetual quest by perfectionists for yet another flawless expression of New California cuisine, which was developed here by founder and chef Alice Waters as a more flavorful, regionalized counterpart to *nouvelle cuisine*. Upstairs is a café for simpler, less expensive dishes such as *calzone*, pasta and salads. The main dining room's fixed-price menu changes nightly as well as seasonally. Most ingredients are organically grown. Reservations are required downstairs; it can be difficult to get a table. Across the Ave. is the **Berkeley Co-op**, a grocery store with a rich stock of gourmet ingredients. This is just one of a host of top-flight specialty food stores within strolling distance of Chez Panisse.

MARIN COUNTY
Map 7E2-3. Across the Golden Gate from San Francisco. US-101 is the axis.
Region served daily from San Francisco by Golden Gate Bridge district commuter ferries and buses.

The current national image of Marin County does not apply to all of the territory within its formal political boundaries. It covers only the mythical part of Marin County, the part where citizens learn self-awareness in salad-making classes, or loll in hot tubs drinking wine and fanning themselves with peacock feathers.

This mythical county has woven itself into the life of a number of real Marin towns, especially **Mill Valley** and **Tiburon**, and, to a lesser degree, **Sausalito** and **San Rafael**. Its influence has not touched the areas to the N and W.

Each of the four towns named has specialty shops and restaurants in beautiful natural surroundings. Marin has some of the Bay Area's greatest natural scenery, especially on the headlands of the **Golden Gate** and above them on **Mt. Tamalpais**.

This part of Marin County exaggerates the San Francisco Bay Area's range of summer micro-climates. On an August afternoon, temperatures in the eastern skirts of Mt. Tamalpais can reach 105°F (40.5°C) while Sausalito stays at 58°F (14°C) under a blanket of fog, although the two points are hardly 10 miles apart. The only advice for roving tourists is to dress lightly and take a heavy sweater.

Marin Headlands

Part of the GOLDEN GATE NATIONAL RECREATION AREA (see SIGHTS A TO Z), these steep hills offer superb views back through the **Golden Gate Bridge** to San Francisco's skyline.

At the outer end of the headlands, the beautifully situated **Point Bonita Lighthouse** is one of California's best spots for whale-watching.

Visitors coming from San Francisco should turn off from US-101 at the Sausalito exit, then turn left into a tunnel after traveling less than 500 yards, to get to a road leading onto the headlands. Once on the headlands, it is possible to drive to an ocean beach at **Fort Cronkhite**, also part of the Golden Gate NRA.

Mill Valley

In and around this affluent commuter suburb there are some fine shops and restaurants. From San Francisco, the SR-1 exit three miles N of the Golden Gate Bridge leads directly to Miller Ave., a main road running N into town.

Mount Tamalpais State Park

Occupying the upper flanks of conical Mt. Tam nearly all the way to its 2,586 feet (788m) peak, this park is a favorite with hikers for its mixture of grassy meadows and redwood-shaded gullies. The 6,200-acre park surrounds **Muir Woods National Monument** and abuts open lands of the Marin Water District, extending hiking possibilities far beyond its own borders. Trails lead W all the way to the Pacific shore at **Stinson Beach**, or NE into water district lands in the warm-weather zone.

Park headquarters is on The Panoramic Highway, which, 3 miles W of US-101, branches off from SR-1.

San Rafael

Marin's largest city and county seat is a spruce commercial center of interest to visitors primarily for two buildings that date from opposite ends of California's history.
MARIN COUNTY CIVIC CENTER 血
At the juncture of US-101 and N San Pedro Rd. on the N side of San Rafael ☎ *Open Mon-Fri 9am-5pm.*

One of Frank Lloyd Wright's last great public buildings. The repeated use of arches and an ingenious metal-skinned tower that hides cooling equipment dominate the building's external appearance. Inside, a towering central court has hanging gardens. There are no guided tours of the building, which houses government offices, but surrounding gardens offer delightful strolls.

MISSION SAN RAFAEL ARCÁNGEL

1104 5th Ave. ☎*(415) 454-8141* 🔳 *Open 6.30am-5.30pm.*

A reconstruction of the mission that was founded in 1817, 20th of the Franciscan chain. It was designed to be no more than a sun-blessed sanitarium for converts whose health had declined in the fogs at Mission Dolores in San Francisco.

Sausalito

Sausalito (it means "Little Willow") plummets from steep hills to a long, curling shoreline that looks back across the Golden Gate to San Francisco. A great majority of the town's shops, restaurants and other attractions are on or near its waterside main street, **Bridgeway**, 2 miles from where a road turns into town at the N end of the Golden Gate Bridge.

A vast concrete shell called **Village Fair** houses a score of specialty shops. Opposite Village Fair and immediately N of the Sausalito-San Francisco ferry pier, a small **boat harbor** makes a pleasant place for yachtsmen to wander. A little fleet of party boats operates from piers in this harbor, going outside the Golden Gate for salmon, striped bass or bottom fish, depending on the season (see *Yellow Pages* under *Fishing parties*). Sausalito's famous community of houseboats is anchored some 2 miles N, where Bridgeway joins US-101.

US ARMY CORPS OF ENGINEERS BAY MODEL

2100 Bridgeway ☎*(415) 332-3871* 🔳 *Open Tues-Sat 9am-4pm. Closed Sun-Mon; major hols.*

This is an enchanting show. Using brilliantly dyed water, tests are carried out on a vast model of San Francisco Bay, San Pablo Bay and the Sacramento River delta, to show everything from the path of the Sacramento River flow to the movement of oil spills. Call ahead to find out if any tests are scheduled. A lively visitor center displays bay flora and fauna and man's effect on them.

Tiburon

One block of Tiburon's original waterside main street has a tight cluster of bars and restaurants with outdoor terraces much patronized by yachtsmen. Seafood is the best choice. Shops and galleries lend variety. On a narrow, steep-sided peninsula, Tiburon and neighboring **Belvedere** have some of northern California's most dramatic residential architecture. Main St., Tiburon, is 4 miles from freeway US-101 via SR-131 (Tiburon Blvd.), or 8 miles from Sausalito by road (but only 2 miles by boat). Red and White Fleet **tour boats** from San Francisco call here.

MONTEREY PENINSULA

Map 9G3. From San Francisco, 94 miles s via US-101, SR-156 and SR-1. Served daily by PSA, United and commuter airlines and Greyhound Lines i Monterey Chamber of Commerce and Visitors and Convention Bureau, PO Box 1770, Monterey 93940 ☎*(408) 649-1770; office at 380 Alvarado St., Monterey.*

Three peninsula towns — Monterey, Carmel-by-the-Sea and Pacific Grove — attract some 6.5 million visitors each year, 105 for each permanent resident. Seascapes from Pacific Grove down to Point Lobos rank among the most beautiful in the world, and the area is a mecca for golf. But variety is what puts the Monterey Peninsula in a class by itself. Seascapes range from wild to settled. Golf comes on a fog-shrouded shore or in sun-baked valleys. The three towns are completely unalike, and their hotels and restaurants excel in different ways.

Monterey looks like a typical, all-business American town, but it is more. It has the region's car dealers, supermarkets and convention hotels. But it has also developed its economically obsolete **Fisherman's Wharf** and **Cannery Row** districts into compelling tourist attractions and created a townwide museum of historic buildings.

Pacific Grove has a prim, Victorian appearance. More purely residential than its neighbors — partly because it sits at the outer tip of the peninsula and partly because a Presbyterian majority kept alcohol and thus tourist development out of the community until the 1970s — Pacific Grove attracts visitors because of the sheer beauty of its rocky shoreline.

Carmel is pure storybook in its quaint prettiness. Buffered from Monterey by the golf greens and great homes of **Del Monte Forest**, the town has managed to keep the scale of everything small, save perhaps the reflected fame of its one-time Mayor, actor/director Clint Eastwood, who legalized take-out ice cream cones and Frisbees in public parks. Eastwood's pub/restaurant, **The Hog's Breath Inn** *(on San Carlos between 5th and 6th Sts.* ☎ *(408) 625-1044),* is worth a visit. Streets without sidewalks or lights dodge around old trees. There are no street numbers for houses or businesses.

Although many residents deplore the fact, Carmel is the most commercial community on the peninsula, its 6-block center packed solid with quiet hostelries, varied restaurants, and galleries and shops carrying everything from tourist kitsch to jewels fit for a crown.

Carmel also has advantages of location. It has a long sandy beach, the implausible beauties of **Point Lobos** and **Del Monte Forest** flank it on either side and share their bracing seaside climate, and, just inshore, narrow **Carmel Valley** refuses admission to the summer sea fogs. Thus its tennis and golf resorts enjoy dry warmth while sea fogs sweep across Monterey and Del Monte Forest.

For all its differences, the Peninsula makes a cohesive whole. A good local transportation system is only the most obvious example of the fact.

The toll road called **17-mile Drive** loops through the private enclave of Del Monte Forest, which separates Monterey and Pacific Grove from Carmel. Along the route are some fine rocky headlands, including **Cypress Point**, three splendid golf courses that delight even touring professionals, and a few over-the-wall glimpses of splendidly grandiose homes built between World Wars I and II.

SIGHTS AND PLACES OF INTEREST

CANNERY ROW
When vast quantities of sardines were hauled in here, the Row lived up to its name. Today it might be called hotel, restaurant and souvenir stores row. Monterey's spectacular **aquarium** (see overleaf) also has its home here.

CARMEL MISSION ✭
w of SR-1 via Rio Rd., or s of Ocean Ave. in Carmel via Junipero St. Open Mon-Sat 9am-5pm;
Sun 1-5pm. Donation expected.

The Basilica of Mission San Carlos Borromeo de Carmelo has few peers and no superiors among the Franciscan missions in California for grace of proportion and refinement of architectural detail. Once badly decayed, it has been restored to excellent condition. Padre Junipero Serra began construction of the second mission in 1771. He lived and worked at Carmel until his death in 1784 and is buried in the chapel here. Two small religious museums adjoin the mission church.

FISHERMAN'S WHARF

Much of the Old Wharf has been converted into restaurants, galleries and curio stores. A small fleet of party boats puts out daily.

MONTEREY BAY AQUARIUM
886 Cannery Row ▨ ☎*(408) 648-4888, (408) 375-3333 for recorded information. Open*
10am-6pm. Closed Christmas ≋ 𝘬 ᴞ ✚

Just a couple of doors up from Doc Rickett's old marine laboratory, celebrated in John Steinbeck's *Cannery Row*, sits the startlingly original Monterey Bay Aquarium. Monterey Bay is one of the most diverse ecosystems in the world, and exhibits in this one-time fish cannery celebrate every aspect of it from forests of towering kelp to a little bubble full of sand dollars. Much of the aquarium is hands-on (pet a stingray!), and even the most formally educational aspects are lively. Highlight of the day is probably the **feeding of the sea otters** at 11am, 2pm and 4.30pm (they move into a more naturalistic home, resembling their native Monterey Bay, in March 1993).

A note of caution: entrance can be difficult on holidays and weekends without advance reservations and tickets.

MONTEREY PATH OF HISTORY

Monterey played a pivotal role in California's development from Spanish to American territory. In tracing a rough oval around downtown Monterey, well-preserved buildings illustrate each major era.

Colton Hall *(Pacific St. near Jefferson St.* ▨ *open Tues-Sun 10-noon, 1-5pm;*
closed Mon, hols) is where settlers framed American California's first constitution. This is where to begin a tour and where to pick up an explanatory map showing the way to other stops along the path: **Customs House**, **Allen Knight Maritime Museum**, **Larkin House**, **Stevenson House** and the **Royal Presidio Chapel**.

PACIFIC GROVE MUSEUM OF NATURAL HISTORY
Forest Ave. at Central Ave. ▣ *Open Tues-Sun 10am-5pm. Closed Mon, hols.*

Just uphill from the beach and butterfly trees at **Lovers Point**, here are well-arranged displays of local geology and animal life.

PACIFIC GROVE SHORELINE

The **Great Tidepool**, immortalized in Steinbeck's *Cannery Row*, is the biggest of a long series of rocky shoals rich in sea life. It is almost due w of Point Pinos Lighthouse. The whole **Pacific Grove** shore w of Lovers Point gives good vantages for watching sea otters, sea lions and scores of shorebirds. It and the adjoining sandy cove of **Asilomar State Beach** are nature reserves where all collecting of life forms is strictly forbidden.

POINT LOBOS STATE RESERVE
w of SR-1, 3½ miles s of Carmel ▨ *Open daily during daylight hours.*

The reserve protects an almost unchanged primitive ecological system containing 300 plants and 250 animal species on 1,250 acres of land and uncounted other species in 750 underwater acres. Of principal interest are groves of Monterey cypresses, sea otters, sea lions and, from November to February, migrating gray whales.

Cars must stay on one long looping road, leaving the richest rewards to visitors who walk the network of trails. When summer crowds overrun parking facilities, latecomers must await their turn at the entry gate.

OAKLAND

Map 7E3. On the E shore of San Francisco Bay at the intersection of I-80, I-580 and SR-17. Served daily by AirCal, PSA, United, Western Airlines, Amtrak and Greyhound Lines. From San Francisco, served by BART light rail trains and A-C Transit buses i Oakland Convention & Visitors Bureau, 1330 Broadway, Suite 1105, Oakland 94612 ☎(510) 839-9000.

Sandwiched between San Francisco and Berkeley both physically and psychologically, Oakland has been hard put to establish a singular identity. It is still primarily an industrial city and not at all a center of tourism. In the 1989 earthquake Oakland was very severely hit.

For visitors, interest comes mainly in the form of an engrossing museum, a vital waterfront and some pleasant parks.

SIGHTS AND PLACES OF INTEREST

LAKE MERRITT
Three blocks away from Oakland Museum, at end of 14th St. ✦
The city park's children's fairyland, bird sanctuary and rental boats make it a respite for restless youngsters who have seen too many paintings at the MUSEUM.

OAKLAND MUSEUM
100 Oak St., Oakland 94607 ☎(510) 834-2413 ▣
On its two lower levels, the museum has a fine permanent exhibition of California's natural and human history. The natural history section approximates a walk from Pacific shore to Sierra ridge line; the human history begins with Native Americans and carries forward to World War II. On the top level a chronology of California art progresses from the certain views of 19thC landscapists to the misty visions of contemporary painters. The museum also hosts major traveling exhibitions.

OAKLAND WATERFRONT
Oakland has a busy deepwater port with some of the most advanced container-ship operations on the Pacific Coast. Each Thursday, the Port of Oakland conducts four free boat tours of its harbor. Tours depart from a pier at **Jack London Square**, a bustling collection of waterfront restaurants and shops at the foot of Broadway. For tour information and reservations, contact **Public Relations, Port of Oakland** (☎ *(510) 444-3188).*

A visit to Oakland can also include neighboring BERKELEY.

SAN FRANCISCO PENINSULA

Map 9F3. Extends 35 miles s from San Francisco along US-101 and I-280. Served daily from San Francisco by Southern Pacific commuter trains (☎(415) 981-4700) and Sam Trans buses (☎(415) 761-7000).

Although there is a long, lightly populated slope facing the Pacific, most locals think only of the narrower San Francisco Bay side when they say "Peninsula." Along the bay shore is a string of towns packed side by side from San Francisco to the Santa Clara Valley. For a place so small, with so few gaps between towns, it is curiously diverse.

Some of the towns are industrial, some middle-class commuter communities, some wealthy enclaves, some a mixture of any or all of the above. For visitors the most interesting districts are **San Mateo-Burling-ame**, near San Francisco International Airport, and **Palo Alto**, adjoining Stanford University. Business travelers flock to electronics and space companies in the geographically imprecise but altogether real **Silicon Valley**, which extends s from Palo Alto to San Jose in the Santa Clara Valley.

SIGHTS AND PLACES OF INTEREST

BAY MEADOWS RACE COURSE
PO Box 5050, San Mateo 94402, adjoining US-101 at the Hillsdale exit 5 miles s of San Francisco International Airport ☎*(415) 574-7223.*
The track is open much of the year for thoroughbred, harness and quarter-horse racing with pari-mutuel betting.

COYOTE POINT MUSEUM ☆
Coyote Point Dr., San Mateo 94010, s of San Francisco International Airport, 4 miles to Poplar Ave. exit from US-101, then follow signs ☎*(415) 342-7755* 🔳 *𝄡 by appointment* ✦ *Open Wed-Fri 10am-5pm; Sat-Sun 1-5pm. Closed Mon; Tues; Jan 1; Dec 25.*
In recent years the decline of San Francisco Bay as a natural environment has been reversed. In a fine bayside park, Gordon Ashby's museum brilliantly displays what is being saved. One huge room contains demonstrations of the Bay Area's six biotic communities, arranged to approximate a walk from ridgetop to tide line, or vice versa. Visitors see living insect communities and films, and games-playing computers that explain what has to be done in nature to assemble the ingredients of a hamburger and how to load Noah's Ark to keep the passengers from eating one another.
(See OAKLAND for **Oakland Museum**, another Ashby design.)

FILOLI 🏛
Canada Rd., adjacent to I-280 N of Woodside ☎*(415) 364-2880* 🔳 *Open Tues-Sat 10.30am or 1pm, by reservation only, mid-Feb to mid-Nov. Closed Sun-Mon; hols; mid-Nov to mid-Feb.*
In 1916, on a 750-acre estate, a locally famous architect named Willis Polk designed a grand house in the style of one built for the Duke of Devonshire by Christopher Wren and Inigo Jones. He surrounded it with Dutch, Spanish and Persian gardens, a knot garden and a stained-glass window garden.

MARINE WORLD AFRICA USA
Vallejo, off Hwy 37 via 101 N or I-80 E, or by high-speed ferry from Fisherman's Wharf, 30 miles NE of San Francisco ☎*(707) 643-ORCA. Open daily 9.30am-6pm summer; Wed-Sun 9.30am-5pm winter.*
A wildlife theme park covering 160 acres of land and water, this is part entertainment, part education, with more than 2,000 animals, including whales, dolphins, elephants, tigers, lions and orangutans. The entrance fee covers some spectacular shows, and the chance to meet animals and trainers. All the usual theme park facilities are here.

NATIONAL AERONAUTICS AND SPACE ADMINISTRATION/AMES RESEARCH CENTER
Moffett Field, adjoining US-101 at Mountain View ☎*(408) 965-6497* 🔳 *Open Mon-Fri at 9.30am, 10.30am, 1 or 2.45pm by appointment only.*
Tours include a wind tunnel, flight simulators and the airfield's flight line, all more exciting than the name promises.

STANFORD UNIVERSITY
General tours by students begin at the Palm Dr. entrance to Main Quad, Mon-Sat 11am, 2.15pm, Sun 2.15pm ☎*(415) 497-2862* 🔳
One of the great private universities in the US, Stanford occupies a sprawling

campus directly w of Palo Alto. The handsome main campus is reached most easily via the Embarcadero Rd. exit from US-101.

The **Stanford Linear Accelerator** *(2575 San Hill Rd., Menlo Park 94025, under a mile east of San Hill Rd. exit from I-280, 29 miles south of San Francisco* ☎ *(415) 854-3300, ext. 2204* 🖸 *open daily by appointment only, closed major hols)* offers a tour lasting about 2 hours that explains Stanford's mile-long nuclear research facility.

The **Stanford University Museum of Art** *(Lomita Dr. at Museum Way* 🖸 ✗ *open Tues-Fri 10am-4.45pm, Sat-Sun 1-4.45pm)* contains an important Rodin collection. Other exhibits include ancient Oriental, Egyptian and primitive art, and early Californiana. The museum also has Stanford family memorabilia.

SUNSET MAGAZINE'S DEMONSTRATION GARDEN

Willow Rd. at Middlefield Rd., Menlo Park 94025, 1 mile w of Willow Rd. exit from US-101, 26 miles s of San Francisco ☎*(415) 321-3600* 🖸 *Open Mon-Fri 9am-4.30pm. Closed weekends; hols.*

One of the Western US's most important publishers of magazines and books on travel, food, gardening and the home maintains a 7-acre show garden open to the public. Along a meandering path, there is a slow shift from groups of plants common to the sw deserts (anchored by a Joshua tree) to those of the Pacific NW (a grove of Douglas firs marks the spot). Tours include editorial offices and demonstration kitchens, as well as the garden.

SANTA CLARA VALLEY

Map 9F3. From San Francisco, 46 miles s on US-101 or I-280. Served daily by AirCal, American, Continental, PSA, Republic, United and Western Airlines, Greyhound Bus Lines, Amtrak, and from San Francisco, by Southern Pacific commuter trains i San Jose Visitors Bureau, Paseo de San Antonio, San Jose 95113 ☎(408) 998-7000.

San Jose has been growing since the 1950s. Now, as the undeclared capital of Silicon Valley, this erstwhile sleepy farm town has passed San Francisco in population. With its companion communities it is double the size. San Jose used the Los Angeles formula of annexing huge swathes of grasslands, then filling them in with new houses and commercial developments. Where old towns existed, San Jose surrounded them. Some capitulated and joined. Some clung to their legal existence. A handful maintained their real identities.

The result of all this is northern California's nearest approximation of the LA style. The vitality is beginning to produce some quality to go along with the ugly and nasty. San Jose and its companion communities have the endless mediocre commercial streets, bewildering traffic jams and smog typical of fast, sprawling, car-oriented growth. But they also have a fine symphony orchestra, excellent shopping areas, attractive wineries and a grand theme park.

SIGHTS AND PLACES OF INTEREST

GREAT AMERICA

PO Box 1776, Santa Clara 95052. The theme park adjoins US-101 at Great America Parkway exit, 45 miles s of San Francisco ☎(408) 988-1800 ■ ⬛ ✶ 🆔 🆑 🆅 *Open daily 10am-10pm third week in May to first week in June; Sun-Thurs 10am-9pm, Fri-Sat 10am-11pm (10am-midnight on July 4) second week in June to first week in Sept; weekends*

10am-10pm second week in Sept to last weekend in Oct and first weekend in Mar to first weekend in Apr. Closed late Oct to early Mar.

Beyond its newest white-knuckle ride, a stand-up, loop-the-loop roller coaster called *Vortex,* and its 2-story carousel, Great America shows off all the clichés of American history in 125 separate attractions and games. Bugs Bunny and other cartoon characters parade 100 acres of grounds, which include reproductions of a New Orleans French Quarter street, a New England seaport and a county fair. A theater, an ice-skating show and a giant-screen movie theater run all day. You can see *Blue Planet,* an IMAX movie of Planet Earth as filmed by US astronauts. Admission covers rides and shows.

MISSION SANTA CLARA DE ASÍS

University of Santa Clara, on The Alameda between Santa Clara St. and Franklin St. ☎(408) 984-4528 ⊡ Open daily.

Founded in 1777, eighth of the California missions, Santa Clara is now part of the campus of the Jesuit Santa Clara University. Affiliated is the **de Saisset Art Gallery and Museum** *(☎ (408) 984-4528 ⊡ open Tues-Fri 10am-5pm, Sat-Sun 1-5pm Jan 15-June 15, June 22-Aug 7, Oct 1-Dec 20; closed at other times and hols),* which has mission artifacts and art exhibitions.

VILLA MONTALVO

Montalvo Rd., Saratoga, $3\frac{1}{2}$ miles NW of Los Gatos on SR-9, Saratoga-Los Gatos Rd., to Montalvo Rd., then 1 mile SW ⊡ (but ⊠ weekends). Gardens open 8am-5pm, galleries open Tues-Sun 1-4pm. Closed Mon, major hols.

Senator James Phelan built Villa Montalvo in 1911 as a private residence and retreat for artists. The art galleries in the house and the 175 acres of superb hillside gardens and woodlands are open to the public.

WINCHESTER MYSTERY HOUSE ⚏

525 S Winchester Blvd., San Jose, directly N of I-280 at first exit W of its junction with SR-17 ☎(408) 247-2101 (recorded schedule) ⊠ ⚲ Open 9am-6pm. Closed Dec 25.

Sara Winchester, Victorian heiress to the Winchester firearms fortune, believed in ghosts and fervently believed that they were out to get her. She sought to confuse them by adding new rooms to her house, making it an ever more baffling maze. Finally it had 160 rooms, 2,000 doors (most led nowhere) and 10,000 windows. There is also a small museum of Winchester firearms.

It has been said that all great cities of history have been built
on bodies of water — Rome on the Tiber, Paris on the Seine,
London on the Thames, New York on the Hudson. If this is a
criterion of a city's greatness, surely San Francisco ranks in the
first magnitude among cities of the world. For never was a
metropolis more dominated by any natural feature
than San Francisco by its bay.
(Harold Gilliam, *San Francisco Bay*)

Farther afield

Roughly equidistant from the city are two natural treasures: YOSEMITE NATIONAL PARK and what Californians refer to as "The Lake" — LAKE TAHOE, America's largest alpine lake.

Turn to pages 144-147 in CALIFORNIA TOURING to run through the persuasive arguments for using a car for an expedition to either Tahoe or Yosemite, or both. And if you are heading for Tahoe's casinos, remember that just a short hop across the state line lies RENO.

This section explores Tahoe and Yosemite, with comments about accommodations and the many opportunities for outdoor sport and adventure. A short supplement on Reno concentrates on the main reason for visiting the place: the hotel-casinos of the "biggest little city."

TAHOE

Map 8D5. From San Francisco, 200 miles E on 1-80 and SR-89 to North Lake Tahoe, or approximately the same distance on 1-80 and US-50 to South Lake Tahoe. South Lake Tahoe served daily by commuter airlines and Greyhound Lines i Lake Tahoe Visitors Authority, 3050 Highway 50, South Lake Tahoe 95706 ☎(916) 544-5050; office in South Lake Tahoe Chamber of Commerce, PO Box 884, Tahoe City 95730 ☎(916) 583-2371; office in Lighthouse Shopping Center at 950 N Lake Blvd. Highway conditions ☎(916) 577-3550. Useful visitor publications: City Escort, Key.

The alpine lake called Tahoe is four places in one: natural wonder, summer resort, ski resort, and gambling resort. Lake Tahoe, the natural wonder, measures 22 miles by 12, and reaches depths of 1,645 feet (501m) from a surface elevation of 6,229 feet (1,899m). But numbers are not the whole story. Tahoe's fame rests upon chill water so pure that few fish can live in it for lack of food, and so clear that glass-bottom boat tours show visitors a rocky lake bed through astonishing depths.

Although the lake itself is alpine by every scientific measure, its setting looks particularly Californian. Dense forests of pine on the surrounding slopes bespeak warm, dry summers. Indeed, in some summers every scrap of snow melts from the 9,000-foot (2,743m) peaks around this basin just E of the Sierra ridgeline. The finest views are from the peaks down to the lake.

Lake Tahoe, the summer resort, divides into the **north shore** and **south shore**. At the north shore, a wealthy elite hides away in expensive, wooded peacefulness. Quiet, low-key **Tahoe City** and posh **Incline Village** are the commercial centers. Populous, popular **South Lake Tahoe** crowds on to a narrow lakeshore shelf and bustles around the clock.

In winter the differences between N and S are less pronounced. A majority of the ski areas, both downhill and cross-country, are in the NW quarter of the basin, where elevation, exposure and snowfall all favor the sport.

Lake Tahoe, the gambling resort, divides W and E along the California-

Nevada state line by law. For serious gamblers, **Stateline**, at the s tip, is the place. Tahoe's biggest hotel-casinos are here. The casinos at Stateline also book top-class entertainers in their lounges and theaters. Toward **North Tahoe**, the casinos and most of the players are less sophisticated.

In fair weather, it is easy to get around the compact Stateline area of south shore on foot. A fair public transit system connects all parts of sprawling South Lake Tahoe as far s as "The Y," where US-50 and SR-89 intersect. North shore also has a modest public transportation system; in spite of it, a car is needed to get around an area with widely scattered attractions.

SIGHTS AND PLACES OF INTEREST
PONDEROSA RANCH
Adjoins Nev SR-28 at s side of Incline Village ☎*(702) 831-0691* ■■ ♪ ▣ ✱
Open June-Sept 10am-6pm; variable hours May, Oct. Closed Nov 1-Apr 30.
The old ranch used in location shooting for the television western *Bonanza* has turned itself into a small theme park by adding an imitation town imitating Hollywood stage sets built for the same program. Visitors can look around the real ranch house, watch staged shootouts, ride old wagons, visit a saloon for a tin cup of sarsaparilla, and fantasize about the Old West on a false-front main street.

ACCOMMODATIONS
Not counting rental condominiums, south shore has 160 hotels and motels with 10,000 rooms. North shore has far fewer hotels and motels, but many more condominiums; locals estimate the two together total about 6,000 rooms.

Summer weekends may be sold out 2-3 months in advance at all of the major hotels and motels on the south shore, and many of the lesser ones. Winter weekends can sell out almost as far in advance in a snowy year. Weekday travelers can shop for special rates in summer and outright bargains from fall to spring. Price levels noted for acommodations are peak; rates can drop by as much as half depending on day, season and length of stay.

Lake Tahoe Visitors Authority *(☎(916) 544-5050)* maintains a reservations service. With a steadier clientele at its summer resorts, a larger population of skiers, and a tighter supply of rooms, north shore is less subject to variations in price. **North Lake Tahoe Visitors Bureau** *(☎(916) 583-3494)* also has a reservations service (mostly for ski packages).

CASINOS
South shore's three major hotel-casinos, **Harrah's** *(☎(702) 588-6611* ▥ *540 rms)*, **Harvey's** *(☎(702) 588-2411* ▥ *543 rms)*, and **Caesar's Tahoe** *(☎(702) 588-3515* ▥ *to* ▥ *446 rms)*, wedge against each other and the California-Nevada state line. At north shore, **The Hyatt Lake Tahoe** *(Country Club Dr. at Lakeshore Blvd., Incline Valley* ☎*(702) 831-1111* ▥ *to* ▥ *460 rms)* has a smaller casino.

RECREATION

Beaches and parks

Tahoe has three fine state parks, two in California, the third in Nevada. A National Forest Service recreation area amounts to a fourth park.

At the SW corner of the lake, the adjoining **Emerald Bay** and **D.L. Bliss State Parks** between them have Tahoe's finest stretch of scenery and one of its most extensive swimming beaches. At the bottom of a steep 1-mile trail reaching the S shore of Emerald Bay is a one-time summer mansion called **Vikingsholm**, a 380-room fantasy patterned on an 8thC Norse fortress. The main swimming beach here is well N of Emerald Bay, at the N boundary of Bliss. Both parks have campgrounds.

Lake tours

Four companies operate daily tour boats from the south shore, three from South Lake Tahoe, the other from **Zephyr Cove**, 4 miles into Nevada. The boats differ — one has a glass bottom, another is a stern-wheeler — but the narrated tours are about the same. Daytime trips to Emerald Bay and Vikingsholm and early evening dinner cruises follow similar routes. Day cruises last about 2 hours, dinner cruises about 3 hours. The tour season runs from May to mid-November; one of the boats also offers a year-round daily ferry service to the north shore.

Rental boats

Both N and S shore marinas offer rental and charter boats of every type from sailboats to fast launches for water-skiing. Consult the *Yellow Pages* under *Marinas* for complete listings.

Although waters generally are calm, Tahoe is large enough for line squalls to produce dangerous waves. When a long, dark wind line appears on the lake, make for the nearest sheltering harbor.

Golf

The Tahoe basin has two tough courses and an easy one open to the public. Another fine course is near Truckee. There are also several nine-hole public courses in the basin.

South shore: Edgewood Tahoe (on loop road behind Sahara Tahoe at Stateline, NV ☎(702) 588-3566), 7,453 yards, par 72, rated 75; Tahoe Paradise (on US-50, 3 miles S of Lake Tahoe Airport ☎(916) 577-0797), 4,100 yards, par 66, rated 60.3.

North shore: Incline Village (955 Fairway Blvd. in Incline Village ☎(702- 831-0246), 7,120 yards, par 72, rated 72. Near Truckee: Northstar at Tahoe (6 miles S of town via SR-267 ☎(916) 562-1010), 6,897 yards, par 72, rated 72.4.

Courses close from November 1-April 24 or later, depending on weather.

Horseback riding

The Tahoe basin has ample country gentle enough for trail rides, but steep enough to make the views rewarding. Local stables offer breakfast rides, half-day trail rides with or without barbecue lunch or dinner, and overnight trips.

South shore stables can be found at Camp Richardson, Heavenly Valley and Zephyr Cove. On the north shore, there are stables at Squaw Valley. Check the *Yellow Pages* for a complete listing.

Skiing

The Tahoe basin has 15 downhill and as many cross-country areas. In most cases, the two come together. North shore, which has the majority of areas, and south shore, which has the majority of accommodations, are linked by buses and a ferry.

South shore: The region's largest and most diverse ski area, **Heavenly Valley**, has its tram base station just a few blocks from the casinos and hotels at Stateline. Cross-country areas are mostly w along US-50.

North shore: The counterweight to Heavenly Valley is **Squaw Valley**. **Alpine Meadows** ranks near Squaw in size and diversity. The two are on parallel spur roads off AR-89 N of Tahoe City. **Sugar Bowl** is a family-oriented area. Incline offers easy skiing and a flashy social scene. Cross-country areas are near these, and along I-80 w of Truckee.

YOSEMITE NATIONAL PARK

Map 8E-F5, 10E-F5. from San Francisco, 184 miles SE via 1-580, 1-205 and SR-120 i Superintendent, Yosemite National Park, CA 95389, or for information ☎(209) 252-0264.

John Muir could never again write calm prose after he saw Yosemite Valley in the mid-18thC. A century later, Ansel Adams could never take a dull photograph of it; glacier-carved granite walls towering 2,000-4,000 feet (610-1,219m) above the narrow floor; light filtering through feathery plumes of water from towering falls; deer grazing in flower-filled meadows.

Only a mile wide and 7 miles long, in a park that takes in 1,189 square miles of the Sierra Nevada's finest high country, the valley is often mistaken for the whole park. With the annual visitor count approaching 3 million, in summertime the crowds, traffic jams and exhaust fumes can ruin what ought to be a memorable experience.

Meanwhile, the rest of the park remains lightly used in spite of its Giant Sequoias, sweeping alpine meadows, crystal-clear streams, and granite peaks reaching elevations of 13,000 feet (3,962m). Some of the names may be familiar: Mariposa Grove, Wawona, White Wolf, Tuolumne Meadows. Wise travelers will fight off the charms of the valley and explore.

SIGHTS AND PLACES OF INTEREST

GLACIER POINT

At 7,214 feet (2,199m), Glacier Point overlooks Half Dome, and is within earshot of Vernal and Bridalveil Falls (see YOSEMITE VALLEY, below). A summer road leads up to it from the valley floor. Many visitors arrange a ride up, then walk back down steep, zigzag **Four-mile Trail** to a point about 2 miles from Curry Village, or **Panorama Trail**, an 8-mile walk which crosses Nevada Falls on the way to Happy Isles Nature Center.

TUOLUMNE MEADOWS

The best known back-country area accessible by road has a lodge at the departure point for long rambles into the High Sierra, including backpacking trips along the famous **John Muir Trail** at the ridge of the Sierras.

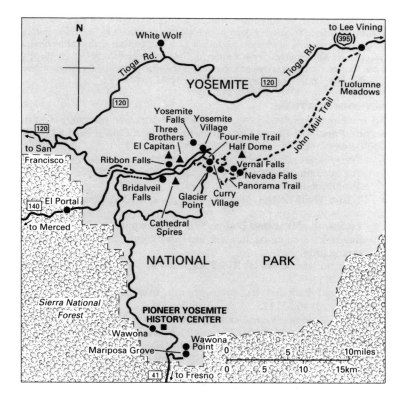

WAWONA

Site of a fine grove of mature Giant Sequoias, Wawona is on SR-41, near the s entrance to the park. The grove, Mariposa, was already mature in 1864 when it became part of Abraham Lincoln's original park grant. Among its thousands of trees, some 200 measure 10 feet (3m) or more in diameter. Visitors must park at the edge of the grove, and walk or take a free tram ride into it.

WHITE WOLF

Another area of sweeping alpine meadows, White Wolf is on the same road as Tuolumne Meadows (see above), but much closer to Yosemite Valley. Any visitor to either of these areas needs to feel comfortable driving on mountain roads; Tioga is no standard highway.

YOSEMITE VALLEY

The great fascinations of Yosemite Valley are its sheer rock walls and the waterfalls that plummet down them. The most famous of the rock walls are Half Dome and El Capitan. Their peers are Three Brothers and Cathedral Spires. Greatest of the falls is Yosemite, which drops 1,430 feet (436m) to its first touch point. After a series of cascades the lower falls plummet another 320 feet (97.5m) to the valley floor. The total distance is 2,425 feet (739m).

Other great falls spill from the ends of their hanging valleys into the great glacial trough of Yosemite Valley. Prime among them are Ribbon, Bridalveil, Nevada and Vernal Falls. All of these landmarks may be seen to awesome effect from either the valley floor or the rim at **Glacier Point** (see opposite).

Three museums or interpretive centers are located in the valley. One is the **visitor center** at Yosemite village, which offers campfire talks and other nature programs, especially in summer. Adjacent to it, the **Indian Cultural Museum** traces native American history in the region. To the E, beyond Curry Village, **Happy Isles Nature Center** has ranger naturalists on hand to answer visitors' questions. It is also a departure point for trails to Glacier Point.

ACCOMMODATIONS
All hostelries and food services within the park are operated by **Yosemite Park and Curry Co.** *(Yosemite National Park 95389 ☎(209) 252-4848).*

- The greatest number and variety of facilities are in Yosemite Valley, but accommodations are available at Wawona, White Wolf and Tuolumne meadows.
- **White Wolf Lodge**, 31 miles from park headquarters, has cabins and tents.
- **Tuolumne Meadows Lodge**, 55 miles from park headquarters near the park's E entrance, has tent-top cabins and a family-style central dining lodge.
- Both the above are on Tioga Rd., SR-120. Both operate summers only.
- National Park Service campgrounds may be reserved through ☎(1-800) 452-1111.
- Many close in winter, but Yosemite's two major hotels — the **Ahwahnee** *(☎(209) 252-4848 ▥ to ▥ 123 rms)* and the **Wawona** *(☎(209) 252-4848 ▥ 105 rms)*—remain open all year. However, they may be fully reserved as much as 6 months in advance.
- **Yosemite Motels** *(☎(209) 742-7106)* provides a central reservation service for motels near the National Park.
- All accommodations may be fully reserved 2 or 3 weeks in advance in summer.

RENO
*Map 8D5. 222 miles E of San Francisco on I-80. Several major airlines serve Reno. Daily Amtrak train each way from Oakland. Greyhound and Trailways bus services **i** Box 1429, Reno, NV 89505 ☎(1-800) 367-7366.*

Reno styles itself as the biggest little city in the world. The intersection of Virginia St. (US-395) with 2nd St. is the hub of its casino district and its modest downtown area. In September, National Championship Air Races are held at Stead Air Force Base.

- The major hotel-casinos with showrooms are:

Bally-Reno 2500 E 2nd St. Reno, NV 89595 ☎(702) 789-2129 ▥ 2,001 rms

Circus Circus 500 N Sierra St. at N Virginia St., Box 5880, Reno, NV 89513 ☎(702) 329-0711 ▥ 1,625 rms, catering especially to families with children

Harrah's Hotel Center and 2nd Sts., Box 10, Reno, NV 89504 ☎(702) 786-3232 ▥ 565 rms

Hilton Flamingo   255 N Sierra St. between W 2nd and Commercial Sts., Box 1291, Reno, NV 89501 ☎(702) 322-1111 ▥ 603 rms

• Other casino-hotels downtown:

El Dorado Hotel   4th St. and Virginia St., Box 3399, Reno, NV 89505 ☎(702) 786-5700 ▥ 406 rms, notable for well-above average restaurants

Fitzgeralds Hotel   255 N Virginia St., Reno, NV 89501 ☎(702) 785-3300 ▥ to ▥ 345 rms

• Other casino-hotels away from the city center:

Ramada Hotel Casino   6th and Lake Sts., Box 681, Reno, NV 89501 ☎(702) 788-2000 ▥ 250 rms

Sundowner Hotel   450 N Arlington Ave., Reno, NV 89503 ☎(702) 786-7050 ▥ to ▥ 550 rms.

• Price bands apply to full-season rates; mid-week and off-season rates can be far lower.

It's a good thing the early settlers landed on the East Coast;
if they'd landed in San Francisco first,
the rest of the country would still be uninhabited.
(Herbert Mye)

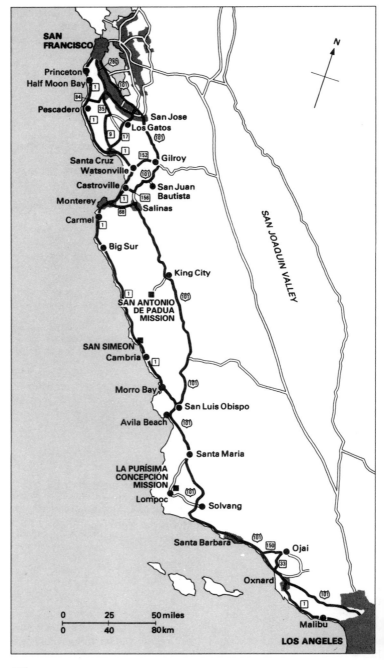

California touring

Those parts of California that are easily accessible from San Francisco divide naturally into three separate touring areas. Any of these areas can be enjoyed alone, but even better perhaps is to move from one area to another, sampling different routes in each. The maps provided in this section give the main roads. Refer also to maps **7-10**.

AREA: COAST SOUTH OF SAN FRANCISCO

This is the most diverse of all California's regions in its nature and in its human development, the one that calls most for thoughtful appraisal of the parts as well as the whole.

For at least half of the 400 miles between San Francisco and Los Angeles, steep hills press hard against the Pacific Ocean shoreline, keeping wild beauty intact, most famously in **Big Sur**, but in other districts as well.

Where the hills do not come so close to the shore, **Santa Barbara** and the **Monterey Peninsula** have grown into two dissimilar but equally urbane oases of civilization. Santa Barbara lies back beneath its reliable sun in conscientious tribute to its Spanish beginnings, while Monterey affects a certain Yankee bustle. Santa Barbara *allows* tourists, while Monterey courts them. In some mysterious way they are mileposts in the psychological shift that differentiates southern and northern California.

Between the extremes of Big Sur wilderness and small city urbanity come all the other shadings of human activity. Within this region, ocean water temperatures change sharply from warm to cold, changing the onshore climate from warm and sunny to cool and foggy, and changing small seaside towns slowly and inconsistently from sleepy resorts to hardworking fishing and/or farming villages. Somewhere among **Avila Beach**, **Cambria**, **Morro Bay**, **Santa Cruz** and **Half Moon Bay** is a town to please any coast watcher looking for an alternative to Santa Barbara or Carmel and the rest of the Monterey Peninsula.

In the chain of coastal valleys, farming is the mainstay all along. Horses and cattle browse the dry, grassy slopes. Down in the bottomlands, crops change in direct cooperation with the weather, from citrus near Santa Barbara to artichokes near San Francisco, with vineyards scattered all along the way. Inland towns most likely to attract a visitor's eye are **Ojai**, **Solvang**, **San Luis Obispo** and **San Juan Bautista**.

Tucked here and there into the landscape are some of the best bits of California history, including William Randolph Hearst's legendary **San Simeon**, and several **Franciscan Missions** less touched by time than those closer to the great urban centers. The most notable missions are **La Purísima Concepción** near Lompoc, and **San Antonio de Padua**, to the w of US-101 near King City.

Spring and fall bring the most pleasant weather to the northern end of the territory. Winter offers nothing more fierce than occasional lingering rain. Summer is the season of fogs along the coast, but a season of heat inland. Toward Santa Barbara the climate stays benign all year around.

Santa Barbara and the Monterey Peninsula both have dozens of hostelries running the gamut from costly resort hotel to plain motel. In the territory between the two cities, both range and numbers dwindle. Most resorts and some hotels are booked solid for a week in advance through the summer; weekend vacancies can be hard to find as much as a month ahead.

Unquestionably, a car is more than merely useful. Santa Barbara has a fine transit system; compact Carmel can be explored satisfactorily on foot. As for the rest, a lack of independent transport is likely to be a substantial handicap.

Coast sampler south of San Francisco

Map 9F3. From San Francisco, SR-1 s to Princeton and Half Moon Bay, then on to Pescadero; from there E on SR-84 to its junction with I-280 for the round trip to San Francisco.

The small fishing and pleasure boat-harbor at **Princeton** has not been varnished for tourists, but keeps strictly to business. **Half Moon Bay** and **Pescadero** are just as single-minded about farming artichokes. Coastside restaurants provide some excellent opportunities to eat fresh local fish. Otherwise, the charm is scenery. SR-1 ("Coast One" to most Californians) follows its up-and-down route across shoreside bluffs. SR-84 climbs wooded hills to join I-280 for the stretch of miles that once won it the title of "The World's Most Beautiful Freeway."

One-day visit to Santa Cruz

Map 9F3. From San Francisco, s via US-101 to SR-17, then w to Santa Cruz. From Santa Cruz, return to San Francisco on SR-1 in clear weather, or via SR-17 and I-280 if the shore is foggy.

One of California's old beach resorts lies just 79 miles s from San Francisco, a surefire lure for families with nostalgic leanings toward oceanfront carnivals, sandy beaches, pier fishing, and similarly uncomplicated pleasures. The trip makes for a very full day, or an easy weekend.

Weekend visit to Santa Cruz

Map 9F3. From San Francisco, s on I-280 to its intersection with SR-84, then w to SR-35, and s on SR-35 and SR-9 to Santa Cruz. Return via SR-1.

The added charms of this indirect route are fine wooded scenery, plus the opportunity to stop off in an excellent grove of coast redwoods at **Big Basin State Park**, and to poke around a couple of old resort towns, **Boulder Creek** and **Bonny Doon**.

Exploring the San Francisco peninsula

Map 9F3. From San Francisco, s on US-101 to its intersection with SR-17, then w to Los Gatos. Double back on SR-17 to its intersection with I-280 for the round trip to San Francisco.

This route, which is all freeway, through densely settled commuter communities, a shade more than 130 miles in length, opens up all manner of urban and suburban opportunities.

For shoppers, this is shopping-mall country. Of particular note are the **Stanford Shopping Center** in **Palo Alto** on the San Francisco Peninsula and **The Pruneyard** in **Santa Clara Valley**. Smaller, and in quieter towns, are **Old Town** in Los Gatos and **El Paseo de Saratoga** in Saratoga, both in Santa Clara Valley.

Toward the head of the list of **gardens** open to the public are Rod McLellan's Orchid Nurseries in San Mateo, Sunset Magazine's Demonstration Garden in Menlo Park, Filoli in Woodside and Villa Montalvo in Saratoga. The first three are on the San Francisco Peninsula; the last-named is in Santa Clara Valley. Sunset and Filoli are only a few minutes apart by car, but any two can be combined easily.

For families, there is an excellent theme park, **Great America**, which is in the Santa Clara Valley close to the municipal boundary between Santa Clara and San Jose. It is accessible from US-101, which allows a swifter return to the city than I-280 if time presses.

Monterey weekend from San Francisco

Map 9F-G3. From San Francisco, s on US-101 to any of the following connector routes: SR-17, which runs w from San Jose to Santa Cruz, from where SR-1 continues s to Monterey; SR-152, which goes w from Gilroy to Watsonville, from where SR-1 continues to Monterey, or SR-156, which quickly connects US-101 with SR-1 at Castroville. To return to San Francisco, follow SR-1 all the way, or reverse any of the above routes.

While it is possible to drive from San Francisco to the Monterey Peninsula and back in a single day, the exercise is futile, for it leaves no time to savor a place that can occupy low-handicap golfers, high-calorie gourmets, art collectors and ocean watchers for days at a time.

The choice among suggested routes is considerable in spite of their overlap. US-101/SR-156 is the quickest way and so gives maximum time on the **Monterey Peninsula**, but it also has the least interesting scenery. US-101/SR-152 does not take much longer, and offers stops in an agreeable wine district called **Hecker Pass**, plus fine coastal hill scenery. US-101/SR-17 offers scenery with reasonable speed on a route that is divided highway (dual carriageway) as far as Santa Cruz.

In any sort of favorable weather, one leg of the journey ought to be along SR-1. The route does not demand much more time than the others, and is impressive for ocean-watching for nearly all its length between Santa Cruz and the city.

AREA: NORTHERN CALIFORNIA COAST

In many ways, a trip along the coast N of San Francisco provides the gentlest introduction to life in California... or the most gradual exit.

Just outside San Francisco is **Marin County**. A certified crucible of The California Life Style, it is not overcrowded except in Sausalito on weekends. Just beyond Marin come the lightly populated vineyard and orchard valleys of **Napa**, **Sonoma** and **Mendocino**, the last outposts of Spanish colonization, where straitlaced farmers mingle with wealthy commuters from Los Angeles and San Francisco over crystal glasses of costly wine. (See WINES AND WINERIES, page 150.) The rock-ribbed **Mendocino Coast** starts looking unlike a California shore. Finally, oak-dotted

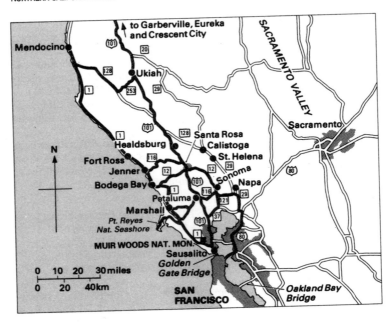

grassy hills give way to redwood forests, and the sparser, earthier population of loggers and commercial fishermen looks and talks like a different society.

The shoreward weather echoes this drift, growing ever cooler, grayer and wetter on the approach to Oregon. In keeping with California habits, however, neither climate nor society follows this pattern rigidly. The inshore farm valleys bake under hot summer suns at least as far as northern Mendocino County, which has a certain notoriety for the size and quality of its marijuana crop. And with or without the aid of funny cigarettes, many of the residents of coastal Mendocino are able to explain a few things about the California Life Style to the good folk of Marin. This mixing helps condense a territory that, although only a few miles wide, stretches 360 miles on its N-S axis.

For travelers, perhaps the best aspect of the N coast is that it offers some of each of its charms within 75 miles of San Francisco. Within this tight compass come wave-beaten headlands, fishing villages, the finest California vineyards and groves of awesome redwoods.

Point Reyes National Seashore, **Muir Woods National Monument**, and the **Napa** and **Sonoma Valleys** can all be visited on day trips from the city. The **Mendocino Coast**, the **Avenue of the Giants** and **Redwood National Park** fall just outside that range, but it is possible to see each of these places to satisfaction on a visit lasting as little as two days.

The one recreation available almost everywhere is **fishing** in all its forms. Boating lakes and golf and tennis clubs can be found here and

140

there, but not amusement parks and posh beach resorts.

These lists announce another truth. This is not grand vacation country for families with children. Even the beaches are perilous for the very young. Heavy surf pounds most of them. Strong currents are common. Where protected water exists, it is too chill, at 52-55°F (11-13°C), for swimming.

Except for Napa and Sonoma, where chic hotels and restaurants fit in with fine wines, accommodations along the coast lean more in the direction of old-fashioned comfort than opulence, more to intimacy than grand scale. North of San Francisco there are but a handful of hundred-room coastal hotels. However, there must be a hundred small hotels in refurbished Victorian houses, or other turn-of-the-century buildings.

In spite of the fact that many vacationers tend to explore the area on day trips from San Francisco, individual hotels are often reserved well in advance by a hard core of visitors who come back to vacation on this coastline year after year and who treasure the region for its quiet, timeless atmosphere.

A car is almost essential. Wineries are scattered throughout the Napa and Sonoma Valleys, as are hotels, restaurants and shops. The Mendocino Coast's visual treasures are spread over about 30 miles of shoreline; its finest hostelries are tucked away in isolation from one another and the sprinkling of towns. Attractions on the Redwood Coast cover an even vaster expanse in much the same fashion as Mendocino. One-day bus tours permit quick sampling of the Napa Valley and some of the red-woods; organized tours are available within the wine valleys for buffs willing to pay a sizable price.

The quickest North Coast sampler

Map *7*E2-3. Across the Golden Gate Bridge, exit from US-101 onto SR-1. After about three miles on SR-1, loop onto Panoramic Highway then Muir Woods Rd., which soon rejoins SR-1. Turning N along the coast, continue on SR-1, then turn off at Point Reyes Station for Point Reyes National Seashore. After regaining SR-1, head inland on Petaluma-Point Reyes Rd., or continue N a few miles and take a similar road from Marshall. At Petaluma, both give access to SR-116, which continues E into the Sonoma Valley. To close the loop, return to US-101 via SR-12, SR-121 and SR-37.

On this short trip it is possible to see a mature grove of coast redwoods in Muir Woods National Monument, a dramatic headland next to some of the roughest seas on the US Pacific coast at **Point Reyes National Seashore**, and a famous wine valley at **Sonoma**.

This drive can be made in either direction. When fog is on the coast, the route as described makes the most sense. The eerie, shifting light and Point Reyes go together. If time presses, good lunches can be had at **Olema** or **Point Reyes Station**, but if it does not, sunshine and warmth await inland. A little cheese factory along the way can supply picnic fare. An even broader variety of picnic foods is to be found on **Sonoma Plaza**, for taking to one of the wineries.

When the coast is clear, the reverse trip works very well. After morning winery tours, gather picnic fare at Sonoma to take to one of the sheltered beaches on the inland side of Point Reyes Peninsula.

Local tour buses serve all three principal attractions, but separately; taking buses takes three days.

Napa Valley day trip

Map 7E3. From San Francisco, across San Francisco-Oakland Bay Bridge, then north on I-80 to SR-37, Columbus Parkway Exit. West on SR-37 about one mile before junction with SR-29, then north into NAPA VALLEY, where SR-29 is the trunk road. While in the valley, SR-29 and Silverado Trail are parallel alternatives, with all of the towns on SR-29. To return, drive south on SR-29, then SR-121, which connects to SR-37. Rather than turning east, go west on SR-37 to US-101 for the round trip to San Francisco.

Some Bay Area oenophiles have logged at least 300 days of winery touring in the Napa Valley and still claim they have not exhausted the possibilities, which puts a heavy burden on a one-day visitor. Nor is winery touring the only way to spend time in this valley. The problem here is not mileage, which is minimal between attractions, but rather electing what to do among all the choices.

The sequence can be inverted. Romantics may wish to use the US-101 in both directions as freeway I-80 has almost no charms and an oversupply of heavyweight trucks. In connection with this trip and the one below, see also Bob Thompson's chapter on WINES AND WINERIES on pages 150-163, with a map on page 152.

Sonoma Valley day trip

Map 7E3. From San Francisco, N on US-101 to its intersection with SR-12 near SANTA ROSA, then E and S along SR-12 to Sonoma town. From town, SR-12 extends a short distance S to a junction with SR-121, which in turn quickly arrives at a junction with SR-37, the connector to US-101 for the return trip to San Francisco.

General Mariano Vallejo would be more than somewhat stunned to see what has happened to the **plaza** he laid out in Sonoma in 1837, but would still recognize several buildings on and near it. This and other historic sites and at least a dozen wineries combine to make a small place worth at least a day's visit at very little expense in driving time.

Sonoma has several distinctive restaurants plus shops that offer every sort of picnic requirement. Several wineries maintain picnic grounds for visitors.

The drive can be made in either direction, depending on whether one wishes to have lunch before or after touring wineries or historic sites. The suggested route assumes touring before eating.

One-day coastal trips north of San Francisco

Map 7E2. From San Francisco, across the Golden Gate Bridge, then N on SR-1 for as far as time permits. Turnbacks crossing the coast hills to US-101 are possible at Point Reyes Station, Marshall, Bodega and Jenner, all easily within one day's driving time.

SR-1 has its most dramatic moments early in its run along the seaward edge of **Marin County**. Thereafter it stays mainly inland, or alongside sheltered bay waters. Its route in Sonoma remains gentle as far as Jenner, as it stays atop low bluffs footed by miles of sandy beach.

Although the road has moments of great natural beauty, much of the appeal in this route lies with the towns of **Marshall** and **Bodega Bay**, honest fishing villages both. This is one loop drive which seems to make less sense if reversed. If one must hurry back it should be on US-101, and not along the winding coast road.

Stroller's Marin

Map 7E3. From San Francisco, across Golden Gate Bridge to exit at N end, which is marked Sausalito. Go through Sausalito, rejoining US-101 for a quarter of a mile to turn off for SR-1, leading to well-marked local road to Mill Valley. From Mill Valley, E on E Blithedale Ave. across US-101, continuing on SR-131 into Tiburon. Return to San Francisco via SR-131 and US-101.

All three of these towns have long shopping streets. Most of the folks in tennis, jogging or sailing gear are locals enjoying their daily routine. Bars and restaurants are plentiful amid select shops. If dramatic residential architecture is of interest, take some time to drive through local streets in all three towns.

Mendocino Coast

Map 7D2. From San Francisco, N on SR-1 to the Mendocino Coast. Return via SR-128 and SR-253 to Ukiah, then US-101 to San Francisco.

The **Mendocino Coast** is just out of one-day range, which provides an unimpeachable excuse to dawdle northward on SR-1, pausing at **Marshall**, **Bodega Bay**, **Fort Ross** and any of dozens of vantage points giving long views of this often dramatic shore.

The return route from the coast to **Ukiah** courses through a small wine valley, the apple-growing town of **Boonville**, and then gets into serious hill country blanketed by second-growth redwood and other conifer forests.

Mendocino town is part artists' colony, part haven for aging dropout flower children, and part retreat for city-weary San Franciscans. Save for Fort Bragg, a sober fishing and lumbering town, the rest of the coast is lightly populated, often shrouded in summer fog; an impeccable environment for low-key Mendocino society. The other attractions are parks.

Redwood Coast tours

Map 7B-C2.

Islands of redwoods dot the coast from **Big Sur** northward, but the grandest groves of these tallest trees on earth lie more than 200 miles N of the city. It is easiest to visit them *en route* to the Pacific Northwest. Several legendary stands can be reached, however, on a two-day excursion from the city, and many in both **Redwood National Park** and **Humboldt Redwoods State Park** fall within a three-day tour.

Eureka, the largest city in the region, is central to both parks. With **Garberville**, it offers the most practical and attractive accommodations for travelers who are planning to turn back to San Francisco. For those continuing northward, **Crescent City** is another useful stopover town. US-101 is the prime route for all of the distance, and the only one for much of the way.

The inland redwoods

For those who would stay warm while they look at redwood trees, the focal point is the **Avenue of the Giants**. Running parallel to US-101 for almost half the distance between Garberville and Eureka, the Avenue connects several outstanding but scattered groves in **Humboldt Redwoods State Park**.

Garberville, astride US-101, 200 miles N of San Francisco, can be reached by car in half a day, even when trailers and other slow vehicles clog some two-lane sections of the highway. Eureka, another 78 miles N, has a wider choice of accommodation in a much cooler climate.

Vacationers without cars can visit the Avenue of the Giants easily by bus. Greyhound runs express buses between San Francisco and Garberville daily. From Garberville, a local company runs bus tours through the redwood park. The driver/guides are knowledgeable locals. It is best to allow three days.

The shoreward redwoods

Redwood National Park stretches for miles from Crescent City S toward Eureka. Many fine stands of trees occupy fog-swept parts of the coastal shelf near Crescent City and the Oregon border, but the finest grove, **Tall Trees**, is near the town of Orick.

This park is almost wholly the province of vacationers with cars. Not only does it sprawl for miles, but the best of the groves are remote from highways.

Crescent City is a sometimes tedious 362 miles from San Francisco. Many visitors aiming particularly to see Redwood National Park drive straight through to Eureka in one day, then explore the park on the way to a second overnight stop in Crescent City. Only 84 road miles separate the two towns.

AREA: TAHOE, YOSEMITE, AND THE SIERRA

The Sierra Nevada holds two great treasures and has held a third. They are **Lake Tahoe**, **Yosemite Valley** (both of which have full sections of their own in EXCURSIONS: FARTHER AFIELD) — and gold.

Trying to assemble these three elements into a coherent whole is futile. Tahoe contains contradictions of its own. It always has been a remarkable alpine lake; it has become an alpine skiing center and — because it straddles the California/Nevada state line — an alpine gambling spot. **Yosemite National Park** is supposed by definition to enshrine nature, although the nature it enshrines is such a powerful magnet that Yosemite Valley endures traffic jams and smog all summer long. The **Gold Country**, once a raw testimonial to the power of money among men, is now an endearing backwater where crowds are more easily avoided than at Tahoe or Yosemite.

These places still link together handsomely, in turn offering anything from modest change of pace to stark contrast, depending on how the visitor chooses to use them. Tahoe still has wilderness all around; in addition to the famous valley, Yosemite encompasses scenic high country open only to hikers. Even the Gold Country has miles of scenic

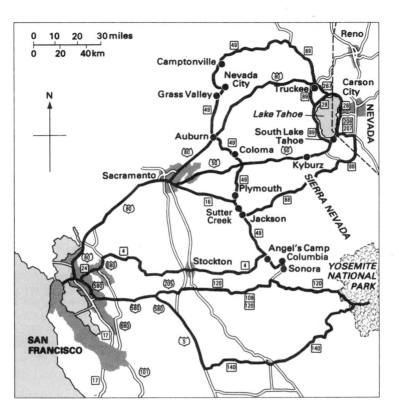

byways in sparsely settled countryside. Conversely, one can mingle elbow to elbow with humanity in Yosemite Valley, at the **gaming tables** on Lake Tahoe's s shore and, not least, in some of the lively Gold Country saloons in Coloma, Columbia, or the many points in between.

Late spring to early fall is the season of sunny, warm weather. September and early October tend to be the peak months for gentle, reliable warmth. Good weather aside, it is worth remembering that photographer Ansel Adams's most powerful views of Yosemite were taken in unsettled spring. Of course, Tahoe has a summer season for lake users, a winter season for skiers, and open season all year for gamblers.

Accommodations are diverse in this part of the world. At Lake Tahoe they range from hotel towers at the gambling casinos to bare-bones motels (see FARTHER AFIELD). Many are booked up on weekends. In the Gold Country, hotels tend to be small and quaint, and are often restored Gold Rush buildings. At Yosemite, rustic is the usual watchword (again, see FARTHER AFIELD).

Starting from San Francisco, it is easy to design loop drives touching any or all of these major attractions. Tahoe is but 180 miles from the city, Yosemite the same distance.

Without a car, much of the Sierra and almost all of the Gold Rush Country is completely out of reach. Although many buses operate daily between San Francisco and Lake Tahoe, they are of little help in getting anywhere beyond the gambling casinos. Only Yosemite Valley lends itself to bus tours. Car drivers pressed for time can plan as little as a day each for Tahoe, Yosemite Valley and the Gold Country.

TAHOE LOOPS

Lake Tahoe lies between two of the easier passes across the Sierra Nevada, which explains the existence of the two major highways, one at either end of the lake. Less easy to explain are the several secondary roads that offer far more diverting and far slower ways to get there from San Francisco.

The quick way

Maps 7-8. From San Francisco, E via I-80 to Sacramento, then to TAHOE via US-50. From Lake Tahoe's N shore, return via SR-89 to Trucker, then I-80.

This route has few points of interest along the way, but serves to get gamblers into the S shore area most directly. The reverse loop better suits those planning to stay at the quieter N shore. The all-freeway drive to Truckee on I-80, 190 miles, takes only a few minutes more than 3 hours; the last leg of the journey into Tahoe takes 15-20 minutes. The return trip combining US-50 and I-80 is a few miles shorter and, in good traffic, quicker. The drive can be made in a long day, but to do so is unwise because too little time is left to enjoy the lake's attractions.

The Gold Country and North Tahoe

Maps 7-8. From San Francisco, E via I-80 to junction with SR-49, then SR-49 E to junction with SR-89 via Grass Valley and Camptonville; SR-89 S to Truckee; from Truckee, take either SR-267 or SR-89 S to Lake Tahoe's N shore. From Tahoe's S shore, return through Sacramento on US-50 and I-80.

Taking the SR-49/SR-89 detour adds only about 60 miles, but a good 2 hours to the driving time. It does, however, add opportunities to explore the **Gold Country**, and to get into more intimate contact with mountain scenery than the I-80 permits. **Grass Valley** and **Nevada City** bear marks from their days as Gold Rush towns.

The Gold Country and South Tahoe

Maps 7-8. From San Francisco, E via I-80 to Sacramento, then US-50 to its junction with SR-16; SR-16 to Plymouth; SR-49 S from Plymouth to Jackson; SR-88 from Jackson E to its intersection with Nevada's SR-206-207, the scenic route into South Lake Tahoe. From Tahoe's N shore, return via SR-267 to Truckee, then I-80.

Taking a set of byways S of US-50 provides what would appear to be almost exactly the same range of opportunities as the loop N of I-80: picturesque **Gold Country** towns and fine mountain scenery. But the experience has at least one substantial difference: where Grass Valley has a fair number of commuters to Sacramento, **Sutter Creek** and

Jackson remain splendidly isolated, and so more timeless in appearance and temperament.

Added time and miles are about the same as for the detour from I-80 on the northern route.

Heart of the Gold Country

Maps 7-8E3-4. From San Francisco, E on I-80, SR-24 (Ashby Ave.), and I-680 to its intersection with SR-4 at Martinez. Continue E on SR-4 to its intersection with SR-49 in the Gold Country. There, turn S on SR-49 as far as Sonora before heading N, on the same road, to Coloma or beyond. Return to San Francisco via I-80, or SR-50/I-80.

While one can speed E on I-80 or US-50 to an intersection with SR-49, a dawdling route such as SR-4 sets a proper mood for travels in the Gold Country. First along levees 20 feet above rich farmlands in the Sacramento River delta, then through drier farm country E of Stockton, it foretells the languorous pace of SR-49 across the Sierra Nevada foothills.

Angel's Camp, Jackson, Sutter Creek, Coloma and Grass Valley between them can tell most of the story through ghost mines, old equipment, antique stores, and quaint hostelries deliberately lacking in swimming pools and televisions.

Yosemite loop

Map 9-10. From Sam Francisco, E via I-580, I-205, and SR-120 to the latter's junction with SR-140 for the last 10 miles to Yosemite Valley. Return via SR-140, I-5, and I-580.

In part, the loop is recommended because the slower, less direct SR-140 has several miles of surpassingly lovely scenery along the **Merced River**. To a greater degree, it is suggested in order to give a small change of scenery along the way. Quite simply, Yosemite is its own reward, and nothing really leads up to it by degrees. The best plan is to get to it with a minimum of distraction, and to savor it for as long as possible.

GRAND TOURS

There is something endlessly beguiling about the idea of Grand Tours. Exhausting to both mind and body, they still appeal because they force so many reactions in so short a time.

The classic Grand Tours spanned the European continent in the days of luxury ships and luxury trains, and took in little more than capitals. California is short on luxury trains and capitals, but the state is big enough and diverse enough to permit several tours that just might qualify as grand.

Tour 1: Great sights of Northern California

Maps 7, 8, 9, and 10. From San Francisco, S on SR-1 to Monterey (see MONTEREY PENINSULA). From Monterey, E on the combination of SR-156, 152, 33 and 140 to YOSEMITE NATIONAL PARK. From Yosemite, N on SR-120 and SR-49 to the Gold

Country. From the Gold Country, ε on SR-88 then ν on Nevada's SR-206-207 to Lake Tahoe. From Lake Tahoe, w on I-80 then ν on SR-12 and SR-29 to the Napa Valley. From the Napa Valley, s via SR-29, 121 and 37, and US-101 across the Golden Gate into San Francisco.

The itinerary anticipates overnight stops on the Monterey Peninsula, at Yosemite, in the Gold Country, at Tahoe, and in the Napa Valley. Except for the long haul between the Monterey Peninsula and Yosemite, daily driving distances are short. Everywhere except at Yosemite the range of accommodations and restaurants is from very expensive to moderate, or even cheap. Yosemite, alas for elegance, is pretty much in the lower half of the range.

The tour forms a loop, so it can be reversed. Most of the territory can be explored from March to November. In high summer, a substantial proportion of the route is subject to temperatures in the 85-100°F (29-38°C) range. Spring and fall are delightful on the coast. Early fall is best for getting the most from the Sierra. Mountain weather makes winter a risky time to follow a tight schedule.

Tour 2: The coast — Los Angeles to San Francisco and back

Maps 9 and 10, and map on page 136. From Los Angeles, ν on SR-1 and/or US-101 to Santa Barbara. From Santa Barbara, ν on US-101 to Avila Beach or Cambria. From that area, ν on SR-1 to the MONTEREY PENINSULA. From Monterey, ν on SR-1 to San Francisco. From San Francisco, s on US-101 to San Luis Obispo. From San Luis Obispo, s on US-101 to Los Angeles. Reverse this itinerary if setting out from San Francisco.

The itinerary anticipates overnight stops in Santa Barbara, Avila or Cambria, and Monterey on the northward leg, and in San Luis Obispo on the southward run. This tour might just as well start in San Francisco as Los Angeles but, either way, when going ν, use SR-1, which clings to sheer cliffs high above the sea for much of the distance between **San Simeon** and the **Big Sur** country, and travel s on US-101.

As in the case of TOUR 1, the basic program allows equally for luxury or budget travel all along. In either case, there are many attractions to choose from. In particular, the long haul from San Francisco to San Luis Obispo can be lightened with visits to **San Juan Bautista** and the **Mission San Antonio de Padua**. Serious eaters should attempt to arrive at mealtimes in **Half Moon Bay/Pescadero** and perhaps **Salinas** and **Solvang**, as well as the stopover towns.

This is an all-year route. Since so many of the attractions are man-made and indoors, winter rains do little to spoil the effects. The emphasis on human contributions does not mean there is no scenery; the shore and several inland valleys have moments of surpassing beauty, but scenery watchers may do best in spring or fall, when coastal fogs are less frequent.

Tour 3: Los Angeles to San Francisco through the Sierra

Maps 7, 8 and 10. From Los Angeles ν on I-5 and SR-99 then w on SR-198 to Hanford. From Hanford, ε on SR-198 into Sequoia National Park. From Sequoia National Park, w and ν via SR-180, 41 and 49 into the Gold Country. From the Gold Country, SR-49 to its junction with SR-89, then double back on SR-89 to Lake Tahoe. From Lake Tahoe, s on Nevada's SR-207-206 to SR-4, w on SR-4,

then s on SR-49 and SR-120 to YOSEMITE NATIONAL PARK. From Yosemite, w on
SR-120, I-205 and I-580 to San Francisco.

The itinerary assumes overnight stops at Hanford, Sequoia National Park, one of the Gold Country towns, Lake Tahoe and Yosemite. Because much of the attraction is scenery, the plan calls for some days of heavy driving. To give variety, the trip loops back on itself, rather than following the straightest possible line. The buttonhook route, having saved the high points for last, does not lend itself to a start from San Francisco; TOUR 4 provides a more attractive option for using the mountains to get from N-S.

A certain variation in the excellence of food and accommodations is to be expected along this route. Hanford and Tahoe contain the brightest opportunities for eaters, with the Gold Country coming not too far behind. Except for Tahoe, where a broad range exists, accommodations are quaint and comfortable rather than luxurious.

Fall weather tends to be sunny but temperate. In summer, much of the route can be very hot indeed. Spring weather puts these mountains in their best light, but chill rains are a possibility.

Tour 4: The San Francisco to Los Angeles all-purpose sampler

Maps 7, 8, 9 and 10. See also maps on pages 136 and 145. From San Francisco, E via I-80 to Lake Tahoe. From Tahoe, s via Nevada's SR-207-206, then w via SR-88 to the Gold Country. From the Gold Country, s via SR-49 and SR-120 to YOSEMITE NATIONAL PARK. From Yosemite, w via SR-41 to San Luis Obispo. From San Luis Obispo, s via US-101 to Santa Barbara. From Santa Barbara, s via US-101 and SR-1 to Los Angeles.

The itinerary assumes overnight stops at **Lake Tahoe**, the **Gold Country**, **Yosemite**, **San Luis Obispo** and **Santa Barbara**. Because these routes cut across some attractive districts, mileages vary from day to day to allow extra time for exploring side roads. The two districts offering particular rewards for digressions from the route are the Gold Country and San Luis Obispo.

The potential for excellent food and accommodation is consistent. Travelers on tight budgets will also find agreeable options all along the way.

Although parts of this tour run through hot summer districts, the area is attractive from May to late fall.

Wines and wineries
by Bob Thompson

Touring the vineyards

In recent years, California wines have caught the fancy of connoisseurs all around the world with their engrossing balance of strength and subtlety.

Nearly all the fine wines come from handsome coastal valleys N and s of San Francisco. Napa is the most famous, but the state offers a long list of other valleys that produce excellent wine and whose vineyards are a pleasure to visit.

Few vineyard regions in the world offer such a warm-hearted welcome to winery visitors. Cellars in every region provide tours for those who wish to learn first-hand how wine is made, and give tastings of their finished products. This public hospitality grew out of necessity. Cellar owners found free tastings for visitors to be one of the few successful ways to reacquaint Americans with wine after national Prohibition had robbed the country of its good taste between 1919 and 1933. The welcome has long since grown into a natural part of vintner/buyer relationships.

Winemaking began in California in the mid-19thC, but today most of the wineries are filled with the latest machinery, made in the US and in Europe. Not that this has meant an end to romantic, castle-like old cellars. On the contrary, they have been refurbished, while quite a few romantic, castle-like cellars have actually been built in recent times.

WHAT'S IN A NAME?
The local system of wine- and place-names is simple. The primary definition of character is by the name of the predominating **grape variety**.

The main whites (with European counterparts) are Chardonnay (white Burgundy), Sauvignon Blanc or Fumé Blanc (dry Graves, Pouilly Fumé or Sancerre), White or Johannisberg Riesling (QbA Rhine or Mosel-Saar-Ruwer), and Chenin Blanc (Vouvray). The first two tend to be dry, the last two just off-dry to outright sweet. Among reds, the major varieties are Cabernet Sauvignon (Medoc), Merlot (St Emilion or Pomerol), Pinot Noir (red Burgundy), and the uniquely Californian Zinfandel.

Less expensive wines called White or Chablis, Red or Burgundy, are blends of several grape varieties, usually made just off-dry, their flavors blandly fresh and fruity.

As for **areas of origin**, the Napa Valley ranks as the most prestigious, with Sonoma a close second. Livermore has a durable reputation for Sauvignon Blanc, and Amador County a similar one for Zinfandel. Other districts gaining attention are San Luis Obispo County's Edna Valley and Santa Barbara's Santa Ynez Valley. Monterey also competes for attention as an up-and-coming district.

In addition to its wines, California has one distinctive beer, Anchor Steam. Steam refers to an almost-lost brewing process, not hot beer. The product is richly flavored and several shades darker than lager.

PLANNING YOUR VISIT

Nearly all of the coastal vineyard valleys lie within a day's drive of San Francisco, and most can be reached in an hour or two. While one-day trips are gratifying enough for casual students, serious wine buffs may wish to spend more time tracking down favorite cellars. Most of the wine towns with large numbers of cellars have excellent accommodations and restaurants.

Veteran visitors recommend planning to visit no more than three cellars in a single day, to avoid sensory overload. Although every season has its charms, April to May and September to November are the great months for photographers and picnickers; harvest time in September and October are the most instructive.

Wineries that welcome visitors are typically open from 10am-4pm. Large wineries with guided tours tend to be open daily. Smaller ones usually close one or two days a week, so a telephone call first to check on opening times is recommended.

For road directions and visiting hours, request a free copy of *California is Wine Country* from the **Wine Institute** *(165 Post St., San Francisco 94108 ☎ (415) 986-0878)*.

✍ **Accommodations Referral of Napa Valley** *(PO Box 59, St Helena, CA 94574 ☎ (707) 963-VINO)* is a referral service for Napa Valley wine country accommodations (free hotline).

The following pages provide both a buyer's guide to excellent bottlings by individual wineries and some suggestions for how to go about touring vineyards and wineries.

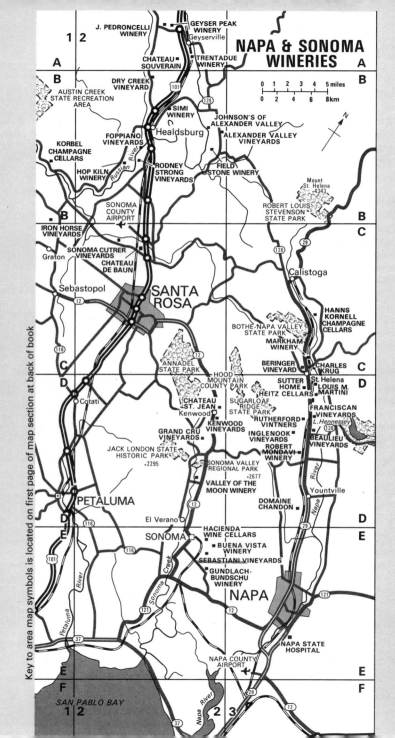

NAPA & SONOMA WINERIES

1 2

A

J. PEDRONCELLI WINERY

GEYSER PEAK WINERY
Geyserville

CHATEAU SOUVERAIN

TRENTADUE WINERY

B

AUSTIN CREEK STATE RECREATION AREA

DRY CREEK VINEYARD

101

128

SIMI WINERY

JOHNSON'S OF ALEXANDER VALLEY

ALEXANDER VALLEY VINEYARDS

KORBEL CHAMPAGNE CELLARS

FOPPIANO VINEYARDS

Healdsburg

HOP KILN WINERY

Russian River

RODNEY STRONG VINEYARDS

FIELD STONE WINERY

Mount St. Helena +4343

ROBERT LOUIS STEVENSON STATE PARK

SONOMA COUNTY AIRPORT

C

IRON HORSE VINEYARDS

SONOMA CUTRER VINEYARDS

Graton

CHATEAU DE BAUN

128

29

Calistoga

Sebastopol

SANTA ROSA

116

HANNS KORNELL CHAMPAGNE CELLARS

BOTHE-NAPA VALLEY STATE PARK

MARKHAM WINERY

ANNADEL STATE PARK

12

HOOD MOUNTAIN COUNTY PARK

BERINGER VINEYARD

CHARLES KRUG

D

St. Helena

SUTTER HOME

LOUIS M. MARTINI

CHATEAU ST. JEAN

Kenwood

SUGARLOAF RIDGE STATE PARK

HEITZ CELLARS

RUTHERFORD VINTNERS

FRANCISCAN VINEYARDS

L. Hennessey

KENWOOD VINEYARDS

GRAND CRU VINEYARDS

INGLENOOK VINEYARDS

BEAULIEU VINEYARDS

128

JACK LONDON STATE HISTORIC PARK
+2295

Cotati

ROBERT MONDAVI WINERY

SONOMA VALLEY REGIONAL PARK
+2677

VALLEY OF THE MOON WINERY

Napa River

Yountville

PETALUMA

116

El Verano

12

DOMAINE CHANDON

29

E

101

SONOMA

HACIENDA WINE CELLARS

BUENA VISTA WINERY

SEBASTIANI VINEYARDS

GUNDLACH-BUNDSCHU WINERY

NAPA

121

Sonoma Creek

Petaluma River

121

37

12

NAPA STATE HOSPITAL

F

SAN PABLO BAY

NAPA COUNTY AIRPORT

Napa River

29

12

37

1 2 **2 3**

A

B

C

D

E

F

0 1 2 3 4 5 miles
0 2 4 6 8km

N

Key to area map symbols is located on first page of map section at back of book

The wine regions

NAPA VALLEY
Map C-E3, page 151. See also map 7E3.
Although other districts are beginning to catch up, the Napa Valley remains California's pace-setter both for wines to drink and wineries to visit.

Human and natural history conspire to give it the advantage. On the human side, this valley has a splendid architectural legacy from its first great era in the late 19thC, and equally splendid buildings have been erected since 1970. It also has numerous fine restaurants and hostelries. Natural history blessed this valley with an intimate scale; vineyards roll across its narrow floor and up onto hillsides that are often a mere 800 yards apart. And yet, for all its smallness, its climate changes so strikingly in the 25 miles from one end to the other that it provides suitable growing conditions for an astonishing variety of grapes. Favored are Chardonnay, Sauvignon Blanc, Cabernet Sauvignon and White or Johannisberg Riesling. Gewürztraminer, Pinot Noir and Zinfandel also do well, but in a more limited way.

Because of Napa's reputation for quality and its proximity to San Francisco (the valley is little more than an hour's drive via I-80, SR-37 at Vallejo, and SR-29 from North Vallejo), it is inundated by visitors all through the year, and many of the smaller cellars have to limit guests to those who have written or made appointments by telephone. However, a considerable number of cellars continue to welcome all comers. The ranks of wineries have now grown to more than 150, so only cellars that can be easily visited receive general description here.

Readily visited (tasting, usually tours)

S. ANDERSON VINEYARD
1473 Yountville Cross Rd., Yountville
☎(707) 944-8642.
Excellent champagne-method sparklers.

BEAULIEU VINEYARD
1960 St Helena Highway, Rutherford
☎(707) 963-2411.
Deservedly famous for pedigreed Georges de Latour Cabernet Sauvignon. Informative tours.

BERINGER VINEYARD
2000 Main St., St Helena ☎(707) 963-7115.
Broad range of always good, often excellent wines. Magnificently overdone Rhenish house and network of tunnels make guided tours picturesque.

BURGESS CELLARS
1108 Deer Park Rd., St Helena ☎(707) 963-4766.
Firm history of producing husky reds, especially Cabernet Sauvignon and Zinfandel. The site, well up Howell Mountain, is worth a visit for itself.

CAKEBREAD CELLARS
8300 St Helena Highway, Rutherford
☎(707) 963-5221.
Steadily mounting reputation for Chardonnay, Sauvignon Blanc and Cabernet Sauvignon. Instructive tours of the handsome cellars are only by appointment.

CAYMUS VINEYARDS
8700 Conn Creek Rd., Rutherford ☎(707) 963-4204.

Amazingly consistent producer of outstanding Cabernet Sauvignon from estate vines.

CHAPPELLET VINEYARD
1581 Sage Canyon Rd., St Helena ☎*(707) 963-7136.*
The winery has established a loyal following with estate-bottled wines from steeply sloping vineyards that look down onto Lake Hennessey.

CHATEAU MONTELENA
1429 Tubbs Lane, Calistoga ☎*(707) 942-5105.*
Picturesque property at foot of Mt. St Helena includes lake with Chinese tea houses on islands. Best known for Cabernet Sauvignon.

CLOS DU VAL WINE CO
5330 Silverado Trail, Napa ☎*(707) 252-6711.*
Outstanding Cabernet Sauvignon, Merlot and Sauvignon; fascinating Zinfandel. The Bordeaux-born winemaker has gone from strength to strength. Unusually informative tours only by appointment.

CODORNIU NAPA
1345 Henry Rd., Napa ☎*(707) 224-1668.*
Producers of *méthode champenoise* sparkling wine, Napa Valley Brut.

CONN CREEK WINERY
8711 Silverado Trail, St Helena ☎*(707) 963-5133.*
Handsome property with reliable record for Chardonnay, Cabernet Sauvignon. Merlot and Sauvignon Blanc introduced in 1986.

DOMAINE CARNEROS
1240 Duhig Rd., Napa ☎*(707) 257-0101.*
The new-in-1987 sparkling wine venture with an imposing cellar that was styled after La Marqueterie at Reims and set among 110 acres of vines.

DOMAINE CHANDON
1 California Drive, Yountville ☎*(707) 944-2280.*
Architecturally superb modern offshoot of Moët et Chandon produces some of California's most stylish sparkling wines. Small fee for tasting. Grand restaurant in grounds.

FOLIE A DEUX WINERY
3070 St Helena Highway, St Helena ☎*(707) 963-1160.*
Tiny, architecturally intriguing newcomer makes impressive Chardonnays.

FRANCISCAN VINEYARDS
1178 Galleron Rd., Rutherford ☎*(707) 963-7111.*
German-owned producer of reliable range has self-guiding tours.

FREEMARK ABBEY WINERY
3022 St Helena Highway N, St Helena ☎*(707) 963-9694 ext. 14.*
Excellent name for Chardonnay, Cabernet Sauvignon and late-harvest Johannisberg Riesling. Excellent place to visit for itself; adjoining restaurants.

GIRARD WINERY
7717 Silverado Trail, Oakville ☎*(707) 944-8577.*
Handsome property still homing in on style.

GRGICH-HILLS CELLAR
1829 St Helena Highway, Rutherford ☎*(707) 963-2784.*
Outstanding reputation for Chardonnay. Informative tours by appointment.

HAKUSAN SAKE
1 Executive Way, Napa ☎*(707) 258-6160.*
No appointment is required for the self-guided tour, which includes a video demonstrating how sake is made.

HEITZ WINE CELLARS
436 St Helena Highway S, St Helena ☎*(707) 963-3542.*
Legendary for Cabernet Sauvignon-Martha's Vineyard; cellar maintains a highwayside tasting room well away from its hidden-in-the-hills winery.

INGLENOOK-NAPA VALLEY
1991 St Helena Highway, Rutherford ☎*(707) 967-3300.*

Steady producer of broad range at various price levels. Best wines are kept in a fine old building that could look at home in St Julien.

HANNS KORNELL CHAMPAGNE
1091 Larkmead Lane, Calistoga ☎(707) 963-1237.
Sehr Trocken is the flagship of a traditional *méthode champenoise* producer who gives excellent tours, then finishes with a flourish of sparkling wines styled after Sekt rather than Champagne.

CHARLES KRUG WINERY
2800 St Helena Highway, St Helena ☎(707) 963-5057.
A steady producer and one of the grand old estates in the valley. Informative tours at historic 1861 winery at St Helena.

LAKESPRING WINERY
2055 Hoffman Lane, Napa ☎(707) 944-2475.
Sound across the board; excellent for Merlot. Tours by appointment.

MARKHAM VINEYARDS
2812 St Helena Highway N, St Helena ☎(707) 963-5292.
Reliable wines across a broad range.

LOUIS M MARTINI WINERY
254 St Helena Highway S, St Helena ☎(707) 963-2736.
The imperishable: an ever-reliable source of stylish, underpriced reds, especially Cabernet Sauvignon and Zinfandel. Fine tours of old-style cellars.

MAYACAMAS VINEYARD
1155 Lokoya Rd., Napa ☎(707) 224-4030.
Mountaintop estate famous for Cabernet Sauvignon and Chardonnay.

ROBERT MONDAVI WINERY
7801 St Helena Highway, Oakville ☎(707) 963-9611.
A great name for Cabernet Sauvignon and Fumé Blanc, and a fine one for the rest of a broad range. Excellent tours of a completely up-to-date winery hidden behind Spanish colonial facade.

MONTICELLO CELLARS
4242 Big Ranch Rd., Napa ☎(707) 253-2802.
Beautiful property much patterned after Thos. Jefferson's Monticello. Excellent wines across the board. There are lovely picnic grounds.

MUMM NAPA VALLEY
8445 Silverado Trail, Rutherford ☎(707) 942-3300.
Producers of *méthode champenoise* sparkling wines.

ROBERT PECOTA WINERY
3299 Bennett Lane, Calistoga ☎(707) 942-6625.
Cellar that has carved out a reputation for Cabernet Sauvignon, Sauvignon Blanc and Muscat Blanc.

JOSEPH PHELPS VINEYARDS
200 Taplin Rd., St Helena ☎(707) 963-2745.
One of the valley's most handsome wineries occupies one of its handsomest sites. Excellent wines all across the board but great reputation for late-harvest Johannisberg Riesling.

PINE RIDGE WINERY
5901 Silverado Trail, Napa ☎(707) 253-7500.
Reputation gains vintage to vintage for Cabernet Sauvignon, Merlot, Chardonnay.

RAYMOND VINEYARD AND CELLAR
849 Zinfandel Lane, St Helena ☎(707) 963-3141.
Excellent wines across the board. Friendly hosts.

RUTHERFORD HILL WINERY
200 Rutherford Hill Rd., Rutherford ☎(707) 963-7194.
Dramatic site, newly dug caves, reliably fine wines make this a premier choice to visit.

RUTHERFORD VINTNERS
1673 St Helena Highway, Rutherford ☎(707) 963-4117.
A good reputation for Cabernet Sauvig-

155

non for a cellar belonging to one of the valley's old hands. His Muscat of Alexandria is sold only at the winery.

ST CLEMENT VINEYARD
2867 St Helena Highway N, St Helena
☎*(707) 963-7221.*
Full-bodied and full-flavored Sauvignon Blanc and excellent Chardonnay and Cabernet Sauvignon. Merlot was added to the roster in 1988.

ST SUPERY VINEYARDS & WINERY
8440 St Helena Highway, Rutherford
☎*(707) 963-4507.*
The state-of-the-art winery was built by a high-powered French business family. They are making Chardonnay, Sauvignon Blanc and Cabernet Sauvignon.

SCHRAMSBERG VINEYARDS
1400 Schramsberg Rd., Calistoga ☎*(707) 942-4558.*
A prime mover in generating new interest in champagne-method sparkling wine in California and still one of the most stylish sources.

SEQUOIA GROVE VINEYARDS
8338 St Helena Highway, Rutherford
☎*(707) 944-2945.*
A rustic winery surrounded by a grove of sequoia trees. Owned by the Allen family, who produce Chardonnay and Cabernet Sauvignon.

SILVER OAK WINE CELLARS
915 Oakville Cross Rd., Oakville ☎*(707) 944-8808.*
Winemaker and partner Justin Meyer specializes in plummy Cabernet Sauvignon made in a handsome stone cellar E of Oakwood.

ROBERT SINSKEY VINEYARDS
6320 Silverado Trail, Napa ☎*(707) 944-9090.*
The elaborate winery is dug into a hillside. It belongs to a Napa physician who makes Merlot, Chardonnay and Pinot Noir.

SPRING MOUNTAIN VINEYARDS
2805 Spring Mountain Rd., St Helena

☎*(707) 963-5233.*
One of Napa Valley's great showplace properties (it featured as Falcon Crest in the TV series). Its Chardonnay and Cabernet Sauvignon are good, sound wines.

STAG'S LEAP WINE CELLARS
5766 Silverado Trail, Napa ☎*(707) 944-2020.*
One of the valley's premier names for Cabernet Sauvignon. Tours by appointment.

STERLING VINEYARDS
1111 Dunaweal Lane, Calistoga ☎*(707) 942-3300.*
Widespread reputation for Cabernet Sauvignon and Sauvignon Blanc. The Greek-Isles-inspired building sits atop a lofty rock and is accessible only by aerial tram. Fee for tram ride. Tours are self-guiding.

STONEGATE WINERY
1183 Dunaweal Lane, Calistoga ☎*(707) 942-6500.*
Small, family-owned cellar that is instructive to visit. Wines are sturdy.

SUTTER HOME WINERY
277 St Helena Highway S, St Helena
☎*(707) 963-3104.*
This one is an anomaly: a Napa winery that makes nearly all of its wine and all of its reputation from Amador County Zinfandel.

TREFETHEN VINEYARDS
1160 Oak Knoll Ave., Napa ☎*(707) 255-7700.*
Handsome estate with excellent reputation. The Chardonnay is outstanding.

VICHON WINERY
1595 Oakville Grade, Oakville ☎*(707) 944-2811.*
Handsomely set, instructive-to-see cellars. Wines excellent, including Botrytis Sémillon.

ZD WINES
8383 Silverado Trail, Napa ☎*(707) 963-5188.*

Producers of Chardonnay, Pinot Noir and Cabernet Sauvignon with Late Harvest White Riesling when there are cool, damp harvests.

SONOMA COUNTY

Map A2-E2, page 151. See also map 7.

Napa's oldest and closest rival is its neighbor to the w. They are similar in vineyard acreage and in their wines, although veteran California tasters can often tell them apart in blind tastings. There is, however, one great difference: where Napa is compact, Sonoma sprawls.

A visitor hoping to see all there is must allow a considerable amount of time for driving as well as for stopping to tour and taste. The largest district follows the Russian River while it runs parallel to US-101 and after the stream turns w toward the Pacific. Some 60 cellars are on or near the freeway between Santa Rosa and the Mendocino County line 30 miles to the n. The much smaller Sonoma Valley has about half of its 20 cellars around the old pueblo town of Sonoma; the remaining ones string out along SR-12 on its way to join US-101 at Santa Rosa. Because of the distances, there is more lovely countryside to explore in Sonoma than there is in Napa. Against that advantage, Sonoma has fewer fine places in which to stay or dine, although the shortage is hardly critical.

Also, fewer Sonoma cellars are household names among California wine buffs, because Sonoma took longer to reawaken from Prohibition. But progress has been swift during the past decade or so, as the following list shows.

Sonoma's greatest reputation is for Zinfandel, which it grows incomparably well. The country also has a first-class name for Gewürztraminer and White Riesling in both conventional and late-harvest styles.

Readily visited (tasting, usually tours)

ALDERBROOK WINERY
2306 Magnolia Drive, Healdsburg ☎(707) 433-9154.
Relative newcomer has earned an early reputation for flavorful whites, especially Chardonnay and Sémillon. Instructive to visit.

ALEXANDER VALLEY VINEYARDS
8644 Highway 128, Healdsburg ☎(707) 433-7209.
Best known for whites. 45-minute educational vineyard walk by appointment.

BUENA VISTA WINERY
18000 Old Winery Rd., Sonoma ☎(707) 938-1266.
Broad range of agreeable wines from a cellar famed as the birthplace of winemaking n of San Francisco.

CHATEAU DE BAUN
5007 Fulton Rd., Fulton ☎(707) 571-7500.
A winery that makes seven wines from one grape, Symphony, a splendidly aromatic cross between Muscat of Alexandria and Grenache Gris.

CHATEAU ST JEAN
8555 Sonoma Highway, Kenwood ☎(707) 833-4134.
A legend for single-vineyard Chardonnay and late-harvest Johannisberg Riesling. The mock-medieval cellar buildings provoke much comment.

CHATEAU SOUVERAIN
400 Souverain Rd., Geyserville ☎(707) 433-8281.
Steady producer of appealing wines. Particularly well known for Colombard

Blanc, which is an overlooked summer sipper. Excellent tours of their modern cellar.

CLOS DU BOIS
5 Fitch St., Healdsburg ☎(707) 433-5576.
Well-established label offers multiple styles of Chardonnay, Cabernet Sauvignon and others.

DE LOACH VINEYARDS
1791 Olivet Rd., Santa Rosa ☎(707) 526-9111.
Year after year, outstanding for Chardonnay, but first-rate across the board.

DRY CREEK VINEYARD
3770 Lambert Bridge Rd., Healdsburg ☎(707) 433-1000.
Has a fine reputation, especially for Sauvignon Blanc. Reds begin to clamor for attention.

FIELD STONE WINERY
10075 Highway 128, Healdsburg ☎(707) 433-7266.
Underground cellar was once an experimental station for mechanical harvesters, field presses and other highly advanced equipment. Now a sturdily independent producer of a broad range of wines.

FISHER VINEYARDS
6200 St Helena Rd., Mayacamas Mountains ☎(707) 539-7511.
Fred Fisher makes excellent Chardonnay and Cabernet Sauvignon at his winery in the high hills between Santa Rosa and St Helena.

FOPPIANO VINEYARDS
12707 Old Redwood Highway, Healdsburg ☎(707) 433-7272.
Steady, old-time producer offers broad range of sound wines, especially reds. The tasting room is an old railroad carriage.

GEYSER PEAK WINERY
22281 Chianti Rd., Geyserville ☎(707) 433-6585.
Sizable producer of sound, often appealing, broad range.

GRAND CRU VINEYARDS
One Vintage Lane, Glen Ellen ☎(707) 996-8100.
Famed for controlled-environment production of late-harvest Gewürztraminer. Generally well regarded.

GUNDLACH-BUNDSCHU WINERY
2000 Denmark St., Sonoma ☎(707) 938-5277.
The company dates back to 1858. Steadily gaining acclaim for Cabernet Franc and Merlot in particular.

HACIENDA WINERY
1000 Vineyard Lane, Sonoma ☎(707) 938-3220.
Produces stylish Gewürztraminer and Chardonnay among other fine wines.

HANNA WINERY
5345 Occidental Rd., Santa Rosa ☎(707) 575-3330.
Dr. Elias Hanna was a heart surgeon in San Francisco before he turned to winemaking. He now makes very successful Chardonnay and Sauvignon Blanc.

HOP KILN WINERY
6050 Westside Rd., Healdsburg ☎(707) 433-6491.
Seeks to make sturdy wines and succeeds; uncommonly interesting Petite Sirah, among others. Isolated cellar has a striking row of towers, once used to dry hops.

IRON HORSE VINEYARDS
9786 Ross Station Rd., Sebastopol ☎(707) 887-1507.
One of the most prestigious sparkling wine houses in California.

JOHNSON'S ALEXANDER VALLEY
8333 Highway 128, Healdsburg ☎(707) 433-2319.
Always sound, sometimes exciting, especially the reds.

JORDAN VINEYARD AND WINERY
1474 Alexander Valley Rd., Healdsburg ☎(707) 433-6955.
The Jordan family build a stunning château-like estate on a hilltop in the Alex-

ander Valley. They make memorable Cabernet Sauvignon and Chardonnay.

KENWOOD VINEYARDS
9592 Sonoma Highway, Kenwood ☎(707) 833-5891.
A family-owned winery going from strength to strength. Sauvignon Blanc is far and away the specialty of the house.

KORBEL CHAMPAGNE CELLARS
13250 River Rd., Guerneville ☎(707) 887-2294.
California's original specialist in *méthode champenoise* sparkling wines is still at it in the original brick building. Informative tours.

LAMBERT BRIDGE
4085 W Dry Creek Rd., Healdsburg ☎(707) 433-5855.
Specialist in Cabernet Sauvignon and Chardonnay, but distinctively flavored wines across the board.

LANDMARK VINEYARDS
101 Adobe Canyon Rd., Kenwood ☎(707) 833-0053.
Focus is on Chardonnay.

LYTTON SPRINGS WINERY
650 Lytton Springs Rd., Healdsburg ☎(707) 433-7721.
Well-founded reputation for hearty Zinfandels.

MARK WEST VINEYARDS
7000 Trenton-Healdsburg Rd., Forestville ☎(707) 544-4813.
Vineyardist husband and winemaker wife pool talents on a picturesque property.

MATANZAS CREEK WINERY
6097 Bennett Valley Rd., Santa Rosa ☎(707) 528-6464.
A winery that has won considerable fame for its Chardonnay, but its Merlot and Sauvignon Blanc are also excellent.

MILL CREEK VINEYARDS
1401 Westside Rd., Healdsburg ☎(707) 431-2121.
Solid all-round list from estate vines.

PAT PAULSEN VINEYARDS
Asti Store Rd., Cloverdale ☎(707) 894-3197.
The television comic writes funny back labels in his role as proprietor, but leaves the winemaking to a serious, skillful aide. Especially known for Cabernet Sauvignon, Sauvignon Blanc.

J. PEDRONCELLI WINERY
1220 Canyon Rd., Geyserville ☎(707) 857-3531.
Underrated, underpriced reds from an old hand in Sonoma winemaking. Whites ever better.

PIPER SONOMA CELLARS
11447 Old Redwood Highway, Healdsburg ☎(707) 433-8843.
Adjacent to Rodney Strong Vineyards and affiliated with it, a Franco-American specialist in *méthode champenoise* sparklers. The self-guiding tour is highly informative.

SAUSAL WINERY
7370 Highway 128, Healdsburg ☎(707) 433-2285.
Veteran growers and winemakers in the region produce steadily across their range, but Zinfandel is the flagship.

SEBASTIANI VINEYARDS
389 Fourth St. E, Sonoma ☎(707) 938-5532.
Best known for thick, plummy reds aged for extra years in wood in the old way. Cellar is a one-man show of carved cask heads. Good tours.

SIMI WINERY
16275 Healdsburg Ave., Healdsburg ☎(707) 433-6981.
Good and growing more stylish by the day. Best known for Chardonnay and Zinfandel, with Cabernet Sauvignon catching up. Informative tours of remodeled stone cellars.

SONOMA-CUTRER VINEYARDS
4401 Slusser Rd., Windsor ☎(707) 528-1181.
The only wine produced is Chardonnay, but it is spectacular.

ROBERT STEMMLER VINEYARDS
3805 Lambert Bridge Rd., Healdsburg
☎*(707) 433-6334.*
A one-man winery with a distinct sense of style.

RODNEY STRONG VINEYARDS
11455 Old Redwood Highway, Healdsburg
☎*(707) 433-6511.*
What used to be Sonoma Vineyards continues to offer a broad range of sound-to-excellent wines, the most prized bearing vineyard names.

TRENTADUE WINERY
19170 Geyserville Ave., Geyserville
☎*(707) 433-3104.*
Small cellar dedicated to producing sturdy wines in the natural, old-fashioned way.

VALLEY OF THE MOON WINERY
777 Madrone Rd., Glen Ellen ☎*(707) 996-6941.*
Old-timer who has upgraded wines from jug generics to pricier varietals, but style is still sturdily rustic.

MENDOCINO COUNTY
Map 7D2.
Mendocino has two distinct small wine districts: one flanks US-101 near the town of Ukiah; the other is well out toward the coast, around a village called Philo. The interior district was best known for French Colombard, but has now established itself as a good source of Chenin Blanc and Johannisberg (White) Riesling. The coastal district, called Anderson Valley, is also known for whites, especially Gewürztraminer and Chardonnay.

Sparse numbers of wineries make these districts more likely candidates for passing-through visits rather than for a settled stay, although Anderson Valley is situated on SR-128 and makes a fine day's outing from any Mendocino Coast town.

Readily visited (tasting, usually tours)

FETZER VINEYARDS
1150 Bel Arbres Rd., Redwood Valley
☎*(707) 485-7634.*
A family-owner winery that has grown rapidly under the direction of nine brothers and sisters and has a broad ranges of wines improving all along the way.

GUENOC WINERY
21000 Butts Canyon Rd., Middletown
☎*(707) 987-2385.*
Once the property of 19thC actress Lillie Langtry, and her likeness is now used on the primary label. Good wines across a broad range.

HANDLEY CELLARS
3151 Highway 128, Philo ☎*(707) 895-3876.*
Owner and winemaker Milla Handley

makes *méthode champenoise* sparkling wines and barrel-fermented Chardonnay, Gewürztraminer and Sauvignon Blanc.

HUSCH VINEYARDS
4400 Highway 128, Philo ☎*(707) 895-3216.*
Wines include their excellent Reserve Chardonnay, only sold at the winery.

MCDOWELL VALLEY VINEYARDS
3811 Highway 175, Hopland ☎*(707) 744-1053.*
Impressive use of solar power is only one aspect of a fascinating building. Wide list of wines consistently good.

NAVARRO VINEYARDS
5601 Highway 128, Philo ☎*(707) 895-3686.*

Distinctive touch with Gewürztraminer and Chardonnay.

OBESTER WINERY
9200 Highway 128, Philo ☎*(707) 895-3814.*
Paul and Sandy Obester are best known for their delicately grassy Sauvignon Blanc.

PARDUCCI WINE CELLARS
501 Parducci Rd., Ukiah ☎*(707) 462-3828.*
One of the original wineries in Mendocino County. The Parducci family still make the wine, which can be outstand-

ing. So too are the tours, the most instructive in the region.

PARSONS CREEK WINERY
3001 South State St., Ukiah ☎*(707) 462-8900.*
Successful Chardonnay and brut sparkling wine.

SCHARFFENBERGER CELLARS
7000 Highway 128, Philo ☎*(707) 895-2065.*
Producer of complex *méthode champenoise* sparkling wines. The winery belongs to the French champagne house of Pommery.

LIVERMORE VALLEY
Map 9F3.
The rocky valley around the town of Livermore, in Alameda County to the s of San Francisco, is one of California's oldest wine regions. It has filled with houses belonging to Alameda County commuters, but it still has vineyards that were famous for Sauvignon Blanc and Sémillon as early as 1880.

Because of all the houses, and because only a handful of wineries operate in the district, it does not lend itself to wine-country touring in the same sense as Napa or Sonoma. The towns of Livermore and Pleasanton, however, lie just off I-580, the connecting freeway between San Francisco–Oakland and the San Joaquin Valley, and visitors are warmly welcomed at its short roster of wineries.

Readily visited (tasting, usually tours)

CHOUINARD VINEYARDS
33853 Palomares Rd., Castro Valley ☎*(415) 582-9900.*
A broad range of wines including Zinfandel and Gewürztraminer.

CONCANNON VINEYARD
4590 Tesla Rd., Livermore ☎*(415) 447-3760.*
Best known for Sauvignon Blanc and Petite Sirah. The label dates back to Livermore's early days.

LIVERMORE VALLEY CELLARS
1508 Wetmore Rd., Livermore ☎*(415) 447-1751.*
A small retirement venture which has established a deserved reputation for

good-quality white wines.

RETZLAFF VINEYARDS
1356 South Livermore Ave., Livermore ☎*(415) 447-8941.*
All the wines are estate bottlings from Robert and Gloria Taylor's 10 acres.

WENTE BROS ESTATE WINERY
5565 Tesla Rd., Livermore ☎*(415) 447-3603.*
Broadly known for steady, agreeable whites, especially Sauvignon Blanc and Sémillon. With Concannon, one of the old-timers. Recent entrant into Champagne-method sparkling wines at separate cellar. Good tours at both; good restaurant at latter.

HECKER PASS
Map 9F3.
About 100 miles s of San Francisco via US-101, Hecker Pass, in southern Santa Clara County, is the last surviving country wine district in the
state. But even here they are in the throes of change: new faces are
making costly varietal wines from distantly-grown grapes. Enough of
the old guard remains, however, to enchant a passer-by with thick,
sturdy reds made in the traditional way in old wooden cellars. Since
few of these wines are generally available for sale, a tour is almost the
only way to find them.

A majority of the small wineries flank SR-152, the Hecker Pass Highway, just w of Gilroy. They make an easy detour from US-101. Alterna-
tively, travelers driving between San Francisco and the Monterey
Peninsula can use Hecker Pass as a scenic ramble through fine coastal
hill country between US-101 and SR-1, the Coast Highway.

Readily visited (tasting, usually tours)

FORTINO WINERY
4525 Hecker Pass Highway, Gilroy ☎(408) 842-3305.
Warm, plump reds dominate the list.

HECKER PASS WINERY
4605 Hecker Pass Highway, Gilroy ☎(408) 842-8755.
Some subtle touches in the reds.

KIRIGIN CELLARS
11550 Watsonville Rd., Gilroy ☎(408) 847-8827.
A broad list of sound wines made by a Yugoslav-trained winemaker who retains
his native sense of style.

THOMAS KRUSE WINERY
4390 Hecker Pass Highway ☎(408) 842-7016.
Steady, sometimes intriguing reds from a small, old-fashioned cellar. Paradoxically,
it started the local revolution from country jug wines to varietal bottle.

SARAH'S VINEYARD
4005 Hecker Pass Highway, Gilroy ☎(408) 842-4278.
A relative newcomer aiming at making fine varietals.

SIERRA FOOTHILLS
Map 8E4.
A sidelight of the Gold Rush of 1849 was a thriving wine industry in the
Sierra Foothills. The focus was on Zinfandel then; it is, once again, in
modern times, though Sauvignon Blanc also weighs heavily in current
totals. Most of the vineyards are between Sutter Creek and Placerville,
and so too are the wineries.

Readily visited

BALDINELLI VINEYARDS
10801 Dickson Rd., Plymouth ☎(209) 245-3398.
Modern cellar makes excellent reds.

BOEGER WINERY
1709 Carson Rd., Placerville ☎*(916) 622-8094.*
A new cellar and a historic one share a site; steady, agreeable wines. Crystal Blush, a fortified dessert wine, is their latest release.

GREENSTONE WINERY
3151 Highway 88, Ione ☎*(209) 274-2238.*
Caters to tourists by its location and the affable style of its wines.

KARLY WINES
11076 Bell Rd., Plymouth ☎*(209) 245-3922.*
Reds are impressively subtle and polished in a region known more for raw power.

MONTEVINA WINES
20680 Shenandoah School Rd., Plymouth ☎*(209) 245-6942.*
The leader in its region's rebirth offers good wines across the board.

SANTINO WINES
12225 Steiner Rd., Plymouth ☎*(209) 245-6979.*
Small, well-equipped cellar has excellent white Zinfandel and late-harvest Riesling made by German-trained winemaker.

SHENANDOAH VINEYARDS
12300 Steiner Rd., Plymouth ☎*(209) 245-4455.*
Rarity of rarities, a cellar willing to put effort into distinctive dessert wines.

OTHER IDEAS

- The **Napa Valley Wine Train** is the lazy way to tour the valley: 36 miles and 3 hours of leisurely travel aboard luxuriously restored turn-of-the-century Pullman cars, wining and dining in style. From Napa Valley Wine Train Station, 1275 McKinstry St., Napa ☎(707) 253-2111 or (1-800) 427-4124.
- **Sonoma Charter & Tours** offers unusual, adventurous tours of the Sonoma Valley, traveling in transportation ranging from limousines to buses. Details from PO Box 1972, Sonoma, CA 95476 ☎(707) 938-4248 or (1-800) 232-7260.
- There are only three periodic geysers in the world, one of them right here in the upper Napa Valley. **Old Faithful Geyser of California** erupts approximately every 40 minutes. At 1299 Tubbs Lane, Calistoga ☎(707) 942 6463 ☒ Open 9am-5pm daily; until 6pm in summer. Picnic area.

For further ideas and information, contact:

- **Calistoga Chamber of Commerce**, Suite 4, 1458 Lincoln Ave., Calistoga ☎(707) 942-6333
- **Sonoma County Convention & Visitors Bureau**, 10 Fourth St., Santa Rosa, CA 95401 ☎(707) 575-1191
- **Sonoma County Wineries Association**, Luther Burbank Center for the Arts, 50 Mark West Springs Road, Santa Rosa ☎(707) 527-7701
- **Sonoma Valley Visitors Bureau**, 453 First St. E, Sonoma, CA 95476 ☎(707) 996-1090

Index

Bold page numbers refer to main entries. *Italic* numbers refer to the illustrations and maps. The GENERAL INDEX begins on page 167.

INDEX OF PLACES

164

GENERAL INDEX

AAA-California, 41, 45
Abstract Impressionist
school, 76
Accidents, automobile, 45
Accommodations *see*
Hotels
Adams, Ansel, 28, **63**,
76-7, 112, 132, 145
Addresses and telephone
numbers, **48-9**
African-American
Historical and Cultural
Society, **69**
AIDS, 12, 33
Air travel/airlines, 35,
48-9
Airports, 37
Oakland International,
35
San Francisco
International, 35
San Jose International,
35
Alcatraz, **62-3**, 68, 78,
107, 118
Alcohol:
duty-free allowances, 34
laws, 46
Allen Knight Maritime
Museum, 124
Alma (scow), 76
Ambulances, 44
American Ballet Theater,
105
American Conservatory
Theater (ACT), 26, 53,
106
American Express:
baggage insurance, 33
charge cards, 34
MoneyGram service, 34
Travel Service Office,
40, 43, 48
travelers checks, 34
American Indian Trade
Fair and Exposition, 53
American Indians *see*
Native Americans
Ames Research Center,
126
Amtrak, 36, 38
Amusement Parks, **118**
Anchor Steam Brewery,
63
Anglin, Clarence, 62

Anglin, John, 62
Animal parks, **117**
Ansel Adams Center, **63**
Anshutz, Thomas, 82
Antique stores, **111**
Aquariums, **117**
Monterey, 117, 123,
124
Steinhart, 54, **65**, 117
Aquatic Park, 55, 70, 76,
107
Aqueduct, Los Angeles,
25
Arboretum, Strybing, 70,
71
Architecture, **29-32**
Army Museum, 59
Arnolds, Charles, 28
Arrowhead Lake, 19
Art galleries, **111-12**
Art Institute, San
Francisco, **75-6**
Arts, **26-8**
Ashby, Gordon, 126
Asian Art Museum of San
Francisco, 54, 82
Automobile Show, 53
Avenue of the Giants,
140, **144**

Baby-sitters, 45
Baggage insurance, 33
Baker, Phil, 64
Bakewell, John Jr, *29*, 67
Balclutha, **63**, 76
Ballet, 26, 53, **105**
Bammies (Bay Area Music
Awards), 52
Bank of America, 25, 58,
66
Bank of California Old
Coin and Gold Exhibit,
59, **63**
Bank of Canton, *30*, 31,
66
Bank of Italy, 25, 58
Banks, 42-3
Barnum and Bailey
Circus, 53
Bars, **102-3**
opening hours, 43
Battle of Harmonicas, 52
Bay Area Rapid Transport
(BART), 38
Bay Bridge, 78

Bay Meadows Race
Course, 52, **126**
Bay Model, **122**
Bay to Breakers race, 52
Beaches, **106-7**, **117**
Baker Beach, 59, 107
Golden Gate National
Recreation Area, 70
map, *20-21*
Northern California
coast, 141
Santa Cruz, 138
Tahoe, 131
Bear Flag Revolt, 22, 24
Bears, 18
Beat Generation, 59
Beaux Arts architecture,
29, 55
Bed and breakfast, **84-5**
Beer, 63, 152
Beer Festival, 52
Beethoven Festival, 52
Belluschi, Pietro, 30, 75
Bengston, Billy Al, 28
Beringer, 31
Berkeley Marina, **119**
Berkeley Municipal Rose
Garden, **119**
Bicycling, **107**
Bierstadt, Albert, 28
Big Bear Lake, 19
Billiards, **107**
Bingham, George Caleb,
82
Blues Festival, 53
Boats:
Balclutha, **63**, 76
boating, **107**
cruises, 55
Lake Tahoe, 131
Northern California
coast, 140
Oakland Waterfront, 125
sailing, 52, **107**
Sausalito, 122
Tiburon, 122
Bonanza (television
program), 130
Books:
background reading, 27
guidebooks, **27**, 47
literature, 26, 27
stores, 26, **112**
Botanical Garden,
Berkeley, 120

167

List of street names

All streets mentioned in this book that fall within the areas covered by our maps are listed below. Map numbers are printed in **bold** type. Some smaller streets are not named on the maps, but the map reference given here will help you locate the correct neighborhood.

Adler St., **6C8**
Alamo Sq., **5E6**
Arguello Blvd., **4B4-E4**
Ashbury St., **4E5-F5**

Baker St., **4B5-D5**
Battery St., **6B8-C8**
Bay St., **4B5-6B8**
Beach St., **4B5-6B8**
Bluxome St., **6E8-D9**
Brannan St., **6E8-D9**
Broadway, **4C5-6C9**
Bryant St., **6E8-D9**
Buchanan St., **5B6-E6**
Bush St., **4D5-6C8**

California St.,
  3D1-6C9
Carl St., **4F4-5**
Castro St., **2C4-D4**
Center St., **6D9**
Chestnut St., **4B5-6B8**
Clay St., **4C4-6C9**
Clement St., **3D1-4D4**
Cole St., **4E4-F5**
Columbus Ave.,
  5B7-6C8
Cosmo Pl., **5C7**
Cyril Magnin St., **6D8**

Davis St., **6C8**
Divisadero St., **4B5-F6**
Dolores St., **5E6-F6**
Drumm St., **6C9**

Eddy St., **4D5-6D8**
Ellis St., **4D5-6D8**
Embarcadero, The,
  6B8-D9

Filbert St., **4C5-6B8**
Fillmore St., **5B6-E6**
Folsom St., **5F7-6C9**
Franklin St., **5B6-E7**
Front St., **6C9-B8**
Fulton St., **3E1-5D7**

Geary Blvd., **3D1-5D6**
Geary St., **5D7-6D8**
Geneva Ave., **2E4-F5**
Ghirardelli Sq., **5B7**
Gold St., **6C8**
Gough St., **5B6-E7**
Grant Ave., **6B8-D8**
Great Highway, **1C2-E2**
Green St., **4C5-6B8**
Grove St., **4E4-5D7**

Haight St., **4E4-5E7**
Harrison St., **5F7-6C9**
Hayes St., **4E4-5D7**
Howard St., **5E7-6C9**
Hyde St., **5B7-D7**

Illinois St., **6E9-F9**
Irving St., **3F1-4F4**

Jackson Sq., **6C8**
Jackson St., **4C4-6C9**
Jefferson St., **5B7**
Joice St., **6C8**
Jones St., **5B7-D7**

Kearny St., **6C8**
Kennedy Dr. J. F.,
  3E1-4E4

Laguna St., **5B6-E6**
Lake St., **3D2-4D4**

Larkin St., **5B7-D7**
Leavenworth St., **5B7-D7**
Lincoln Ave., **4B4**
Lincoln Blvd., **3A3**
Lincoln Way, **3F1-4F4**
Lombard St., **4B5-6B8**
Lyon St., **4B5-D5**

Maiden Lane, **6D8**
Marina Blvd., **4B5-5B6**
Mariposa St., **6F8-9**
Market St., **5F6-6C9**
Mason St., **5B7-6D8**
Masonic Ave., **4D5-E5**
McAllister St., **4D5-5D7**
Merchant St., **6C8**
Minna St., **5E7-6C9**
Mission St., **5F7-6C9**
Montgomery St.,
  6B8-C8

New Montgomery St.,
  6D8
Nob Hill, **6C8**
North Point St.,
  4B5-6B8

O'Farrell St., **5D7-6D8**

Pacific Ave., **4C5-6C8**
Pagoda Pl., **6C8**
Parnassus Ave., **4F4**
Pine St., **4D5-6C9**
Polk St., **5B7-E7**
Post St., **4D5-6C8**
Potrero Ave., **2C5-D5**
Powell St., **6B8-D8**
Presidio Ave., **4C5-D5**
Redwood Alley, **5D7**

175

Sacramento St.,
  4D4-6C9
Sansome St., 6B8-C8
Santos St., 2E4
Scott St., 4B5-E6
Skyline Blvd., 1E2-F2
Sloat Blvd., 1D2-3
South Dr., 3E2-3
Stanford St., 6D9
Stanyan St., 4D4-F4
Steiner St., 5B6-E6
Stockton St., 6B8-D8
Sutter St., 4D5-6C8

Taylor St., 5B7-6D8
Telegraph Hill Blvd., 6B8

Townsend St., 6E8-D9
Turk St., 4D4-6D8
Twin Peaks Blvd., 1D3

Union Sq., 6D8
Union St., 4C5-6B8
United Nations Plaza, 5D7

Vallejo St., 4C5-6B9
Van Ness Ave., 5B7-E7

Waller St., 4E4-5E6
Washington Sq., 6B8
Washington St.,
  4C4-6C9
Waverly Pl., 6C8

Numbered streets:
2nd St., 6C8-D9
3rd St., 6D8-F9
4th St., 6D8-E9
5th St., 6D8-E9
8th St., 5D7-6E8
11th St., 5E7
14th St.,
  4F5-5E7
16th St., 5F6-F9
20th St., 2D4-C5
24th St., 2D4-5
6th Ave., 3C3-F3
8th Ave., 3C3-F3
10th Ave., 3C3-F3
34th Ave., 1C2-D2

KEY TO MAP PAGES

KEY TO MAP SYMBOLS

Area Maps

- =O= Superhighway (with access point)
- = Main Road / Four-Lane Highway
- ▬ Other Main Road
- ▬ Secondary Road
- ▬ Minor Road
- 🛡66 Interstate Highway
- 🛡1 US Highway
- ㉗ State Highway
- - - - Ferry
- ▬ Railway
- ✈ Airport
- ✦ Airfield
- - - - State Boundary
- - - - National Park Boundary
- ■ Place of Interest
- 𝒜 Good Beach
- ▨ Forested Area
- 5▶ Adjoining Page No.

City Maps

- ▨ Place of Interest or Important Building
- ▢ Built-up Area
- ▨ Park
- ⊥ ⊥ Cemetery
- ▬ Railway
- Ⓜ Muni Metro Station
- ◈ BART / Muni Metro Station
- ◈ BART Station
- - - - Cable Car Routes
- 𝒊 Tourist Information
- ⬛ Parking / Garage
- ⊞ Hospital
- ✉ Post Office
- → One-way Street

```
0    10   20   30   40   50miles
|----|----|----|----|----|
0      20   40   60    80km
```

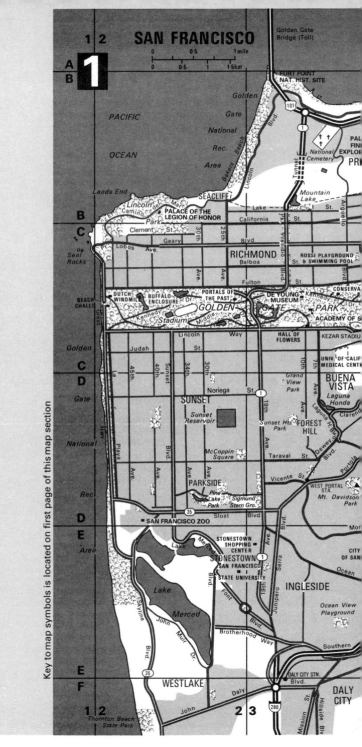

SAN FRANCISCO

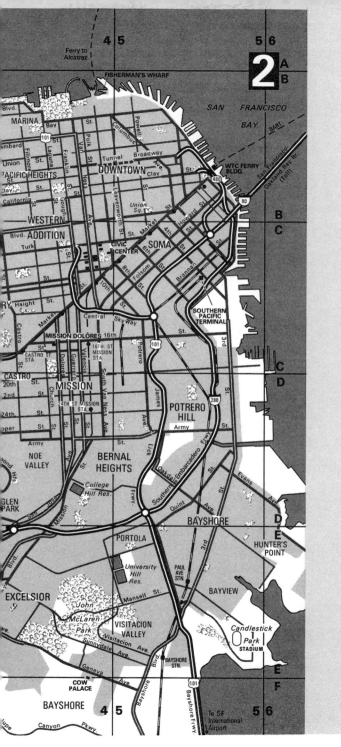

GOLDEN GATE
BRIDGE (TOLL)

Fort Point Nat.
Hist. Site

LINCOLN BLVD

STOREY AVE

RALSTON AVE

KOBBE AVE

HITCHCOCK

CRISSY FIELD AVE

LINCOLN BLVD

PARK

GOLDEN GATE
NATIONAL
RECREATION AREA

B
C

BAKER
BEACH

LINCOLN BLVD

PERSHING DR

WASHINGTON BLVD

CHINA BEACH

EL CAMINO DEL MAR

US Public Health
Hospital

PARK BLVD

Mountain
Lake

C
D

ROCHAMBEAU
PLGD.

RICHMOND
PLGD.

LAKE

CALIFORNIA   STREET

DUPONT
PLGD.

CLEMENT   STREET

CLEMENT

RICHMOND

GEARY   BOULEVARD

ARGONNE
PLGD.

ANZA

PARK   PRESIDIO   BOULEVARD

30TH
29TH
28TH
27TH
26TH
25TH
24TH
23RD
22ND
21ST
20TH
19TH
18TH
17TH
16TH
15TH
14TH
12TH
11TH
10TH
8TH
AVENUE

FUNSTON

BALBOA

CARILLO

D
E

31ST
AVENUE

30TH
AVENUE

FULTON
PLGD.

FULTON   STREET

F.K.

CROSS OVER DRIVE

Portals of
the Past

KENNEDY   DRIVE

OVER   DRIVE

Golden Gate
Park Stadium

MIDDLE   DRIVE

STOW
Stow
Lake

De Young Museum
& Asian Art Museum

Japanese
Tea Garden

Aca
of Sc

Strybing
Arboretum

GOLDEN   GATE

MARTIN

Hall of
Flowers

E
F

MARTIN   LUTHER   KING   DRIVE

LINCOLN   WAY

1 2

28TH
AVE.

25TH
AVE.

22ND
AVE.

19TH AVENUE

18TH
AVE.

14TH
AVE.

IRVING

11TH

SUNSET

2 3

0   250   500   750   1000 yds
0   250   500   750   1000m

CIVIC CENTER BUILDINGS
1. City Hall
2. Civic Auditorium
3. Main Library
4. Brooks Exhibit Hall (underground)
5. War Memorial Opera House
6. Louise M. Davies Symphony Hall
7. Veteran's Building
8. State Office Buildings
9. Federal Buildings

Underwater World   35

33
31
29
27
23
19
17
15

TELEGRAPH HILL
Coit Tower
PIONEER PARK
WASHINGTON UNION

GRANT
EMBARCADERO
SANSOME STREET
BATTERY STREET
STREET
GREEN STREET
VALLEJO STREET

B
C

SAN FRANCISCO BAY

BROADWAY
AVENUE
PACIFIC
JACKSON
SIDNEY WALTON PARK
US Custom House
Jackson Sq.
PORTSMOUTH SQ.
CHINATOWN
Tien Hou Temple
Transamerica Pyramid
Bank of California
ST. MARY'S SQUARE
PINE STREET
BUSH ST
Ferry Building World Trade Center
EMBARCADERO SKYWAY
EMBARCADERO PLAZA PARK
WASHINGTON
CLAY ST.
FRONT
DAVIS
EMBARCADERO
Rincon Annex

14

UNION SQUARE
MONTGOMERY ST
Sheraton Palace
POWELL STREET
Transbay Transit Terminal
MISSION STREET
BEALE ST
FREMONT
SAN FRANCISCO OAKLAND BAY BRIDGE
FIRST

24

26
C
28
D

Moscone Convention Center

30
32
34
36
38
40

SOUTH OF MARKET
Ansel Adams Center
80
SOUTH PARK
BRYANT STREET
SOUTH BEACH

D
E

JAMES LICK SKYWAY
Southern Pacific Terminal
TOWNSEND STREET
EMBARCADERO SKYWAY
CHINA BASIN

48

Hall of Justice
KING STREET
EMBARCADERO
3RD
Mission Rock Terminal
50
52

BRANNAN
STREET
54

6TH STREET
OWENS STREET
280
STREET

E
F
64

JAMES LICK FRWY
16TH STREET
STREET
JACKSON PARK
17TH STREET
MARIPOSA

8|9

9|10
CENTRAL BASIN

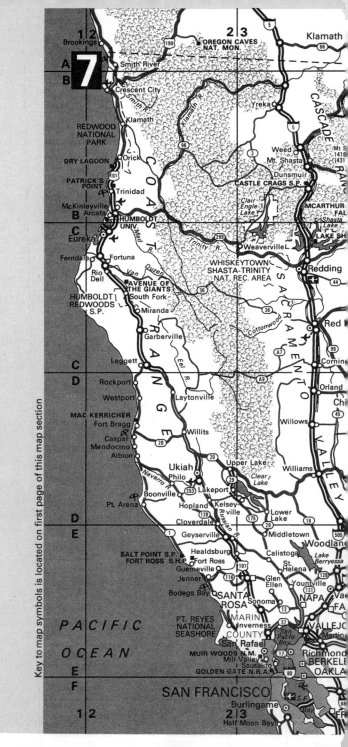

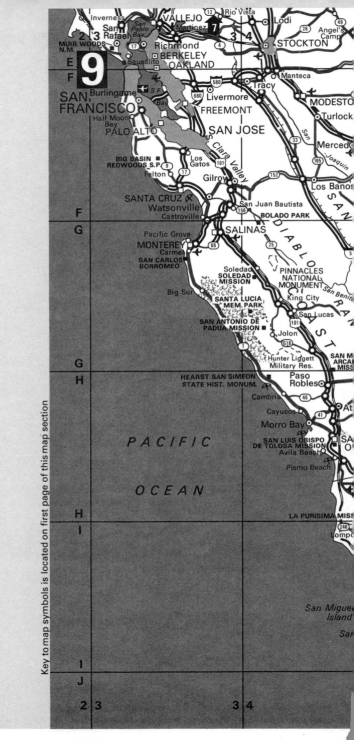

What readers from all over the world have said:

• "The book *(Hong Kong, Singapore & Bangkok)* was written in such a personal way that I feel as if you were actually writing this book for me." (L.Z., Orange, Conn., USA)

• "Your book *(Florence and Tuscany)* proved a wonderful companion for us in the past fortnight. It went with us everywhere...." (E.H., Kingston-on-Thames, Surrey, England)

• "I feel as if you have been a silent friend shadowing my time in Tuscany." (T.G., Washington, DC, USA)

• "We followed your book *(Los Angeles & San Francisco)* to the letter. It proved to be wonderful, indispensable, a joy...." (C.C., London, England)

• "We could never have had the wonderful time that we did without your guide to *Paris.* The compactness was very convenient, your maps were all we needed, but it was your restaurant guide that truly made our stay special.... We have learned first-hand: *American Express — don't leave home without it.*" (A. R., Virginia Beach, Va., USA)

• "Much of our enjoyment came from the way your book *(Venice)* sent us off scurrying around the interesting streets and off to the right places at the right times". (Lord H., London, England)

• "It *(Paris)* was my constant companion and totally dependable...." (V. N., Johannesburg, South Africa)

• "I could go on and on about how useful the book *(Amsterdam)* was — the trouble was that it was almost getting to be a case of not venturing out without it...." (J.C.W., Manchester, England)

• "We have heartily recommended these books to all our friends who have plans to travel abroad." (A.S. and J.C., New York, USA)

• "Despite many previous visits to Italy, I wish I had had your guide *(Florence and Tuscany)* ages ago. I love the author's crisp, literate writing and her devotion to her subject." (M. B-K., Denver, Colorado, USA)

• "We never made a restaurant reservation without checking your book *(Venice).* The recommendations were excellent, and the historical and artistic text got us through the sights beautifully." (L.S., Boston, Ma., USA)

• "We became almost a club as we found people sitting at tables all around, consulting their little blue books!" (F.C., Glasgow, Scotland)

• "This guide *(Paris)* we warmly recommend to all the many international visitors we work with." (M.L., Paris, France)

• "It's not often I would write such a letter, but it's one of the best guide books we have ever used *(Rome)* — we can't fault it!" (S.H., Berkhamsted, Herts, England)

What the papers said:

• "The expertly edited American Express series has the knack of pin-pointing precisely the details you need to know, and doing it concisely and intelligently." (*The Washington Post*)

• "*(Venice)* ... the best guide book I have ever used." (*The Standard* — London)

• "Amid the welter of guides to individual countries, American Express stands out...." (*Time*)

• "Possibly the best ... guides on the market, they come close to the oft-claimed 'all you need to know' comprehensiveness, with much original experience, research and opinions." (*Sunday Telegraph* — London)

• "The most useful general guide was *American Express New York* by Herbert Bailey Livesey. It also has the best street and subway maps." (*Daily Telegraph* — London)

• "...in the flood of travel guides, the *American Express* guides come closest to the needs of traveling managers with little time." (*Die Zeit* — Germany)

What the experts said:

• "We only used one guide book, Sheila Hale's *Amex Venice,* for which she and the editors deserve a Nobel Prize." (Eric Newby, London)

• "Congratulations to you and your staff for putting out the best guide book of *any* size *(Barcelona & Madrid)*. I'm recommending it to everyone." (Barnaby Conrad, Santa Barbara, California)

• "If you're only buying one guide book, we recommend American Express...." (*Which?* — Britain's leading consumer magazine)

American Express Travel Guides

spanning the globe....

EUROPE
Amsterdam, Rotterdam
 & The Hague
Athens and the
 Classical Sites ‡
Barcelona & Madrid ‡
Berlin ‡
Brussels #
Dublin and Cork #
Florence and Tuscany
London #
Moscow & St Petersburg *
Paris #
Prague *
Provence and the
 Côte d'Azur *
Rome
Venice ‡
Vienna & Budapest

NORTH AMERICA
Boston and New
 England *
Los Angeles & San
 Diego #
Mexico ‡
New York #
San Francisco and
 the Wine Regions
Toronto, Montréal and
 Québec City ‡
Washington, DC

THE PACIFIC
Cities of Australia
Hong Kong & Taiwan
Singapore &
 Bangkok ‡
Tokyo #

* Paperbacks in preparation   # Paperbacks appearing January 1993
‡ Hardback pocket guides (in paperback 1993)

Clarity and quality of information, combined with outstanding maps — the ultimate in travelers' guides

Buying an AmEx guide has never been easier....

The *American Express Travel Guides* are now available by mail order direct from the publisher, for customers resident in the UK and Eire. Payment can be made by credit card or cheque/P.O. Simply complete the form below, and send it, together with your remittance.

New paperback series (£6.99)   # Available from January 1993

☐ Amsterdam, Rotterdam
& The Hague
1 85732 918 X

☐ Brussels #
1 85732 966 X

☐ Cities of Australia
1 85732 921 X

☐ Dublin & Cork #
1 85732 967 8

☐ Florence and Tuscany
1 85732 922 8

☐ Hong Kong & Taiwan
0 85533 955 1

☐ London #
1 85732 968 6

☐ Los Angeles & San Diego #
1 85732 919 8

☐ New York #
1 85732 971 6

☐ Paris #
1 85732 969 4

☐ Rome
1 85732 923 6

☐ San Francisco and
the Wine Regions
1 85732 920 1

☐ Tokyo #
1 85732 970 8

☐ Vienna & Budapest
1 85732 962 7

☐ Washington, DC
1 85732 924 4

Hardback pocket guides (£7.99)

☐ Athens and the Classical Sites
0 85533 954 3

☐ Barcelona & Madrid
0 85533 951 9

☐ Berlin
0 85533 952 7

☐ Mexico
0 85533 872 5

☐ Singapore & Bangkok
0 85533 956 X

☐ Toronto, Montréal
& Québec City
0 85533 866 0

☐ Venice
0 85533 871 7

While every effort is made to keep prices low, it is sometimes necessary to increase them at short notice. American Express Travel Guides reserves the right to amend prices from those previously advertised.

Please send the titles ticked above.   **SFW**

Number of titles @ £6.99 ☐   Value: £

Number of titles @ £7.99 ☐   Value: £
Add £1.50 for postage and packing   £   1.50

Total value of order: £
I enclose a cheque or postal order ☐ payable to Reed Book Services Ltd, or please charge my credit card account:

☐ Barclaycard/Visa   ☐ Access/MasterCard   ☐ American Express

Card number ☐☐☐☐☐☐☐☐☐☐☐☐☐☐☐☐☐☐☐☐☐☐

Signature _____   Expiry date _____

Name _____
Address _____

_____   Postcode _____

Send this order to American Express Travel Guides, Cash Sales Dept,
Reed Book Services Ltd, PO Box 5, Rushden, Northants NN10 9YX.